YANKEES AT THE COURT

The First Americans in Paris

Yankees at the Court

THE FIRST AMERICANS IN PARIS

by Susan Mary Alsop

Doubleday & Company, Inc., Garden City, New York

Design by Beverley Vawter Gallegos

For my beloved grandson,

William S. Patten, Jr.

Contents

Illustrations

John Adams (*Harvard University Portrait Collection*)
Arthur Lee (*Independence National Historical Park Collection*)
Abigail Adams (*New York State Historical Association*)
John Jay (*Diplomatic Reception Rooms, Department of State*)
Sarah Livingston Jay (*From the author's collection*)
Street scene (*Bibliothèque Nationale, Paris*)
William Carmichael (*Frick Art Reference Library*)
Robert Livingston (*Diplomatic Reception Rooms, Department of State*)

after page 248

George Washington (*Pennsylvania Academy of the Fine Arts*)
Marquis de Lafayette (*Anne S. K. Brown Military Collection, Providence, Rhode Island*)
Marquise de Lafayette (*Courtesy of the Vicomte de Noailles*)
Conde de Floridablanca (*Courtesy of El Banco Urquijò, Madrid*)
Comte de Rochambeau (*Anne S. K. Brown Military Collection*)
Surrender of Lord Cornwallis at Yorktown (*Yale University Art Gallery*)
Signing of the Treaty of Peace (*Diplomatic Reception Rooms, Department of State*)

Acknowledgments

THIS BOOK COVERS a period, 1775–85, that has been so well explored by students of American history that I would not have ventured to embark upon it had I not been fortunate enough to obtain some original material. I owe my first thanks to Madame Ida Le Clerc, the descendant of the Chevalier de Bonvouloir, to the late Monsieur Jacques de Beaumarchais and my dear friend his widow, to the Earl and Countess of Mansfield, whose ancestor was the Viscount Stormont, Franklin's contemporary and antagonist, and to Mrs. Joan Auld, the charming archivist who drove the precious boxes of Stormont papers to Edinburgh herself in order that I could be the first student to study them since the Mansfield muniments had been listed. In Paris, Leray de Chaumont's descendant, the Comte Philippe de Bausset, was good enough to offer me more original material, and in America my greatest debt is to Professor Richard B. Morris of Columbia University, who permitted me to draw unremittingly on his knowledge and kindness, as well as allowing me access to the John Jay papers. Olivier Bernier was another source of strength; he kindly came all the way up to Maine when I was starting my research to teach me about French habits and customs of the eighteenth century, and I have quoted what he told me frequently.

My thanks are also due to William Clark, Nancy and David Perth, Louise and Jean-Louis de Rougemont, Claude-Anne

Lopez, Meredith Frapier, Cécile de Durfort, Anne Rain, Pierre Lemoine and his assistant, Guy Kuraszewski, Lino S. Lipinsky Orlov, Arnold Whitridge, Denise Azam, Lilianne de Rothschild, Jean-Jacques Journet, Ene Sirvet, Lucius Wilmerding, Jr., Richard Helms, Walter Pforzheimer, C. M. Harris, Joseph Alsop, Briton C. Busch, David Schoenbrun, William S. Moorhead, Evangeline Bruce, Katherine Winton Evans, Lynn Pedigo, Anne Brown, Richard B. Harrington, Clement E. Conger, Gail Serfaty, Georges Vernes, Pierre Vernes, Corinne Zimmerman, G. Vitelli, Frances FitzGerald, Marilyn Gillet, George M. Cheston, Carmen Marañon Urquijò, Yolande Collins, Dr. Charles Ryskamp and the staff of the Pierpont Morgan Library, especially Jane Shoaf, the staffs of the Library of Congress (especially the Manuscript Division), the New York Public Library, the New York Society Library, the Public Libraries of Washington, D.C., the Bibliothèque Nationale, the London Library.

Mary Buell, my research assistant, bore the brunt of the hard work and my debt to her is great, as it is to my ever-patient and supportive editor, Carolyn Blakemore, her assistant James G. Moser, Alex Gotfryd, and to Ken McCormick, who also kept his wise and compassionate eyes on my work. Evelyn Tehaan typed the manuscript, a difficult job for which I am very grateful.

YANKEES AT THE COURT

The First Americans in Paris

Prologue

It is impossible to exaggerate the reluctance of our colonial forebears to revolt against England. The word "revolution" calls instantly to mind dedicated conspirators, aflame with a passionate sense of nationalism: Greek, Irish, Russian, French—the list could be expanded indefinitely. This burning desire for independence was not felt by the American colonists until 1775 and even then it developed slowly.

Thomas Jefferson was tortured with doubt only months before he picked up his brave pen to write that sublime state paper: The Declaration of Independence. Sitting alone at Monticello on August 25, 1775, he revealed his thoughts to a Tory kinsman, John Randolph: "I hope the returning wisdom of Great Britain will e'er long put an end to this unnatural contest," and he described himself as one of those *who still wish for a reunion with their parent country.** Then he burst out at the end of the letter: "But, I am still one of those too who, rather than submit to the right of legislating for us assumed by the British parliament, and which late experience has shown us they will so cruelly exercise, would lend my hand to sink the whole island in the ocean."[1] A more anguished ambivalence of mind is hard to imagine.

It must not be forgotten that, during the 1760's, the reins of government lay loosely on the shoulders of George III's Ameri-

* *Author's emphasis.*

can subjects. No other colonies had been permitted so much autonomy, so great a degree of home rule. With the exception of the Negroes and the Indians, they were very free, perhaps freer than the English themselves. Taxes were light; in Connecticut no taxes were levied for three years running, except local rates for roads and schools.[2]

Then there was the sentimental bond between the two nations. The New Englander Oliver Wolcott summed up his exasperation with the British government well when he wrote in 1776, as he watched his country slip into what was in fact a civil war of the bitterest kind: "The Abilities of a Child might have governed this Country, so strong has been their attachment to Britain."[3]

Of course they were attached, for they had no history of their own. Americans had been brought up on the stories of British heroes. The tale of King Alfred and the cakes, the drama of Drake and the Spanish Armada, were as much a part of their lives as was the English currency that they used every day, the imported English clothes that they wore, the strong, coarse English needles with which the fishermen repaired the sails of their boats, and the delicate, fine-pointed products of Sheffield used by those who could afford them to darn the English damask tableclothes which dressed their dining tables, the better to show off the gleaming products of the London silversmiths. It is a lonely and frightening business to throw off heritage and habits, as dissidents throughout the ages have discovered.

No dissident felt the wrench of civil war more painfully than the British-trained officer George Washington. Obeying the call of the Second Continental Congress, he marched north to Boston to assume command of the army in June 1775, but a letter to his wife showed how heavy was his heart. When he was young he had always spoken of England as home. A detail that illustrates how hard it was to break lifelong habits is that, as late as January 1776, the health of King George was drunk nightly in the officers' mess at Washington's headquarters; as was the custom in all military outposts of the British Empire throughout the world.[4]

What then were the frictions that led to what Jefferson had called "this unnatural contest" in his unhappy letter to his kinsman? It all started as a dreary commercial and legal squabble. The British government had a case that seemed clear to it: surely it was fair that the colonies should assume part of the debt for the recent and very expensive wars† by which the expansion and security of the colonies had been won at the expense of the French. To this effect, a series of revenue acts were passed by Parliament, of which the heaviest and most unpopular was the Stamp Act of 1765.

The colonists saw no reason why they should be taxed to pay for a war that had been imposed on them, however much the British successes had been to their advantage. The resulting hue and cry brought about the repeal of the hated Act in the following year, 1766.

This victory was greeted with demonstrations of gratitude and loyalty throughout the colonies, almost hysterical in their enthusiasm. But the joy was short-lived. The King and his ministers were not monsters of evil, in fact the young George III was an attractive man who probably would have been immensely popular had he made an American tour, as British monarchs do today. It is easy to imagine him as Farmer George, shooting wild turkey with his Virginia hosts and pleasing them with his genuine interest in the production of tobacco.

But the King remained in London and, only a year after the repeal of the Stamp Act, he and his ministers annulled the effect of their propaganda success with the passage of the foolish and shortsighted laws known as the Townshend Acts which imposed heavy duties on English goods entering the country, such as paint, glass, paper, and tea. The interim ministry of the Duke of Grafton had just been joined by a brand-new Chancellor of

† *The Seven Years' War is the easiest name to employ for the global conflict that ended in 1763 and which included the French and Indian War in North America.*

the Exchequer, Lord Townshend, who was clever, arrogant, and eager to make his name. It was said that the speech in which he introduced his Acts was delivered in a roseate glow produced by a bumper of champagne. To the rage of the Whig opposition, the measures were at first a financial success and were highly applauded by British public opinion until, as in the case of the Stamp Act, they became impossible to enforce because of the outrage of the colonists. So they too were rescinded in 1770, with the exception of the tax on tea. To London this did not seem an important exception.

While the struggle over pounds, shillings, and pence dragged on year after wearying year, loyal and respectful American lawyers worried over their duties to the Crown: "The Parliament unquestionably possesses a legal authority to regulate the trade of Great Britain and all her colonies. . . . We are but parts of a whole," wrote John Dickinson of Pennsylvania in 1767.[5] Dickinson was a true patriot but, to him and to other thinking men, the useful umbrella phrase so familiar to us from our schoolbooks, "No taxation without representation," raised complicated issues. Men on both sides of the Atlantic in the eighteenth century believed in the rule of law; and as one reads the lists of the provincial colonial assemblies, again and again one is struck by how many of the members were lawyers. What is more, these men were as soaked in the words of the great English jurists, from Coke to their own contemporary, Mansfield, as were the London barristers sitting in the Inns of Court three thousand miles away.

While these serious men wrestled painfully with their conflicting ties, Sam Adams' Sons of Liberty saw things in a clearer and simpler light. The British were wrong; they were right and it was up to them to become an increasingly effective underground force. Indeed, they became one and, although their leaders kept the mobs in check so that little blood was shed, they all the same looted, rioted, and pillaged the homes of British customs officials and those of British officers on garrison duty.

Emboldened by their success in forcing the repeal of the

Stamp Act, the patriots staged two violent protests in 1770 against the Townshend Acts. The first, in New York in January, was a serious riot in the course of which infuriated British soldiers cut down a liberty pole and made a pile of the pieces in front of the headquarters of the Sons of Liberty. One man was killed during the ugly confrontation that ensued. The second, two months later, the so-called Boston Massacre of March 5, was no massacre at all. The always unpopular British redcoats were provoked into firing into a mob and four people were killed. The radical Samuel Adams jumped on the incident and exploited it for all it was worth but, in the trial of the responsible British officer, Captain Preston, two fine young lawyers, John Adams and Josiah Quincy, defended him against the charge of murder. He and the other British soldiers involved were acquitted. It was on this day that Lord North's ministry repealed the Acts that had caused the trouble, with that aforementioned exception of the tax on tea.

Three years later, in December 1773, that tax provided the grounds that the radicals had been looking for in order to force the issue of taxation without representation once and for all. In protest against it, the Sons of Liberty created that famous incident known as the Boston Tea Party. Disguised as Indians, they crept aboard the East India Company ships at night and threw 342 chests of expensive tea into the harbor. The King, maddened beyond endurance, wrote to his Prime Minister, Lord North: "The dye is now cast. The Colonies must either submit or triumph."[6]

The British reprisals took the form of the severe laws known as the Coercive, or Intolerable, Acts. Boston was closed to trade until the tea was paid for. Closing the port meant strangulation for a town which depended on the sea in order to breathe and live. The other colonies rallied to the side of Massachusetts and, on September 5, 1774, fifty-five delegates gathered in Philadelphia to consult. During the course of this First Continental Congress, the members tried hard to find a just path to conciliation.

Even then there was no sense of inevitability about the course of events. The most distinguished and intelligent men in America sat for six weeks seeking a way to "preserve and confirm the liberties that they already had as colonials."[7] Certainly they did not see themselves as demanding independence, and John Adams and Thomas Jefferson wrote pamphlets at the time advocating what we would call today Dominion status within the British Commonwealth. Probably, if the Whigs had been in power, they would have accepted the terms; for years the House of Commons had reverberated to the thunder of some of the greatest orators in British history as they warned of the fatal effects of dealing harshly with the colonists. The leaders were Lord Rockingham and the great Edmund Burke; Lord Shelburne and Lord Dartmouth fought and argued too.

The snail-like slowness of events, which stretched over a period of ten years (1765–75), must have put a greater strain on the participants than would have a sudden crash like the fall of the Bastille. Even after hostilities began in April 1775, with skirmishes between British troops and Massachusetts militia at Lexington and Concord followed by the first real battle on June 17 at Bunker Hill, it was over a year before the colonies could force themselves to declare independence.

It is hard to comprehend how a revolt which originated as a "squabble about who should pay the bills"[8] evolved into "so momentous an event that characters as unlike as Pitt, George III, Fox, and Adams felt that it was a climacteric in the world's history. . . . Things can never be the same again, they proclaimed with unanimity."[9] In 1976, on the occasion of our Bicentennial Celebration, an Englishman was still asking why "the very natural determination of the Boston grocers not to pay an extra penny for a pound of tea was transformed by the Founding Fathers into a declaration of the Rights of Man which included Life, Liberty and the Pursuit of Happiness. And it was of course for these Rights and these high ideals that the American colonists saw themselves fighting and dying. . . . We need to remember also that these universalist ideals were almost immediately transformed into a very strong nationalism. . . . In fact, the American Revolution had created a new nation with a distinctive political philosophy. How did this national way of political life appear to its founders, and how was it perceived by the Old World looking across the long and dreary expanses of the Atlantic Ocean?"[10]

To answer the first part of this important question: During the hangover period that followed the heady wine of the battle of Bunker Hill, which had been a numerical victory for the Americans, this "national way of political life" looked perfectly terrifying to its founders. The better-educated among them saw the difficulties ahead and the reason for their slowness to proceed was not cowardice, it was an awareness of their appalling weakness.

John Adams had set off for the First Continental Congress with little confidence in himself or in the colleagues he was about to meet. He wrote in his diary: "This will be an assembly of the wisest Men upon the Continent, who are Americans in Principle, i.e., against the Taxations of Americans, by Authority of Parliament. I feel myself unequal to this Business. A more extensive Knowledge of the Realm, the Colonies, and of Commerce, as well as of Law and Policy, is necessary, than I am Master of."[11]

A few days later he took a long, farewell walk through his beloved, stony Massachusetts fields, and his apprehensions increased: "I wander alone, and ponder. I muse, I mope, I ruminate. I am often in Reveries and Brown Studies. The objects before me are too grand and multifarious for my Comprehension. *We have not Men, fit for the Times.*‡ We are deficient in Genius, in Education, in Travel, in Fortune—in every Thing. I feel unutterable Anxiety. God grant us Wisdom, and Fortitude!"[12]

The introspective Adams was even gloomier as he sat in the Second Continental Congress during the following summer. The novelty of the conception of independence still alarmed the moderate members of that body, and their lack of unity was typ-

‡ *Author's emphasis.*

ically demonstrated on June 3, 1775, when two new committees were formed: one to prepare a petition of conciliation to the King; the other to raise money to buy ammunition with which to make war. It was a dispiriting time as the colonists waited for a reply to their last, futile attempt to persuade the British to redress their grievances: the crucial paper known as the Olive Branch Petition.

Benjamin Franklin had worked harder than anyone else to prevent the break. A letter from him to Lord Howe illustrates the pain he felt: "Long did I endeavour, with unfeigned and unwearied Zeal, to preserve from breaking that fine and noble China Vase, the British Empire; for I knew that, being once broken, the separate Parts could not retain even their Shares of the Strength and Value that existed in the Whole, and that a perfect Reunion of those Parts could scarce ever be hoped for. Your Lordship may possibly remember the tears of Joy that wet my Cheek when, at your good Sister's in London, you once gave me the Expectations that a Reconciliation might soon take place."[13]

It was only rarely that Franklin permitted himself so sentimental a letter. He had returned from England in June prepared for the inevitable and had immediately thrown his great heart and his great powers into the cause of independence. During the summer he wrote at length and enthusiastically to friends in Europe describing the perfect state of unanimity in the colonies. In modern history there is no more expert master of propaganda than Benjamin Franklin; even his hoaxes were believed because he wrote so reasonably and convincingly.*

But the jokes had been for a sunnier time. Now his letters were serious ones, addressed to men who had access to high

---

* Signing himself "A Traveller," Franklin wrote, apropos of Parliament's Woolen Act, that superficial readers believed the American sheep gave scarcely any wool at all, not enough for a pair of stockings a year. Whereas the truth was that the tails of American sheep were so laden with wool that each animal trailed behind it a cart or little wagon to support its tail and keep it from dragging on the ground. Catherine Drinker Bowen, The Most Dangerous Man in America, p. 202.

places. For instance, on December 12, 1775, in a graceful letter to a prince of Spain, Don Gabriel de Bourbon, he suggested
an alliance for the benefit of the two countries.[14] The audacity
of proposing that a great power like Spain should ally herself
with the feeble, unarmed American colonies in order that both
together should be strong must have astonished Don Gabriel,
but a cardinal principle of Franklin's diplomacy was that the
weaker the hand, the stronger should be the bluff. He hoped
that his words stressing the strength of purpose of the Americans would be believed, circulated, and discussed abroad. He
was convinced that it was only a question of time before the revolution would begin to pick up an irrevocable momentum.

Thanks to the inconceivable stupidity of the King and his
ministry, the momentum was indeed building. The icy rejection
of the Olive Branch Petition was followed by the passing of an
Act prohibiting all trade and commerce with the Thirteen
Colonies; thus was strangled the last hope of reconciliation.
From now on the Americans were proclaimed rebels. Insult was
added to injury when, following the burning of Falmouth in
October by the British, it was learned that German troops had
been engaged as mercenaries to put down the rebellion. As a result, the unhappy climate of uncertainty that had prevailed
throughout the summer of 1775 in Philadelphia underwent a
remarkable change.

George Washington had written a modest letter to his wife
when he assumed command of the army in June in which he
said that he had used every endeavor in his power to avoid the
appointment, "but as it is a kind of destiny that has thrown me
upon this service, I shall hope that my undertaking is designed
to answer some good purpose."[15]

"A kind of destiny." The Congress sensed what Washington
had meant. There was no sparkling, flashing moment with
trumpets calling a nation to arms, but the delegates were
released from sterile argument into concerted action, and action
was what they understood best.

They were exceptional men, these colonial merchants, doctors, lawyers, country squires. Too few in number for any one of them to afford himself the luxury of specialization, each lent his hand to whatever seemed the paramount concern at the time. Immediately the researcher picks up the accelerated tempo from the record of the late-autumn debates. Gone were the delicious four o'clock dinners that had been generously provided by the beautiful Philadelphia hostesses during earlier sessions. There was now no time for leisurely meals, nor did anyone appear to have regretted them as the brisk winds of late autumn blew through the brick-lined streets of the town. Gone were what John Adams had fretfully referred to as the "nibblings and quibblings" of Congress.[16] They were angry men now, with everything in the world to do at once; and, miraculously, they did it.

John Adams himself was a good example. This forty-year-old lawyer, who knew nothing of armed ships, found himself working from seven in the morning to ten at night on the committee formed to create an American navy; he had not a moment left in his day to write the familiar complaining letters home. At last he was fully engaged, with the wind behind him.

The seventy-year-old Franklin, whose experience as printer, journalist, scientist, and philosopher had not included the study of war, was making a model of a pike for the use of infantrymen. He convinced the Committee of Safety to adopt it. It also occurred to his quick mind that bows and arrows might be a useful innovation for an army that lacked muskets and ammunition; to persuade the Congress of their worth, he quoted eloquently in Latin from Polydore Vergil. His other committees included one to replace the royal postal system with an American post office, another to arrange for the printing of a new currency, and another to organize the manufacture of saltpeter.

One especially interesting committee engaged the attention of Dr. Franklin, who was its leader. It was known as the Committee of Secret Correspondence, and was the forerunner of our modern State Department. It had been formed at the end of November 1775, as the delegates to Congress, groping their way toward independence, perceived that, there being no hope of reconciliation with England, the colonies in their weakness must seek the aid of friendly powers abroad. Besides Franklin, there were four other members: John Dickinson of Pennsylvania, John Jay of New York, Thomas Johnson of Delaware, and Benjamin Harrison of Virginia. Of the group, only Franklin had served in England as colonial agent and so had some knowledge of foreign affairs. The others were provincial novices, wholly ignorant of negotiation beyond the boundaries of their own colonies. But they were remarkably able men, accustomed to swift improvisation as the circumstances demanded. These founders of our country were not proud, nor were they unduly modest in their versatility. If some among them were to be obliged to become diplomats while other colleagues struggled over the manufacture of saltpeter, so be it. They got on with the job. The job of the Committee of Secret Correspondence and what it led to is the story that I shall try to tell.

I have already attempted to answer the first part of the question asked by my English friend quoted above: how did the future look to the men who had been forced to turn what had started as a "squabble about who should pay the bills" into a devastating civil war? To reply to the second part of the question, how was the struggle "perceived by the Old World looking across the long and dreary expanses of the Atlantic Ocean?" the story must begin in France.

🌿 I 🌿

Paris and Versailles

THE FRENCH, led by their philosophers, had early adopted the American cause with enthusiasm. Never had there been such a multitude of "philosophes" as in the eighteenth century. La Mettrie, Voltaire, Diderot, d'Alembert, Grimm, Helvétius, Holbach, Rousseau were some of the most famous names, but there were many others.

They must not be thought of as living in ivory towers, talking to each other in abstruse language. Metaphysics and systems of philosophy seemed to them useless. They left the schools behind them and came into the social arena, writing clearly so that any educated man could understand them. Far from being heavy, their works were often diverting; they took the form of novels, short, pungent essays, witty dialogues. Boldly they evaded the heavy censorship of the times and, if they could not publish in France, they published in Holland or, as in the case of Voltaire, sometimes wrote under another name. They admired the practical sciences and to them mathematics, physiology, chemistry, physics, and astronomy were as much a part of philosophy as abstract thought.

Bursting with vitality, they were a potent social force; their political thinking was imbued with confidence and hope. While they differed on the means, their common doctrine was a belief in the perfectibility of man, *provided* that he learned to exchange reason for superstition.

No more stirring example of courageous optimism exists than in the backbreaking work of the editors and writers who attempted to harness all human wisdom within the massive volumes of the *Encyclopédie,* which began to be published in 1751 by Diderot and d'Alembert. Man was by nature good, wrote the authors, and capable of achieving happiness once ignorance and false theory were abandoned. The contributors were a galaxy of the most brilliant men in France, working as a team. "There were Turgot and Montesquieu on politics and history; Rousseau on music; Buffon on natural history; Marmontel on comedy; Quesnay on agriculture; and Holbach on chemistry. Condorcet and Voltaire contributed occasional articles. . . . The theme was that the universal aim was happiness, guided and controlled by reason."[1]

Church and State rose together to harass the Encyclopédistes for their irreverence and their anti-clericalism, but they plunged on, volume after volume, to the plaudits of the Paris salons and of their admirers who bought pirated editions in Switzerland and spread them throughout Europe.

It was a marvelous, ebullient, effervescent time, but by the early 1770's the endemic French craving for novelty began to rise to the surface. The French were a little weary of eloquence, a little impatient of the lack of practical results after a half century of assurances that reasonable men could achieve happiness. Where was this happiness? The new reign of the young Louis XVI had opened as a golden age, but in day-to-day life the French found themselves as frustrated as before, tied and bound by the inequalities and injustices of their outdated system. Would the promises of the philosophies never be fulfilled? They longed for something concrete and tangible to adore.

Miraculously, they found it in an astonishing phenomenon across the Atlantic. Book after book about America began pouring off the presses in the 1770's. One of the most popular was that of the Abbé Raynal, whose highly inaccurate work went into eighteen editions.[2] The good Abbé seized the reader's imagination with descriptions of a marvelous New World, peopled with inhabitants who were happy, tolerant, simple, and reasonable; philosophers to a man. To make this idyllic state sound plausible, he added page after page of impressive facts and statistics, and no one could argue with them as no one had verified his facts. Raynal was perfectly trusted as he wrote of the customs of this western Utopia. For instance, he spoke of the complete religious tolerance in the colonies, while actually religious tolerance was observed only in Pennsylvania and Rhode Island (1770–74).

Little sentimental anecdotes made his picture all the more believable, as small human stories are always what people remember best about history, and the saintly Abbé had a stock of them. There had been Polly Baker, for example, a poor girl who was accused and convicted of having had six illegitimate children in Puritan New England. The court which tried her was so touched by her honesty and simplicity that they let her off with a blessing and wished her well. From this moving tale Raynal drew impressive conclusions about the generous humanitarianism of the New England jury system. It brought tears to the eyes of the readers and deeply embarrassed Benjamin Franklin, who met Raynal later in Paris and felt obliged to confess to him that there never had been such a person as Polly Baker. He, Franklin, had invented her when, as a young journalist, he found himself desperate for copy. The Abbé exclaimed with a laugh, "Oh, very well, Doctor, I had rather relate your stories than other men's truths."

The abbés were prolific; never was penned a more controversial case for the remarkable flora and fauna of America than that of the Abbé De Pauw.[3] The great French naturalist Georges de Buffon took the trouble to contradict what seemed to him the outrageous inaccuracies in De Pauw's popular and picturesque work but, as neither author had the evidence on which to confirm or deny their respective claims, Buffon generously gave up the argument, stating that probably De Pauw had mixed up the continents of North and South America, as anyone might.

Besides the books, the newspapers were full of stories about

America. A model educational system "à la Rousseau" was described; the Quakers were praised to the skies for having freed their slaves, and the newly founded American Philosophical Society was said to offer corrupt and futile Europe a moral lesson with its plain and practical wisdom. Even the official papers glorified the colonies. On April 4, 1775, the most important newspaper in Paris, the *Gazette de France*, ran a singular article based on the observations of navigators who knew North America. It appeared that an innate love of liberty exuded from the very soil, the sky, the lakes, and the forests of the vast continent, and the climate made this emotion as contagious as might be fever rising from a swamp. A European had only to be transported there in order to alter his convictions and become a new and better man.

There was nothing that the French, in their euphoria, would not believe about this Utopian state, and the best of it was that it had all been imagined and described by their own writers, so that they could take an almost possessive pride in the achievement of the dream. For the sentimentalists, who had grown weary of the rationalism of the midcentury, the American Indian provided an ideal example of Rousseau's Noble Savage theory, i.e., that men are born innocent and good and become depraved by civilization.

The enthusiasm filtered down from the educated classes to the man in the street, and was redoubled by news of the oppression of the colonists by their English masters. Lexington and Concord were hailed as victories so important that they might as well have been great battles, instead of skirmishes, and they were reported not only by the Paris press but by newspapers as far away as the *Courrier d'Avignon* and the *Gazette de Leyde*. Marseilles, in particular, became a hotbed of pro-American sentiment; by 1776 a club was founded there at which the members met monthly to discuss news from the colonies and to study the virtues of the institutions of the "insurgents."*

* *The name "insurgents," first used by the* Gazette de France *in preference to* "rebels," *soon became part of the language.*

This wave of emotional sympathy was canalized and focused for the benefit of America by the resolute statesman who had been called to Versailles to advise the twenty-year-old Louis XVI: Charles Gravier, Comte de Vergennes. No one was less sentimental about the colonies than this Foreign Minister; Thomas Jefferson, who later knew him well, wrote from Paris to James Madison in 1784: "He is a great minister in European affairs, but has very imperfect ideas of our institutions, and no confidence in them. His devotion to the principles of pure despotism renders him unaffectionate to our government. But his fear of England makes him value us as a make-weight. He is cool, reserved in political conversations but free and familiar on other subjects, and a very attentive, agreeable person to do business with."[4]

Jefferson was perfectly correct; Vergennes cared nothing for the cause of American liberty, but was implacably dedicated to another cause: that of redressing the balance of power. The humiliating peace imposed on France by the British in 1763 following the Seven Years' War was a source of bitter resentment to this proud Frenchman. He understood the importance of propaganda quite as well as Franklin did. The pro-American articles in the official *Gazette de France* were directly inspired by him, although he would have been revolted by the sentimentality of them. It is easy to imagine his disgust as he read the pieces about the Noble Savage. Like Dr. Johnson, who snubbed Boswell sharply when he raved about the islanders of the South Seas ("don't cant in defence of savages"),[5] he would have been immensely irritated by Rousseau's contention that primitive man was more virtuous than civilized man. Vergennes believed in civilization.

However, anything was grist to the mill of this diplomat turned propagandist. Knowing that he had very little time ahead of him, he tossed fuel on the flame of public opinion and let the fire blaze as he turned his attention to the difficult task of convincing the King and the Cabinet of the wisdom of his American policy.

The King had come to power on May 10, 1774, replacing a grandfather who had left him the task of governing a great nation whose people were the most discontented in all Europe. He read an interestingly self-critical line in Louis XV's will: "I have governed and administered badly, which is due partly to my own lack of skill and partly because I have been badly advised."[6] This surprising confession must have seemed to the new King almost an order to replace the ministers who remained from the preceding reign.

A lonely young man, the monarch had been left an orphan at an early age and brought up by a governor whom he loathed. His only companions had been two younger brothers. They hardly troubled to conceal their jealousy of his position and their contempt for his awkward, shy ways. His confidence was further eroded by his inability to consummate his marriage to a beautiful and glamorous young princess; a failure that was known throughout France. It was a period of scurrilous verses, and the cruelty of the jokes about the supposed impotence of Louis XVI was as humiliating as the well-meaning act of an abbé who publicly threw himself across the King's path as he left the royal chapel, begging to be allowed to teach his ruler certain remedies which would increase the chance of procreation.

He was horribly inhibited in his relations with his wife. Who was there in the family to offer him affection and advice? The closest adult relatives near him were his maiden aunts, Mesdames Victoire, Sophie, Adélaïde, and Louise. These ladies lived in spinsterly splendor (with the exception of Madame Louise, who became a Carmelite nun) in the palace of Versailles, which had been torn apart to make apartments that they considered fitting for them. Cross, bigoted, and suspicious, the aunts, nevertheless, were fond of their nephew and, when he went to see them for advice two days into his reign, they were delighted to help him.[7]

Madame Adélaïde, the most powerful of the four, produced from the recesses of her musty treasures a very important document indeed: a list made by her brother, the Dauphin, father of

Louis XVI, of the names of the men he trusted to help his son when in time he should come to the throne. To the King, this list from the other side of the grave was sacrosanct, and it was from it that he formed his new Cabinet. Having had their day, the aunts disappeared from French history forever, regretted, it is feared, by no one.

As the King deliberated, the courtiers and ex-ministers held their breaths. One of them, the Prince de Montbarey, wrote in his memoirs, "Quivering and vibrating, the whole Court waited, their agitation mixed with fear, to see which direction the King would take."[8] They did not have long to wait. That very night, May 12, a messenger was sent to summon the Comte de Maurepas from his exile at Pontchartrain. He was named Minister of State, roughly equivalent to Prime Minister today. It was an excellent choice.

Maurepas was a wise old bureaucrat of seventy-four, the descendant of a long line of public servants. He counted nine ministers among his ancestors. Having served Louis XV, in the family tradition, as Minister of the Navy, he had lost his position due to a bitter feud with Madame de Pompadour and had been living with his wife in the country, comfortably off but without children. It was said that he too was impotent, but about whom was there not malicious gossip? Everyone agreed that they were a happy pair, and that Maurepas was still one of the most amusing men in France. He was known as "le charmeur." A small man, he carried himself with dignity and seemed instantly at home in whatever circumstances he found himself.

The Prince de Montbarey noted that Maurepas hadn't been back at Versailles for fifteen minutes before one felt that he had never left his chair.[9] There is something reassuring about the sound of the ménage; he with his jokes and his vast experience, she with the comfortable ways of a housekeeper of the grande bourgeoisie, devoted to her husband and her cat. Unfortunately, the cat was soon shot by the King, who had the habit of wandering about the terrace of Versailles on moonlit nights shooting

stray cats. He felt very badly about this accident. It may even have drawn him closer to the Maurepas', whom he soon installed in the apartments directly above his own. They had formerly belonged to Madame Du Barry, the last mistress of Louis XV, and were connected with the King's suite by an inner staircase.

Lovely, cozy rooms they were; up in the attics with low ceilings and deeply embrasured dormer windows that seemed to invite a guest to pull up an armchair or a pile of cushions in order to watch the milling scene in the courtyard below. Only in the library was the paneling gilded. The other rooms were painted by the Martin family, whose skill as decorators has never been equaled. The effects they created were so artless that they appeared to have sprung from the paintbox of a talented child. Into a polychrome door panel went dozens of green and blue tones; and a delicate little lacquered wreath of wildflowers crowning a small overmantel could require up to forty layers of varnish and three months' work. From this charming eyrie the Mentor, as Maurepas was soon called, would descend several times a day to advise his pupil.

The great Duc de Choiseul, former Minister of Foreign Affairs, fully expected to be summoned again; it was he, after all, who had made the Austrian alliance which culminated in the marriage to Marie Antoinette, and he was still a popular figure. When he entered the Cour de Marbre at Versailles to see the King, his carriage was full of flowers flung to him by the fishwives of Paris, much to the irritation of Louis XVI, who met him with one icy sentence: "Well, Monsieur de Choiseul, I see that you have lost a great deal of hair since we last met." Then he turned on his heel and the disappointed statesman, knowing that he had met defeat, ordered his coachman to be ready to take the road the next morning at six for Chanteloup, his estate in Touraine. On the magnificent property was the seven-story Chinese pagoda that the Duke had built during his banishment. Between 1770 and 1773 he had engraved on its walls the names of 210 of the faithful who came to see him, all distinguished persons. The names of his more humble visitors were not recorded on this monument to Choiseul's enduring popularity.

It is hard to think of a more dangerous man to have had in opposition to the new reign than the Duc de Choiseul; besides which the decision went entirely against the wishes of Marie Antoinette, something which her husband almost never did in regard to appointments. But on the sacred list entrusted by Louis XVI's father to Madame Adélaïde, another name had been written beside the title of Minister of Foreign Affairs. For this position, the Dauphin had recommended the comparatively unknown, unglamorous professional diplomat, the Comte de Vergennes.

No greater contrast to the Duc de Choiseul can be imagined. That "grand seigneur" had all the dash and style that the eighteenth-century French expected and admired in the great officers of state that surrounded the throne. A clever man, he also possessed enormous experience of the world. Choiseul would probably have been an energetic and effective minister had he come to office in 1774, for he was eager to overcome the failure of his earlier policy which had led to the disastrous Seven Years' War.

Yet Vergennes, whose conversation was heavy, whose jokes were few, whose middle-class features and corpulent fifty-five-year-old form lacked any semblance of grace, was a great Foreign Minister. Underestimated in his own country, he is hardly known in the United States of America, whose debt to him is immeasurable. He was a human and affectionate man and a shrewd judge of character. Maurepas and he were not intimate, but each closely observed the monarch and both developed a genuine affection, paternal in nature, for him who they saw was trying desperately to do his best.

When Louis XVI succeeded to the tarnished throne of his grandfather, his greatest desire was to govern according to the wishes of his people. A hard-working, serious young man, he read with care the papers that were given to him by his ministers and, even though he saw Maurepas and Vergennes every day, he found time to keep up a voluminous correspondence with them. Nothing could be more erroneous than to imagine the King always out hunting or working on locks in his carpentry shop.

Chroniclers of the Court of Versailles have written much of the *lever* or ceremonial rising of the sovereign from his canopied bed in the morning, assisted by his officers of state, each with his appointed task of handing the King one of his rich garments. This absurd procedure did take place, just as it always had since the days of Louis XIV, usually at eleven-thirty or even later in the morning. But the monarch was not lolling about until the procession of courtiers arrived at his bedchamber. In fact, the King got up between six and eight, donned a plain suit, often gray, and set to work in his office. If the Queen happened to be at the Trianon, which she grew to love so much, he would walk across the park to breakfast with her; a hasty meal before return- ing to his papers and his ministers, from which he would turn wearily to the silly business of going back to bed and suffering the tedium of the traditional *lever*.

Then, magnificently dressed in a brilliantly embroidered suit, ornamented with the diamond star of the Saint-Esprit, he would lumber on his way to join the Queen and her ladies in the Galerie des Glaces, that awe-inspiring room which runs across the endless western façade of the palace. The graceful Marie Antoinette was admired by all as she glided across the shining floor to meet him, but he looked to an observer "like a peasant slouching along behind his plow. Nothing whatever grand or royal in his bearing. He made awkward signs with his head from right to left, speaking to a few ladies whom he knew, but never to young ones. He was so shortsighted that he couldn't recognize anyone three feet away, and was further handicapped by not seeming to know what to do with his sword."[10]

To the French people, this clumsiness was not apparent. They adored their young sovereigns; and the early years of the reign were a halcyon time, full of hope and promise. Crowds lined the streets, cheering wildly, as the richly ornamented car- riage crossed Paris, bearing the smiling couple, dressed in white.

The populace could not have guessed how alone the King was as he prepared himself for his first major policy decision: the American question. He had been secretive since he was a boy. Discussion of state affairs with the Queen was impossible, not only because they did not interest her but because, like the good daughter that she was, she obeyed the orders of her formidable mother in Vienna implicitly and saw the Austrian Ambassador, Count Mercy-Argenteau, every day. The King knew that this shrewd diplomat conveyed to Empress Maria Theresa every thought that went through the Queen's head, every item of news that she had gathered, and had implanted in the butterfly mind the importance of her mother's orders: "To be a good Queen of France, my daughter, you must be a good German." So the King's private correspondence with Vergennes and Maurepas was filed away in a secret place with his own hands after he had read them; the information they contained was for him alone.

The Comte de la Vauguyon, Louis XVI's governor, had been ordered by the Dauphin to erase any sense of pride and arrogance that he might develop as the heir to the throne. Unfortunately this hard and tactless tutor thoroughly succeeded in destroying whatever self-confidence his pupil might have possessed. Yet, like many insecure people, he was capable of fits of obstinacy, digging in his heels with mulish stubbornness. Vergennes, observing him closely, perceived the answer to the central problem of dealing with his confused, unhappy master.

While, on the one hand, the King did not have the confidence to make his own decisions, on the other he resented having his prerogative preempted. It was all-important to him that the world should have the impression that the final decision had been his alone. Once this was believed, *above all by himself,* he could be as courageous as he was tenacious.† This crucial psychological point has confused some scholars to this day who

† *General de Gaulle put it well, but it is hard to translate his subtle observation:* "Louis XVI n'avait pas la passion du pouvoir, mais il avait la jalousie de la décision."

claim that it is to the King, not to Vergennes, that the United States owes her debt. Unquestionably Louis XVI must be recognized for his valor, for once he had been shown the road, he stayed the course, which was not an easy one.

Versailles and Philadelphia

THE COMTE DE VERGENNES was a man of equable temper who adored his fat, unfashionable wife, was devoted to his two sons, got on well with his colleagues, and, in general, liked and trusted his subordinates. But the Comte de Guines, French Ambassador to the Court of St. James's, he detested. Guines owed his high diplomatic post to Marie Antoinette. The Queen was not interested in foreign policy, but she liked helping her favorites and Guines made her laugh. Once, when she was recovering from the measles and obliged to seclude herself at the Petit Trianon for fear of infecting the King, she asked for permission to have a merry band of attractive men to serve her as entertainers during the dull weeks that lay ahead. Louis XVI, evidently feeling that there was safety in numbers, agreed cheerfully enough. Guines was one of the chosen companions.

Guines was very much the dandy, despite his enormous girth. At Versailles his wardrobe included two pairs of breeches, one for the days when he would have to sit down and one, much tighter, for the days when he would remain standing. "In the morning, before helping him to dress, his valet would ask, 'Will Monsieur be sitting down today?' The Duc de Lévis recounts, 'When he was to remain standing, he climbed onto two chairs and descended into his breeches, which were held up by two of his servants.'"[1]

Everything about him was anathema to that very professional diplomat, Vergennes.[2] For one thing, while in London as ambassador, he was involved in some distinctly shady financial speculations and his affair with the English beauty Lady Craven was notorious even by the easy standards of eighteenth-century society. But the minister, unable to touch Guines while the Queen protected him, was obliged to content himself with making an occasional snubbing comment in his private letters to the King. "It appears to me that to be an ambassador is not his vocation," he wrote on January 31, 1776.[3]

More important than Guines's private life was the unevenness of his political reporting. Although not stupid, he possessed the defect of being overly impressed by the opinion of the last man he had talked to; an evening with one of the Tory ministers could produce a jeremiad about the invincible strength of the British forces in America, just as the Whig opposition could persuade him two days later of the exact contrary. His dispatches seemed so emotional[4] to Vergennes that the King and he grew to depend increasingly on the brilliantly written letters of their secret agent in London, Caron de Beaumarchais. These were consistently optimistic and interventionist. Vergennes, however, knew that they were not unbiased, as Beaumarchais was influenced by his greatest English friend, the pro-American Whig leader John Wilkes.

Much as he loathed Guines, Vergennes would have considered it his duty to pore over his dispatches line by line. The embassy was after all his official source of intelligence for American affairs. During the reign of Louis XV it had been routine for his Minister of Foreign Affairs, the Duc de Choiseul, to send French agents to America in order to keep Versailles in touch with the situation in the colonies, but the custom had fallen into disuse. As the year 1775 progressed, the question of France's role in the gathering storm across the Atlantic became a critical policy issue. Consequently, both Vergennes and the London embassy were in agreement on the necessity of sending someone across the ocean to test the temper of the Americans on the spot.

Who but the fatuous Guines should suggest the very fellow? Vergennes must have almost forgiven the ambassador his revoltingly tight breeches as he read his competent letter. The proposed agent was called the Chevalier Julien Achard de Bonvouloir and, wrote Guines enthusiastically, he not only was a gentleman and a retired officer of the well-known Régiment du Cap, but he had just returned from America, where he had excellent sources of intelligence in Philadelphia, New York, Boston, Providence, "and Rhod-Island." Guines even knew all about his family; his cousin was the Marquis de Lambert and his two estimable brothers were both distinguished officers in the French army. What luck to have found this trustworthy man who was both willing and anxious to show his zeal by going back to the colonies. Unfortunately, he was lame as the result of a childhood accident, but quite up to doing what was necessary.

Very pleased with himself, the smug ambassador signed off and sat back in his large, gilded armchair to await orders. The orders to go ahead came from Versailles with amazing speed for those days, especially in view of Vergennes's heavy burden of work. To the dispatch from London written July 28, the minister replied on August 7; and one must count at least five days for the diplomatic courier to have traveled from England. Evidently the matter of obtaining intelligence from America had assumed the highest priority, for Vergennes in his letter referred to the King in terms that showed he had not just been consulted pro forma but had taken an active part in the decision.[5] Vergennes began the letter by saying that he had looked up Bonvouloir and could find no record of his having served in the Régiment du Cap but, despite this discrepancy, he would accept him as an agent and was enclosing what Guines had requested: a commission in the infantry and a gracious message from the King expressing his gratitude to the officer for undertaking this service for his country. The suggested salary of 200 livres was also agreeable to the ministry.

It seems astonishing that so prudent a man as Vergennes

should have entrusted a delicate assignment to an agent about whom he knew almost nothing, but Frenchmen familiar with the colonies were rare in 1775 and he was in enough of a hurry to take what he could get. That he considered the matter important is unquestionable, for his correspondence with Guines over the details comprises nine letters. The instructions were clear and icy cold. Above all, the spy was to understand that he could compromise no one but himself. Should he get into trouble, he would not receive the slightest help from the French government. He was not to carry any written instructions, nor was he to present himself as an official emissary. In conversation with the American leaders, he was to follow his verbal orders exactly: (1) he must obtain the maximum amount of intelligence on the state of affairs, (2) he was to assure them of the profound sympathy of France for their cause and to make it clear that the French had no intention of interfering in Canada, and (3) he was to offer them the use of French ports for their ships once they had attained independence. On completion of his task, a full report must be dispatched with celerity and with the utmost precaution to ensure its security.

Guines replied with another unctuous letter, attempting to justify his choice of Bonvouloir. He really had been in the Régiment du Cap, as a volunteer. Unfortunately, later he had wasted his share of the family fortune and caused his excellent brothers great concern; however, in spite of his faults, they were still devoted to him. After all, it was only "this class of man" who could be expected to agree to take such a risk; and it had been really touching to see the spy's face when he received the King's message of thanks. He had been quite overcome with gratitude.

No doubt Julien de Bonvouloir was grateful for the King's message, and for the 200 livres, although it was a meager wage for such an assignment. A good Paris chef received 1,500 livres a year in 1775; and the Queen had, that same winter, called the 250,000 livres she paid a Paris jeweler for a pair of bracelets a trifle.[6] But it seems likely that his joyful countenance was primarily prompted by what he had in his pocket: an honor he had always wanted, a commission as an officer of the French army. He was the black sheep of a family of the minor nobility who had served the King since an Achard de Bonvouloir had marched with Charles Martel to beat back the Moorish invaders at Poitiers in 732. Badly educated, physically handicapped, scorned by his father, at twenty-six Bonvouloir was now given the opportunity of his life.[7]

A hundred days later, following a horrendous voyage, Bonvouloir landed in Philadelphia and rushed to his contact, Francis Daymon. French-born Daymon, as librarian of the "Library Company" founded in 1731 by Franklin and a group of his friends, was a respected figure in Philadelphia. He had just been named Secretary of the Continental Congress when Bonvouloir arrived, introducing himself as a French officer on sick leave anxious to serve the American cause. Within a few days, thanks to some words whispered in the ear of Dr. Franklin by Daymon, Bonvouloir was occupying the time and attention of the five members of a most important committee of the Congress: the Committee of Secret Correspondence.*

There was every reason for the busy and harassed delegates to receive the shabby stranger. Their committee had just been formed on November 29 "for the sole purpose of corresponding with our friends in Great Britain, Ireland and other parts of the world." Such were the rather grand instructions of Congress. But who were the friends who would wish to correspond with the faraway, weak, rebellious American colonists? The Whigs in England sympathized, but their party was out of power. Franklin, resourceful as always, had written to his well-informed friend at The Hague, Charles Dumas, to ask his advice as to

---

* The committee kept this name until April 17, 1777, when it was officially renamed the Committee for Foreign Affairs. It was often referred to as the "Secret Committee," which is incorrect. The committee, appointed in 1775 to import gunpowder, was known as the Secret Committee because this importation had to be done clandestinely. There is a good deal of confusion about the two committees. Robert Morris and Arthur Lee were very imprecise when referring to them, as are the Deane Papers and the Revolutionary Diplomatic Correspondence.

which, if any, Court represented in that capital might consider assistance or alliance. But it would take some time for even the helpful Dumas to assess the situation and to reply to the appeal, and time was in short supply.

During the autumn various adventurers from the French West Indies had appeared in Philadelphia to offer their services to the small American army, but a handful of untrained volunteers was of little interest to men who were tossing in their beds at night as they estimated the dwindling supply of saltpeter in their arsenals or, like Benjamin Franklin, calculated the chances of pitting bows and arrows against British cannons.

Massive help was needed, and at once, now that America was cut off from its normal supplier, the mother country. France and Spain were the traditional enemies of England, so it was natural for the colonists to pin their hopes on these two powers, but they lived in agonizing uncertainty about the intentions of Paris and Madrid.

As it turned out, it was to be France that would save the United States from defeat at the hands of Great Britain. Unquestionably, the War of Independence would have been lost by 1778 without French aid. The fine epic glows with famous French names of which Lafayette's is the best known. Who has heard of the Chevalier de Bonvouloir? Yet it was his humble mission that launched American diplomatic history.

Bonvouloir's three meetings with the committee took place at Carpenter's Hall between December 18 and 28, 1775, with Francis Daymon acting as interpreter. It was the committee's first confrontation with a foreign agent and what transpired was, and remained, truly secret. "At our night time meetings," wrote the agent in his report, "each one of them took a different route through the darkness to the indicated rendezvous."[8] For the Americans, there must have been a schoolboy cloak-and-dagger thrill about stealing through the dark streets of Philadelphia on a winter night to meet with a mysterious stranger. Later, Franklin was asked by a suspicious Rhode Islander if it was true that there had been meetings with a French envoy that winter.

He replied, with a splendid example of the Franklinian diplomatic style, as innocent as it was bland: "How could such a Thing be before Independency was declared?"[9]

Due to the clandestine nature of their business, none of the Americans present left a record of his impressions of the agent at the time, but many years later, John Jay described him to his son William as "an elderly lame gentleman, having the appearance of an old, wounded French officer." Curious that he should have said this, for Jay was just thirty at the time of the meetings, and Bonvouloir was only twenty-six. But the recollection was that of a very old man. What is important is that, despite the shabby, worn appearance that he presented, at his climacteric moment of his hitherto unsuccessful life, Julien Achard de Bonvouloir showed resourcefulness and skill. He must have had presence also, for the members of the committee hung on his words.

He introduced himself as a French officer, passionate for the colonial cause. While he spoke purely as a private citizen, he had just come from Europe, where he had certain high-placed friends to whom he felt it his duty to report any requests that the Congress might care to make of them.

The Americans, led by Benjamin Franklin, received this ambiguous introduction with straight faces, and proceeded to provide "the private citizen" with all the intelligence that a foreign government might want to know. In return they had some questions of their own:

> *Monsieur de Bonvouloir is begged to examine the following proposition, under the understanding that we are speaking as private individuals to each other:*
>
> 1. *Can he tell us what the views of the Court of France are in regard to the North American colonies? Are they favorable, and if so, how can we obtain official confirmation of this?*
>
> 2. *Could we find in France two competent engineer officers, well recommended and reliable? What steps should we take to obtain them?*

3. *May we obtain from France arms and other necessary munitions of war in exchange for the products of our country? And may we have free entry into the French ports?*

Bonvouloir, in his answers, stuck exactly to his instructions, with one exception: he said that he did indeed think that it would be possible to send over French engineer officers, possibly many more than the two for which the committee had asked. This must have greatly encouraged the committee, for General Washington was desperate for engineers.

Throughout the three long evenings of conversation, the Americans were flattering to the envoy. The compliments that were rained on him may have been the first that he had ever received. It must have been almost irresistible to offer more than the careful hints of future help that he had been told to extend. But, pressed by Benjamin Franklin as to the possibility of a treaty of alliance, defensive and offensive, between the two countries, Bonvouloir backed off sharply, while employing deferential and sympathetic words. The temptation to please the great man might well have seduced a more sophisticated negotiator. It was an astonishingly competent performance for the black sheep of the Achard de Bonvouloir family.

The interviews were concluded on December 27. The practical result on the American side was that it was clear to the Committee of Secret Correspondence that France was behind them and that no time must be lost in dispatching an official envoy to Paris in order to expedite the desperately needed aid.

On the French side, the result was dramatic. Bonvouloir wrote his report in haste, forgetting the orders Guines had given him to pen the secret parts in milk. There are almost no crossings cut or signs of rewriting in the long, poorly written document—just the mark of the hot shovel which the irritated Guines must have attempted to apply to what he had expected to be milk.[10] To carry his report, Bonvouloir found a trusted Frenchman who was sailing immediately for Calais, where he promised to deliver the paper to Guines's agent there for transmission to the London embassy.

Bonvouloir returned from the port with a light heart. Having handed his precious envelope to his friend aboard the *Saint-Jean* weighing anchor for France, he settled down to wait at the house of his fellow countryman the sieur Legros, calculating that in three or four months he would receive a reply from the Court of France. He would not have been human if he had not hoped for some lines of praise and thanks for a mission accomplished. He waited in vain.

The *Saint-Jean* made a safe and rapid crossing, and the dispatch was handed to the Comte de Guines at Calais as he passed through on his return from London to Paris. From Bonvouloir's point of view the timing was most unfortunate, for the ambassador had just made an incredibly stupid diplomatic gaffe in London. Interfering in matters that were not his business, he had informed his colleague the Spanish Ambassador to London that, in case of war between Spain and Portugal, France would stand aside, thereby abrogating her sacred treaty obligations to Louis XVI's uncle, the King of Spain. Of course, the Spanish Court let out a howl of protest and Vergennes, springing like a jaguar, advised the King of France that Guines must be recalled at once.

When the dispatch from America was handed to him at Calais, the once fashionable ambassador was on his way to banishment. *Disgrâces*, as the French called banishments, fill the pages of eighteenth-century memoirs and are written up dramatically:

"On hearing of his *disgrâce* the Duke, who is religious, behaved with Christian submission; when they went to tell the Duchess she thought, from their faces, that her son must have died."[11]

Let it not be thought that *disgrâce* sent the victims to die under a torrid sun in some faraway spot like Devil's Island, the notorious penal colony. In the eighteenth century it meant banishment to the provincial estates of the noble in question, as far away from Paris as possible. Louis XIV had been terrified by the civil war of the preceding century known as the Fronde. His policy was to defang future nobles by chaining them to his side at Versailles. Robbed of real power, they were given pretentious titles and handsomely paid positions which were meaningless. There was even a department especially established for their entertainment. Known as the Menus-Plaisirs, it arranged fêtes and balls and theatricals which were the most sumptuous in history. Only the many minor noble families, like the Achard de Bonvouloirs, lived permanently in the provinces, but they were poor and without influence.

Louis XIV's successful policy had played on the French love of fashion. Versailles was the center of the world, with Paris amusing as a change. Life in the provinces was dowdy and dull —out of the question. "Living in their beautiful houses in the beautiful French countryside, with the administration of huge estates to interest them, these exiled nobles were considered, and considered themselves, as dead.† In fact, they generally became either very fat or very thin, and departed life rather quickly."[12]

Such was the gloomy prospect before the ex-ambassador as he embarked on the endless drive from Calais. His coach had six horses with eighteen others waiting for him at relay stations. It is unlikely that he thought very much about his servants, sitting up front on seats that had no springs, instead were simply boards laid across wooden struts. For them such a journey was infinitely more exhausting than riding horseback would have been, yet they dared not complain as Guines pressed on, annoyed if the courier riding half an hour ahead failed in his duty, which was to make arrangements at an inn for the night. Two other couriers rode beside the coach and were responsible for the safety of the master.

As soon as he reached Paris, Guines sent Bonvouloir's report

† *The Duc and Duchesse de Choiseul might be considered an exception to the rule after their banishment to Chanteloup, for they remained popular in their exile. But Choiseul longed for another job, and was deeply disappointed by the King's choice of Vergennes as Minister of Foreign Affairs. (See Chapter I.)*

to Vergennes. He was either too tired or too angry with the Minister of Foreign Affairs to bother to redraft it before handing it over as he had promised Bonvouloir he would. However, he was intelligent and patriotic enough to appreciate the importance of the badly written document. He accompanied it with long commentaries of his own and added a warmly phrased paragraph suggesting that the agent had done very well. Unable, because of his rage with Vergennes, to sign off according to the usual formula, "I am your very humble and obedient servant," etc., he did not sign it at all. Vergennes received the report on February 27, 1776. He read black-and-white confirmation of what until now had only been suppositions and hopes.

"Everyone here is a soldier, the troops are well-clothed, well-paid, and well-armed. They have more than 50,000 regular soldiers‡ and an even larger number of volunteers who do not wish to be paid. Judge how men of this caliber will fight. They are more powerful than we could have thought, beyond imagination powerful, you will be astonished by it. Nothing shocks or frightens them, you can count on that. Independency is a certainty for 1776, there will be no drawing back. . . ."

Where did Bonvouloir get his inflated figures on the strength of Washington's army? Possibly from the enthusiastic Daymon, possibly from having misunderstood the fast-spoken English of the members of the Committee of Secret Correspondence. It doesn't matter. What was critical was the effect of his optimistic intelligence on Vergennes. By coincidence, within three days of receiving it, the minister was in possession of a memorandum to the King from the agent in London, Beaumarchais. Beaumarchais's paper, known to history as "La Paix ou la Guerre," was an impassioned plea for support of the Americans written by an alchemist with words. By contrast, Bonvouloir's effort was a clumsy one from the literary point of view. Perhaps its very simplicity and honesty had its own impact.

‡ *"Washington's army reached its first peak of strength with 18,000 in the summer of 1776. It fell to 5,000 by the end of the year, rose to a little more than 20,000 in mid-1778, and then declined." Douglas Southall Freeman,* George Washington, *Vol. IV, p. 622.*

In any case, the two documents taken together precipitated events, for two crucial state papers were drawn up by Vergennes for presentation to the King and the Cabinet. Known as the "Reflections" and the "Considerations," their effect on the divided Cabinet and the young King was tremendous. Beaumarchais's influence and brilliance were then, and were to continue to be, an essential contribution to the great debate that took place over the question of supplying clandestine aid to the colonies at the risk of war with England, but Bonvouloir's arguments and his statistics on the strength of the Americans were quoted word for word by Vergennes in his famous "Reflections."

He had arrived at a chilling conclusion with regard to England's foreign policy: "England is the natural enemy of France; and she is an avid enemy, ambitious, unjust, brimming with bad faith: the permanent and cherished object of her policy is the humiliation and ruin of France."[13] This was what Vergennes had been saying privately for years. His first memorandum to the King, written in December 1774, had throbbed with rage at the humiliation of France in 1763, and he was known to have said to a friend, "I tremble, I shake, I even turn purple at the very thought of England."

It is a sad footnote to history that Bonvouloir never knew that his report had been read, let alone had affected French history. His seventeen despairing letters to Guines from America went unanswered and he died of fever in India at the age of thirty-four. His brothers' children and their descendants were brought up in the belief that he had been a worthless uncle. Does he deserve more? Certainly not if the measure is endurance. But in the dim candlelight of Carpenter's Hall in December 1775, Julien-Alexandre Achard de Bonvouloir flew like the firefly which has its one moment before it is consumed by the flame. It would be a pity were he to be forgotten.

The Comte de Guines was not banished to a melancholy existence on his remote estates, there to grow thin and finally die of boredom. Thanks to Marie Antoinette he was made a duke, thus jumping two rungs on the ladder of nobility and prestige.

Immensely rich, he kept up a fine house in Paris as well as an establishment at Versailles, and later married his daughter to the heir of one of the greatest houses of France.

What the Comte de Vergennes felt about this is not recorded, but in the early spring of 1776 he had other things on his mind. He requested the King to summon the senior members of the government for what today would be called an emergency session to discuss assistance to the colonies. The essence of his thinking can be condensed to a few lines: The American rebels had determined to persist in their struggle but, without French support, they would fail, for the English were decided to prevent their independence at no matter what cost. As it was the duty of France to weaken the venomous power of England whenever the occasion presented itself, so the cause of American independence must be favored. France would gain both politically and commercially.

The ministers who filed into the Cabinet de Conseil, as the Cabinet Room was called at Versailles, were Maurepas; Vergennes; Anne-Robert Jacques Turgot, Comptroller of Finances; the Comte de Sartine, Minister of the Navy; and the Comte de Saint-Germain, Minister of War.

The Council Chamber lay immediately next to the King's state apartments, overlooking the Cour de Marbre. Louis XVI had only to open the door from his bedchamber to enter the glorious gold and white paneled room. A round table, covered with a cloth of sky-blue satin embroidered in gold thread, occupied the center. At the high windows hung curtains of the same rich material, pleated and befringed. A gilded armchair awaited the King; but the attendant ministers had to put up with folding stools, made as comfortable as possible with tasseled downy cushions. Should their aching backs cause their attention to wander, they had their choice of regarding a rather intimidating porphyry bust of Alexander the Great, stern-eyed and martial, or letting their tired eyes roam over the irreverent rococo gold panels which were among the masterpieces of the architect Jacques-Ange Gabriel and his wood-carver Rousseau. In the center of each was a medallion containing fat and merry cherubs playing at being state counselors, their tiny golden arms embracing documents, books, and seals, tools of their trade. One central infant stood holding his small finger to his lips, and his look was a grave one, as befitted this emblem of discretion.

The six men in the room listened soberly as the Minister of Foreign Affairs explained the importance of the recent intelligence estimates and spoke of the need for action. Vergennes was taking a tremendous chance, and they all knew it. It was well enough to state so simply that it was the destiny of France to humble England by any means available, and that the rebellion of the colonies offered a golden opportunity to redress the balance of power, but the risks were enormous. What if the "insurgents" failed in their effort and were persuaded to jettison the difficult aim of independence for the more comfortable solution of reconciliation with the mother country? This could mean war between France and a Great Britain that was *united* with the colonies, and it would be a war fought primarily at sea. Sartine was Vergennes's man, eager to back him, but he knew that the navy wasn't ready. Thanks to an energetic shipbuilding program, they were a long way from the unhappy days of 1756 when France had last gone to war with a miserable fleet of 25 ships, but the minister was obliged to reserve his judgment and ask for more time.*

That experienced old soldier, the Comte de Saint-Germain, was even more reluctant than his colleague Sartine. He was immensely proud of his army, a magnificent fighting force crowded with young men who were longing for action after thirteen years of peace. But the Minister of War was singularly nonbellicose. It was said that he loved his soldiers so much that he could not bear to think of one of them getting hurt. Such sentimentality was surely pure gossip, but he was sixty-eight years old and perhaps his successor, the Prince de Montbarey, was right when he said that Saint-Germain had come to the office

---

* He made the most of it. Two years later, in 1778, the fleet consisted of 264 warships, of which 78 were fine ships of the line.

ten years too late. His appearance was martial, with a lean, upright figure and cool, steady blue eyes, but his opinion could not be shaken. Clandestine aid to the American colonies might lead to war. The risks were too great, and his vote was a firm nay.

Maurepas the Mentor, the senior by six years of the Minister of War, also favored caution, but Vergennes's arguments had impressed him. He waited to hear what Turgot, the Comptroller of Finances, would say. Turgot, at forty-seven, was the most attractive man in the room, and surely the most unhappy. One of the foremost economists of his time, he was also a great administrator who had put his physiocratic theories into practice when, as *intendant*, he governed for fourteen long years one of the most over-taxed and poorest provinces of France. As a free-trader, his influence on Adam Smith in England was as important as it was on his followers at home, and his reputation as a reformer had caused his appointment to be internationally acclaimed by the philosophers of both countries. He too was a philosophe, and a contributor to the *Encyclopédie*. There was nothing this vigorous man did not find time for between tearing off dissertations, pamphlets, and books on every subject from the evils of the *corvée*† to his famous work, *Réflexions sur la Formation et la Distribution des Richesses*. He was one of the most popular figures in the salons of Paris.

This brilliant scholar, this accomplished man of the world and gifted administrator was an idealist whose heart was deeply stirred by the ideals represented by America. "America is the hope of the human race, and can become its model," was his beautiful phrase. As the committee of ministers assembled in the Council Chamber deliberated the implications of Vergennes's program, if there was one among them who would have liked to support it, it was Turgot, yet he could not. Aware that France, with a national deficit that year of 20,000,000 livres, required the most draconian of financial reforms, the most stringent economies, he trembled at the prospect of further weakening

† *Forced labor.*

the tottering structure of the ancien régime by adding to it the burden of aid to the colonies which might well lead to war.

When this meeting, the first of many held that spring, gave Turgot the opportunity to impress the King with the dangers that he felt so strongly, he missed his opportunity for a curious reason. It was admitted by his friends and his enemies alike that as a dinner companion there was no man more witty, more entertaining than Turgot. But the charm and gaiety for which he was famous in intimate company deserted him when he was among strangers or men he did not know well. He became arrogant, haughty, pedantic. To the King, who had much admired Turgot when he appointed him, he talked like a schoolmaster, and the King could not bear to be lectured at. Perhaps he felt he was back in his unhappy boyhood with his alarming governor. Also, understanding little of economics and finance, he may have suspected that Turgot was talking down to him. What Louis XVI responded to best was the respectful, but paternal, tone employed by Maurepas and Vergennes, or the delightful, bubbling wit of Beaumarchais, whose playwright's pen illuminated the heavy state papers that he was forced to study.

Ultimately it was the King who had to decide between his divided Cabinet. Months of exhausting negotiation with the reluctant Spanish government had at last elicited the offer of a secretly given million livres for the Americans, on the understanding that the actual supplies must come from France so that the King of Spain could not be implicated. Vergennes had wrung from the unhappy Turgot the promise of a second million from the French themselves. As a result, on May 2, 1776, he was in a position to write a crucial letter, terse and businesslike in style, to Louis XVI.

The first sentence read: "I herewith lay at Your Majesty's feet a paper which will authorize me to furnish the English colonies with a million livres." He went on to say that "in order that this operation should not be penetrated" (a curiously modern turn of phrase!), any letters on the subject would not be written by Vergennes himself, nor by any of his assistants or secretaries, all of whose hands were too well known, but would be dictated to his fifteen-year-old son, whose handwriting was unknown.‡[14]

The King wrote *"approuvé"* on the margin of the May 2 letter and further directed that the secret aid should be channeled to the colonies by Beaumarchais, acting for a bogus commercial firm to be known as Roderigue Hortalez et Cie. Thus, even before the Declaration of Independence had been signed, the first of the vast loans and subsidies that were to ensure that independence had been authorized.

Beaumarchais himself should have written the extraordinary story. The author of *The Barber of Seville* and *The Marriage of Figaro* would have done it justice. We have the Foreign Minister of France, Vergennes, famous for his caution, taking a gamble on which his country depended, largely in the belief that the playwright could carry it off. The very name Roderigue Hortalez et Cie is sheer Beaumarchais in its theatricality. We have two improbable co-conspirators, the flashy courtier-ambassador Guines and his courageous agent Bonvouloir. We have the young King of France, who loathed deception and trickery, acceding to the plan against the advice of his Minister of War, his Minister of the Navy, and his Comptroller of Finances, the great Turgot. Backed by the support of Vergennes and Maurepas, Louis XVI went ahead, fully aware that clandestine aid to the colonies might well bring on war with England long before France's forces were ready to fight.

And what was happening in the remote colonies across the Atlantic?

‡ *This top secret letter is in fact written in a hand so nearly resembling Vergennes's own that one could easily confuse the two writings.*

III

Philadelphia, New York, and Paris

THE COMMITTEE OF SECRET CORRESPONDENCE had lost little time in pursuing the encouraging news that Bonvouloir had given them. Someone must be sent to France; not yet an official ambassador, but a competent envoy who, under cover of being a commercial agent, could discreetly present to the French government the military needs of the Congress. This job was not one that would demand a man of the caliber of Franklin, Jefferson, Adams, Morris, or Jay; the statesmen who were to represent America abroad after independence was achieved. These men were up to their eyes on the various committees on which they served, carrying increasingly heavy loads of responsibility. They could not be spared; but by a lucky chance the respected Silas Deane, who had been a delegate from Connecticut to both the First and Second Continental Congresses, was available and willing. The choice of the committee fell on him.

Deane was then in his early forties. The son of a blacksmith from Groton, Connecticut, he had graduated from Yale in 1758, after which he taught school and studied law. Two fortunate marriages had brought him wealth and position; the former came to him from the rich widow Mehitabel Webb, the second he achieved by marrying, after his first wife's death, Elizabeth Saltonstall, the granddaughter of a former governor of Connecticut.

John Adams met him in 1774 when he paused in Hartford on his journey from Boston to Philadelphia for the First Continental Congress. He wrote that Deane, a man of liberal education, was now in trade, by which he meant that he was a merchant. What struck Adams was that Deane and his two stepsons, the Messrs. Webb, were calmly prepared to abandon their highly successful livelihood if it would profit the Congress.

"Mr. Deane says that the sense of Connecticut is, that the resolutions of the Congress shall be the laws of the Medes and Persians; that the Congress is the grandest and most important assembly ever held in America, and that the *all* of America is intrusted [sic] to it and depends on it."[1]

This sounds very like Silas Deane, the enthusiast to whom it never occurred to be embarrassed by emotional patriotic declamation and who meant every word that he said. The inhibited Adams would never have employed such rhetoric, but he was so favorably struck by it that he wrote down every word. All his life, John Adams was acutely, albeit furtively, romantic. Listening to the busy, practical delegates from Connecticut expound their views, he felt like a different man from the one who had written despairingly so short a time before: "We have not Men, fit for the Times. We are deficient in Genius, in Education, in Travel, in Fortune—in every Thing. I feel unutterable Anxiety."

The diary entries between Boston and New York show a new, sanguine Adams. He was touched and flattered by the reception given to his delegation as it moved through the colony. Following a splendid party on August 15, 1774, in Middletown at the beautiful house of Mr. Richard Alsop, they proceeded to the home of the Deanes at Wethersfield. "There we stopped, and were most cordially and genteely entertained with Punch, Wine, and Coffee."[2] It was a fine day and Adams thought that the view from the steeple of Wethersfield Meeting House was "the most beautiful prospect in the world; at least that I ever saw."[3] New Haven produced a wonderful celebration. "As we came into the Town all the Bells in Town were sett to ringing, and the People, Men and Women, and Children, were crowding at the Doors and Windows as if it was to see a Coronation. At Nine O'Clock the Cannon were fired, and about a Dozen Guns I think."[4]

Such demonstrations of respect to the beleaguered Massachusetts Bay Colony sent Adams across the border into the province of New York exhilarated, eager to see more. He had questioned Deane about the men he would meet there: the delegation that would be waiting to greet the Bostonians. Deane, with his usual confidence-inspiring certainty, made it sound delightfully easy. He knew everyone, and Mr. Adams was sure to make friends with them. There would be three merchants: Philip Livingston, Isaac Low, and John Alsop. Mr. Alsop was the brother of Mr. Richard Alsop, who had entertained them so handsomely. Then there were two lawyers: James Duane and John Jay.

It is sad reading to follow the diary from then on. John Adams, that crustacean figure now so nearly enticed from his shell, began by admiring New York. The houses were bigger and grander than those of Boston; he liked the fact that the brick was painted. The streets were wide and elegant, the English silver teapots of the hostesses finer than those with which he was familiar. He did his best to enjoy the sightseeing, but the earnest entries soon became mechanical and joyless; one can only suspect that the New Yorkers overdid the parties:

"A more elegant Breakfast I never saw—rich Plate—a very large Silver Coffee Pott, a very large Silver Tea Pott—Napkins of the finest materials, and toast and bread and butter in great Profusion. After breakfast, a Plate of Beautifull Peaches, another of Pairs and another of Plumbs and Muskmellen were placed on the Table." Not a word of pleasure or praise for this feast.

The fun had gone. Silas Deane and the Alsops of Connecticut had receded into a past that was replaced by: "Phill. Livingston* a great, rough, rappid Mortal. There is no holding any
Conversation with him. He blusters away. Says that if England
should turn us adrift we should instantly go to civil Wars
among ourselves to determine which Colony should govern all
the rest. Seems to dread N. England—the Levelling Spirit &.
Hints were thrown out of the Goths and Vandalls—mention
was made of our hanging the Quakers, &."[5]

Finally: "With all the Opulence and Splendor of this City,
there is very little good Breeding to be found. We have been
treated with an assiduous Respect. But I have not seen one real
Gentleman, one well bred Man since I came to Town. There is
no Modesty—No Attention to one another. They talk very loud,
very fast, and alltogether. If they ask you a Question, before you
can utter three Words of your Answer, they will break out upon
you, again—and talk away."[6]

This bitter indictment of the New Yorkers was the outburst
of a tired man on a hot August day who had had enough of the
rich, with their elaborate silver services and their exotic fruits.
The exuberance of New York entertainments has often shocked
visitors from foreign parts. In fact, only the Livingstons were
very rich. A couple of years later, William Eden, head of the
British Secret Service, asked for "An estimate of the Value of
the real Estates in the possession of those Gentlemen of New
York known to be Rebels."[7] Among those gentlemen whom
Adams met, John Alsop was worth only 900 pounds to the Livingstons' 10,000. The Jays are down for 5,000 pounds, perhaps
because John Jay had married a Livingston, a niece of the intolerable Philip; he who had hinted to John Adams that the New
Englanders were like the barbarian Goths and Vandals.

In later years, Adams was to become the lifelong friend of
some of these men. John Jay, for example, had been dismissed
in a diary sentence as a hard-working young lawyer said to be a

---

* Philip Livingston, delegate to First Continental Congress, brother of
William and Peter Livingston.

good speaker. By 1776, Adams and Jay were already friendly as the Committee of Secret Correspondence prepared to send Adams' friend Silas Deane across the Atlantic. Events were to bring them even closer.

Adams was not on the committee. Some thought that he would rather they had asked him to join it than Robert Morris, a newly appointed member, but it was Benjamin Franklin who made the decisions. It was he who drew up Deane's instructions, although they were signed by the whole committee.

Jay's role was to enlist the services of a renegade brother, Sir James Jay, who, throughout his career, was to be an embarrassment to his respectable family. Knighted by George III as a reward for having raised 10,000 pounds for King's College (now Columbia University), he had returned from England with a degree in medicine from Edinburgh University and an impressive record as a practicing London physician. Unfortunately, there then ensued a squabble with the governors of the college about what had actually become of the money. Sir James was cleared, but the row left a shadow on his name. He was more than delighted to have an opportunity to prove what a flaming patriot he had become in 1776.†

Sir James's medical knowledge turned out to be extremely useful. The Committee of Secret Correspondence was as innocent of the techniques of intelligence as it was of those of diplomacy, but the members knew that sophisticated Europeans employed such devices as invisible ink and ciphers. James Jay produced some ink that impressed everyone and Silas Deane was given a supply to take with him.‡ John Jay retained the chemical solvent which would make the agent's reports readable. He and Robert Morris studied the matter of codes and ciphers and became very pleased with their prowess. "Once, in a letter to John Jay, Robert Morris spoke of an innocuous letter from 'Timothy Jones' [Deane] and 'the concealed beauties therein,'

† *Later he changed sides several times and John Jay cut off relations with him.*
‡ *General Washington ordered quantities of it and distributed it freely to his spies before the Battle of Long Island.*

noting 'the cursory examinations of a sea captain would never discover them, but transferred from his hand to the penetrating eye of a Jay, the diamonds stand confessed at once.' "[8]

Silas Deane sailed in March 1776. Never in history has an envoy been sent out less well prepared than he. He had not the faintest idea of what to expect of the French, nor could he speak their language. All he knew was what was expected of him. The Committee of Secret Correspondence had instructed him to buy clothes and arms for 25,000 men, as well as munitions and artillery. If possible, he was to obtain these goods on credit, otherwise by direct purchase. It would have been helpful for this middle-aged Connecticut Yankee merchant to have had some knowledge of the climate of opinion in Paris and, above all, some idea of the personalities and histories of the men he was about to meet. But no one in America knew enough to brief him. He wrote his wife: "I am about to enter on the great stage of Europe, and the consideration of the importance of quitting myself well, weighs me down . . ."[9]

Traveling by a roundabout route, Deane reached Bordeaux at the end of May. After a few weeks there posing as an agent interested in buying goods for the American Indians, he took the road for Paris, entering the city on July 8 by the Porte d'Orléans. There stood a small, rather squalid customhouse where the guards poked through his luggage with long, sharp steel needles in order to make sure that he was not carrying contraband. They were very polite to him, as the French were in those days to all foreigners, and he was soon free to cross the city to his hotel on the rue St.-Guillaume.

How lonely he must have felt. It would have been nice to find a line from his wife, Elizabeth, giving family news, or even a crisp letter sent by fast packet from John Jay, perhaps enclosing further instructions from the Congress. There was nothing. In the opening sentences of a letter written months later by Deane, he expressed the terrible sense of isolation from which all American envoys abroad during the War of Independence suffered.

Dear Jay,

> *If my Letters arrive safe they will give you some idea of my situation, without Intelligence, without Orders, and without Remittances, yet boldly plunging into Contracts, Engagements and Negotiations, hourly hoping that something will arrive from America.*[10]

Such were the difficulties of communication that Deane, complaining later in the letter that he had hardly a drop of Jay's brother's ink left with which to write a dispatch, was totally unaware of what the summer had been like for his correspondent. In June, the British fleet entered New York Harbor. The first order of business for the patriot colonists was to round up the Tory enemies within the gates, and there were many of them. Philip Livingston, John Jay, John Alsop, and Gouverneur Morris undertood the successful operation under General Washington's orders. Among those arrested was the mayor of New York City, David Matthews. He was sent off to jail, along with a number of others who had been enlisted to help the British fleet.

The provincial assembly of New York, which we would today call the state legislature, fled first to White Plains and later in the summer up the Hudson River to Fishkill. Jay, as a conscientious member of that body, had to move with it, leaving behind his own family and his wife's family, both of whom lived in the path of the advancing British forces. Their safety was Jay's responsibility. He was especially concerned about his blind brother and sister, Peter and Anna Maricka, who lived with their aging parents at Rye. As Silas Deane knew none of the details of that horrendous time, it is no wonder he grew impatient.

Although without news or guidance from home, Deane was not left long to cool his heels at the hotel on the rue St.-Guillaume. All three men he had been instructed to contact upon his arrival in France responded immediately. There were two Frenchmen, both friends of Franklin, Dr. Barbeu Dubourg and Monsieur Jacques Donatien Leray de Chaumont, and one native of Massachusetts, Dr. Edward Bancroft. The last, upon receiving Deane's letter in London, along with thirty pounds for his traveling expenses, jumped out of bed where he lay "burning under the paroxysm of a Quotidian Intermittent fever"[11] and came racing to Paris.

In recommending Barbeu Dubourg, Franklin was lamentably out of touch. Dubourg was a well-meaning, but bumbling, old fool; worse than useless as an intermediary with the French government. Leray de Chaumont, a prominent pro-American financier, was to prove himself a true friend, but his time had not yet come. There was little at the moment that he could do to help. Dr. Bancroft became Deane's confidant and adviser from the start. Such was his zeal that, by the time Franklin and Arthur Lee joined Deane to form a triumvirate of American envoys known as the Commissioners, he was indispensable. He remained a hard-working paid member of the United States mission for many of those difficult years.

Dr. Bancroft, whom Franklin had known in London, had been a pupil of Deane's during the latter's early career as a schoolmaster. He had been born in Westfield, Massachusetts, educated as a physician in England, had traveled widely, and was an inventor and scientist, specializing in dyes and poisons. A fellow of the Royal Society, he was considered to know political London as well as he knew the scientific world, besides which he was urbane, charming and cosmopolitan; just the sort of man the innocent Deane required to take him through the brambles and thickets of diplomacy. It is quite clear from the committee's instructions to Deane that his colleagues considered him a babe in the woods. For example, he was ordered not to wander around Paris sightseeing on arrival, "as so many foreigners are tempted to do," but to stay put until his wise advisers came to tell him how he should best approach his task.

Possibly one of the most agreeable men of his time, Bancroft got on with everyone, except for Arthur Lee, a paranoid whom Franklin accused of having a sick mind. Franklin himself was devoted to Bancroft. One of the last letters he wrote from Philadelphia before his death in 1790 was an affectionate note to the doctor. John Adams, normally suspicious and reserved, took to him at once, and Jefferson regarded him as a true friend.

It was not until the second half of the nineteenth century that historians uncovered the unhappy fact that this seemingly honorable and patriotic gentleman was one of the most able British spies of all time. When his namesake, George Bancroft, guessed the true story in 1866, a fellow American historian, Dr. Francis Wharton, came screaming back at him with a defense of the spy in his classic *Revolutionary Diplomatic Correspondence of the United States*. It contained the following tragically ironic passage:

> It may hereafter appear, on the unearthing of the secret service papers of the British foreign office, that this (that of a spy) was really Bancroft's position. But if it be so, he presents a case of which history affords no parallel. To believe him guilty of such atrocious and yet exquisitely subtle perfidy we must believe that, ingenuous, simple-hearted and credulous as he appeared to the general observer, occupying to Franklin and to America a position not unlike what Boswell did to Johnson and Corsica, though with certain scientific aptitudes to which Boswell laid no claim and with an apparent occasional heroism of which Boswell was incapable, he was, nevertheless, a dissembler so artful as to defy the scrutiny of Franklin, with whom he was in constant intercourse; an intriguer so skillful as, without money or power, to deceive Vergennes and the multitudinous police with which Vergennes encircled him; a villain so profoundly wary as to win the confidence of Paul Jones . . . a double traitor, whose duplicity was so masterly as to be unsuspected by the British court, which held him to be a rebel; and by such men as Lafayette, as John Adams, as Jefferson . . . this amusing combination of apparently absolutely inconsistent characteristics may exist in bewildering harmony in the character of Edward Bancroft; but such a phenomenon should not be believed to exist without strong proof.[12]

The proof of treason has been available for some time to students, but the feat remains miraculous. In view of the efficiency of the French Secret Service, it is hard to believe that it never caught up with Bancroft, who, for eight years, went to the south side of the Tuileries gardens, one of the most public places in all Paris, every Tuesday night before half past nine and inserted a sealed bottle into a hollow tree that stood there, to be picked up by a British agent. It is still difficult to pin down the exact date when he became a traitor. The first written evidence we have from him is dated December 1776, when he agreed to accept from the British government 500 pounds down and 400 pounds per annum for services rendered. Dr. Bancroft cared a great deal about money. He wrote an eloquent appeal to the British Foreign Secretary, the Marquess of Carmarthen, in 1784, stressing his need for a permanent pension of 500 pounds in view of the eight years he had worked in France, beginning when he joined Silas Deane in July 1776. It would appear almost certain that he made his decision sometime during that month.

A week after his arrival, Silas Deane went to Versailles to see Vergennes accompanied by the ubiquitous Dr. Barbeu Dubourg. Dr. Bancroft had been invited by Deane to join them, but he modestly declined on the grounds that he might be in the way. After all, Deane could tell him all about it when they rejoined that night at their hotel. It would be interesting to know where the meeting took place. In order to avoid the Argus-eyed agents of the British Ambassador, Lord Stormont, it would not have been in the minister's office. More likely it was held at his private residence, "La Solitude," which was only a ten-minute drive from the ministry. Conrad Alexandre Gérard, Vergennes's *premier commis* (first clerk—analogous to Under Secretary of State today), translated as Vergennes spoke no English and Deane, no French.

From the first it was apparent that Barbeu Dubourg, eager as he was to serve as intermediary between Deane and the French in matters of business, did not suit Vergennes, who had already settled on Caron de Beaumarchais. Acting through the fictional firm of Roderigue Hortalez et Cie, he was to be the instrument employed. A crucial decision was made regarding the arms to be shipped to America via the bogus firm. The French agreed to provide them from the King's arsenals, with the express understanding that the royal coat of arms, the fleur-de-lys, must first be removed from them.

News of the Declaration of Independence having not yet reached Paris, Vergennes asked Deane a hard question: What was to stop the colonies from splitting away from each other after independence was declared instead of remaining united as one nation? (Gérard's exact notes read: "What if they differ among themselves?") On Deane's answer depended the success of the mission. He did well.

"He fulfilled his instructions not only with shrewdness, but with a conviction of argument which could only have been expounded by a believer: a true patriot. The impression that he must have hoped to achieve had been accomplished. The minister turned to Gérard and told him to take note of the address of the envoy, adding to Deane that he would be delighted to receive him often personally. As this would be difficult, he hoped that Deane would keep in touch with Gérard, on whom he could count absolutely. If something urgent came up, Vergennes himself would be immediately informed. The interview was over."[13]

The American found some words to excuse his manners, which were, according to the record, "not at all what Monsieur de Vergennes would expect, but perhaps he would pardon them coming from the envoy of a new country unaccustomed to court etiquette." This again is typical Deane. His honesty and simplicity of expression must have been what won his case, but he would never have understood that.

His first meeting with the Minister of Foreign Affairs concluded, what a relief it must have been for Deane to have someone waiting to whom he could confide every detail of the momentous day. "No one has a clearer head than Dr. Bancroft,"

John Adams was to remark approvingly. We can be sure that he kept it very clear indeed that night, although he was a bon vivant who knew his way about the best restaurants of Paris and probably insisted on celebrating the success of Deane's meeting with Vergennes.

The next weeks were busy ones for Deane. Beaumarchais called to discuss business arrangements on July 18, and again on the nineteenth. Because of his total ignorance of European affairs, Deane came to rely heavily on Bancroft, who, he reported to Congress, "was rendering the greatest service." Much impressed by the doctor's wide range of information, Deane was soon using his concurrence to clinch an argument: "Dr. Bancroft was full with me in this opinion."[14] Depending on him as he did, it was a blow when Bancroft announced in mid-August his intention to return for a time to London on private business. He promised, however, to keep Deane informed of any English affairs that might interest the Committee of Secret Correspondence.

If Bancroft had not already gone over to the British, it is certain he did so now. Upon his return to London, he went to see Paul Wentworth, the British Secret Service's chief agent for France. Wentworth had been trying to recruit Bancroft for some time, according to the latter's letter of 1784 to Carmarthen. The report that Bancroft turned over to him described Deane's instructions, the interview with Vergennes, the plans concerted with Beaumarchais. Too important for Wentworth to handle, or even for his chief, William Eden, the able Undersecretary for Foreign Affairs and head of the Secret Service, it was sent directly to the Cabinet and the King.

George III, like his French counterpart, was a hard-working young king. He took a keen interest in his Secret Service, which was an important adjunct of the Foreign Office with an annual budget of 80,000 pounds, an enormous sum for those days.

It is interesting to note that an intelligence report from Paris, some of which were over thirty pages in longhand, might come to Eden at 4 P.M., be digested by him and sent to the palace that evening where it was read at once by the King. His comments, often shrewd and pithy, are frequently dated ten or eleven o'clock that same evening.

Unfortunately the judgment of the eager, energetic monarch was flawed by his strong personal views of the agents whose reports he studied so carefully. In his opinion a man who speculated on the stock exchange could not be trusted. It would be a wild exaggeration to suggest that the American colonies were lost because of George III's prejudice against "loose-living gamblers," as he called certain of his spies, but the point is not unimportant.

Faithful to his promise, Dr. Bancroft wrote weekly to Deane in Paris offering all sorts of London news and gossip which greatly impressed the latter. Deane could not have guessed that much of what he read was public knowledge and of the most trivial importance. He wrote to the committee in Philadelphia that no one had better intelligence in England, "but it costs something." Blinded as Deane was by the brilliance of his friend, he was still a Yankee trader intent on getting full value for his limited funds. However, if Bancroft had to pay highly, as he alleged, for the intelligence he was gleaning, the information must have been valuable. Deane was grateful to have found such a dedicated and industrious source.

The British Secret Service had no reason to object to the unimportant information passed to Deane by their new agent. "The occasional reports he sent regarding the despatch of troops were probably made deliberately and with the knowledge of the English authorities, for all real information of this nature was guarded most carefully even from most members of the Cabinet."[15] Bancroft even arranged to have himself arrested because of his letters to Deane, which greatly upset his trusting friend. Writing to the committee of the occurrence, he said: "This worthy man has been confined in the Bastile of England . . . I feel for Dr. Bancroft more than I can express—he deserves much from us. Consequently [he] will be pursued with the utmost vigor by them."[16] Having warned Deane that he feared he might not be allowed to remain much longer in London, Bancroft returned to Paris for good that winter. Clearly, he would be more useful there to the British.

The absence of his one companion that summer and fall would have been all the more disappointing for Silas Deane had he not been busy setting up the agreements with Caron de Beaumarchais and his fictitious commercial house, Roderigue Hortalez et Cie. The two men had already met in Bordeaux, where Beaumarchais happened to be on a mission to buy gunpowder when Deane arrived from America. Arthur Lee had been the agent with whom Beaumarchais had been dealing in London but, when he read Deane's instructions from Congress, he at once established a relationship with the new envoy which was to be a close and fruitful one.

The terms of the agreement were simple enough. Deane had been ordered to "purchase military stores on terms of liberal credit, payable in American produce."[17] Theoretically, the ships which had carried the supplies across the Atlantic would return to France laden with tobacco, indigo, and other goods. Under the contract drawn up with Beaumarchais, "the supplies were to be furnished to Congress, at its risk, f.o.b. France, and to be paid for later—the date not fixed—in produce and money."[18] Thinking he had a good, practical business deal, Beaumarchais raised additional capital, over and above the two million livres provided by France and Spain, and proceeded to rent the enormous house known as the Hôtel des Ambassadeurs de Hollande as his headquarters. He also advanced credit to charter vessels to carry the goods to America.

They were in business. It must have been a delight to work with the optimistic Beaumarchais. He would say to Deane: "Congress is talking about 25,000 men? Let's make it supplies for 30,000, to be on the safe side. One hundred field guns? Oh, make it 200. As for payment, either pay me the going price in America when the stuff arrives, or pay cost plus price in France, all in commodities. When the war is over we can put to Congress the question of my commission."[19]

Pierre Augustin Caron de Beaumarchais, son of a watchmaker and a watchmaker himself, was a controversial figure in his own time and remains one today. His friend in adversity, the writer Gudin de la Brenellerie, said, simply, that it was not possible to see him without loving him. On the other hand, one of the most distinguished modern American eighteenth-century historians, the late Julian P. Boyd, refers to the author of *The Marriage of Figaro* as an "adventurer, quondam blackmailer, and suspected murderer."[20] He almost certainly was not a blackmailer or murderer, but that he was an adventurer is undeniable.

As attractive to women as he was to men, Beaumarchais was assisted by a disparate collection from both sexes in his vertiginous climb to fame. His skill as a watchmaker brought him into notice at Court. His passionate love of music and his cool assurance charmed King Louis XVI's mean-minded aunts, Mesdames Adélaïde, Louise, Victoire, and Sophie, even though they seldom looked kindly upon a member of the petit bourgeoisie. He played the harp for these formidable Mesdames. This was rung one up the ladder. His marriage to Madame Franquet, the widow of an old Court official, was rung two. Madly in love with the handsome young man, she managed to arrange for him to take over the office that had been held by her late husband. This seemingly meaningless position carried with it the patent of nobility, and Pierre Augustin Caron, *fils d'horloger* (son of a watchmaker), became Caron de Beaumarchais, a small title, but it was rung three. His wife died a year after the marriage.

Next step on the ascent to fame came with *Eugénie*, his play that was produced for the first time on January 29, 1767. Marriage to a rich young widow, Madame Lévêque, followed the next year. Partnership with the greatly respected banker Pâris Du Verney brought him possession of a large part of the forest of Chinon in Touraine. His letters to his wife[21] from Chinon show his ineradicable love of novelty which strikes the student of his life again and again. He was the happy forester, missing and loving his family, but absorbed from dawn to dark: "Imagine, 200 workers in the forest to see today, their cuttings to be examined—new roads to the river to be cleared—the old ones to be repaired. My room has for furniture a bad bed, where I sleep soundly, four straw chairs. . . ." Never did Beaumarchais sound more content.

In 1770, when he was thirty-eight years old, everything went to pieces. His wife died, following the birth of their first child, a boy. He was accused of having poisoned her, an accusation all the more unlikely as her fortune had been left to her as a life annuity. But people overlooked this and remembered instead the sudden death of his first wife. Then came the death of his partner, Pâris Du Verney, which led to a notorious suit brought against Beaumarchais by the heirs, known as the Procès Blache, followed by a second suit leading from it, the Goëzman case.

After several years of litigation, Beaumarchais was imprisoned in 1773, discredited, his case seemingly hopeless and his fortune lost. Public opinion was against him. Except for a tiny group of literary friends, *"la bande joyeuse"* as he called them in his memoirs, and his own loving relations, he was a social outcast. One of the nastiest attacks, openly published, came from his former protectors at Versailles, Mesdames, who announced that they wished to having nothing more to do with their former harp teacher.

Down and out and privately in despair, to judge from his letters to his devoted family, Beaumarchais fought to save himself with his pen. Through his clever use of it, from a pariah he became the idol of every thinking Frenchman. Legal cases such as his were presented to the supreme judiciary body, the *parlement*, in the form of memoirs or reports written by the adversaries. Applying his own case to universal justice, Beaumarchais went after Maupeou, the detested chancellor of the *parlement*, with savagery, bitter humor, and a brilliance of style that was applauded by all France, where the legal system was deeply unpopular. An incredible change of opinion took place overnight; Voltaire, following the drama from his retreat at Ferney, wrote to d'Alembert:

Louis XVI
King of France, 1776

Marie Antoinette
Queen of France

Tomb of the great philosoph

an-Jacques Rousseau

Charles Gravier, Comte de Vergennes
The great Foreign Minister of France during the War of Independence

Benjamin Franklin
by Jean-Baptiste Greuze, 1777

A café on th

...levards of Paris

Hôtel de Valentinois

The magnificent residence in Passy of Franklin's mission in France

"What a man! He brings everything together, jokes, serious subjects, reason, gaiety, strength and—touching things—every possible kind of eloquence. Yet he isn't trying to be eloquent. He teaches his judges a lesson, and confounds his adversaries."[22]

Horace Walpole wrote to the famous hostess Madame du Deffand from England: "I have received the Beaumarchais memoirs, and am in the third . . . I have forgotten to describe to you the horror which overtakes me on reading about judicial proceedings in your country. . . ."[23]

She replied on February 26, 1774: "We are expecting a great event today: Beaumarchais' judgement. M. de Monaco has asked him to come in this evening to read us his comedy which is called 'The Barber of Seville' . . . it may be that instead of having supper with us he will be condemned to banishment or even the pillory; I will let you know tomorrow."[24]

Unfortunately for Madame du Deffand, Beaumarchais was too tired to appear at the Prince de Monaco's soirée. He wrote his host a polite note of regret and then went to his sister Madame Lépine's to fall into the sleep of utter exhaustion, having decided to kill himself if sentenced to the pillory. They woke him up there to tell him the results. Both he and his adversary had received the same sentence, known as *le blâme*. This decision meant the loss of civil liberties but, in the atmosphere of euphoria that prevailed the next day, the sentence was taken as a triumph.

"All Paris came to call on him, and the Prince de Conti and the Duc de Chartres gave a brilliant party in his honor. . . . Monsieur de Sartine [Lieutenant General of the Police of Paris] teased him, 'It isn't enough just to be *blâmé*, you must also try to be modest.'"[25] In that same year, with the advent of Louis XVI, Beaumarchais's enemies in the magistrature lost their power.

The following year *The Barber of Seville* was produced and its author was sent to London on a bizarre mission involving a former secretary of embassy and minister plenipotentiary called the Chevalier d'Éon. This individual had been replaced following a violent row with another French diplomat, the Comte de Guerchy, but he remained in London. About 1771, the gossip going the rounds of English society was that the Chevalier was not a man, but a woman. Bets on the matter were placed in the clubs.

The case of an unimportant transvestite would never have come to the attention of Vergennes had it not been that during the reign of Louis XV contingency plans had been drawn up for the invasion of the British Isles. These were never used but, instead of being filed in a secret Foreign Office archive, they remained in London. In 1775, the Chevalier d'Éon revealed to the French government that he had them. Now, he said he did indeed desire to change his sex, but he would need a large sum of money in order to live as a lady of rank should. If the French government was unable to fulfill his requirements, it would surely interest the British to buy the plans, plus a lot of other official papers of a delicate nature he happened to have kept in a trunk in case they might turn out to be useful. Vergennes dispatched Beaumarchais to buy off the Chevalier. He was, after all, known to be attractive to women, if indeed the Chevalier was a woman. It was a long, tedious business. Some think that Beaumarchais fell in love with his client,[26] but such a supposition is very unlikely. He at last succeeded in getting the papers back, for a sum, and the Chevalier returned to France to live for thirty more years, dressed in skirts.*

By 1776 Beaumarchais was completely rehabilitated in the eyes of the law and deeply involved in a new career, that of secret agent. He had always said he would have liked to have been a diplomat had he received the proper education and, as a result of his London mission, he had developed a passionate interest in the American colonies. It was then he began writing the arresting appeals to the King and to Vergennes that were so important in the decision to aid the Americans. The latter, recognizing the magic of his pen and the effect it could have on the

---

* A postmortem established that the Chevalier was a man.

King, used his agent's gifts to the full, with the complete accord of the Chief Minister, Maurepas.

One French historian[27] has used an ecclesiastical expression, "touched with grace," to describe Beaumarchais's dedication to the American cause. Certainly his writing is inspired, but his direct descendant, the late Monsieur Jacques de Beaumarchais, himself a distinguished ambassador of France and student of his illustrious ancestor, put it this way: "He was always a mixture of commercialism and idealism. At the beginning he probably thought that he would make a good thing out of the American connection. He didn't. But unquestionably idealism came into it later."[28]

This seems a fair and balanced assessment of a complex man who found himself, in the summer of 1776 in Paris, in partnership with a Connecticut merchant whose French was nonexistent, as was Beaumarchais's English, and whose knowledge of Europe was as limited as his eagerness was great. What an odd couple! It is thanks to their joint effort that the Battle of Saratoga was won; the pivotal engagement of the War of Independence. For this triumph, America owes a debt to Silas Deane which has never been acknowledged. But the senior partner was Caron de Beaumarchais. The creator of *Figaro* was to have as many problems as his stage character, but to the end of his life he was delighted when he was addressed, half in jest, half seriously, as "Beaumarchais, *l'Américain,*" his nickname in Paris.

❧ IV ❧

Conspirators and Ambassadors

IT SEEMED AT THE TIME a risky operation; in retrospect it
seems lunatic. Beaumarchais was engaging in a commerce which
was officially prohibited and, despite the fact that he was in
close touch with Vergennes—they met twice a week and their
correspondence during twelve years totaled 1,000 letters[1]—he
was perfectly well aware that, at the least hint of indiscretion,
the government arsenals from which he drew his supplies for
America would be closed to him. The French government simply could not afford to be caught aiding the Americans. As this
would have meant the outbreak of a war for which they were
not yet prepared, it was imperative that every weapon sent to
the colonies should appear to have been purchased through the
commercial firm of Roderigue Hortalez et Cie.

Beaumarchais and Deane were supposed to take what they
could get surreptitiously and only in installments from the
different state arsenals, find the ships to carry the consignments,
and load them in French ports without the British being aware
of the fact that so much as a pin was being transported. Pins
and needles were indeed items in the cargoes. It is often forgotten how desperate was the need in the colonies for the ordinary
things of daily life which had in the past been imported from
England. "Picks, spades, pickheads, hatchets, Bill-hooks, iron
pincers, shears, hammers" figure in the invoice of the *Amphitrite,* one of Beaumarchais's ships, which also carried "52 guns,

their carriages and fore-carriages, 20,160 four-pound cannon-balls, 12,000 weight of gunpowder, 9,000 Grenades."[2]

For Silas Deane the worst of it was that, under the extremely vague orders that he had been given by Congress, he was supposed to procure the ships, should the French agree to sell him the supplies, but how could he do so without any knowledge of the French language or the French merchant marine? Partner Beaumarchais took up the burden without a word of complaint. Trusting in the honesty of Congress to defray his expenses later, he bought or chartered the ships, eventually establishing a fleet of forty vessels. Other pro-American entrepreneurs, of whom by far the most important was Leray de Chaumont, gambled their fortunes on the cause, but it was Beaumarchais with whom Deane dealt on a day-to-day basis. Together the two men would go up to the ports during the autumn of 1776 and the ensuing winter and watch as the ships were loaded; first innocent items of trade were packed by day, then the weapons of war by night, and in the dawn another layer of goods that would not arouse the suspicions of English spies. Sometimes the ships had to be loaded three or four times, due to the interference of the French port authorities, who were under strict orders to cancel the sailing of any cargo that could cause diplomatic embarrassment. It was nerve-wracking work, and grew more so as the autumn brought rumors of bad news from America.

At least Deane had the compensation of Beaumarchais's companionship and his eternal optimism. Once, in a low moment, when the vigilance of the British navy, assisted by Bancroft's messages from Paris, had caused particularly troubling losses of ships and war supplies, the playwright had an inspired idea. A Polish primate had died in France and his body was to to be sent back to the Baltic on a funeral ship. With due solemnity it was placed aboard one of Beaumarchais's ships at Marseilles, the *Hardie,* which was painted black and white for the occasion and decorated with painted tears.* (Why not crosses? But the record reads: *"en noir et blanc avec des larmes."*)

* *I owe this amusing example of Beaumarchais's imagination to Mr. Lucius Wilmerding, Jr.*

The *Hardie* was allowed to proceed unmolested through the Mediterranean and pass under the guns of the British fortress of Gibraltar, which were reverently silent. Once out into the Atlantic the captain appeared to lose his way, and when next heard of, the *Hardie* was in Charleston, South Carolina, landing a rich cargo of munitions for Washington's forces in the South. There is no record of what happened to the coffin of the Polish bishop. Perhaps it was buried in some peaceful, palmetto-shaded graveyard by the grateful South Carolinians.

Beaumarchais appears to have annoyed Vergennes only once during this period. To while away a dull interval between the frenetic loadings of his ships, he brought the whole company of the Comédie-Française up to Le Havre in order to rehearse a new production of *The Barber of Seville*. As the distinguished cast included the most famous actors and actresses in France, their arrival caused a sensation in the seaport town. Vergennes was outraged. Did Beaumarchais not know the meaning of the word "discretion"? Had he forgotten that he was a secret agent?

The playwright was momentarily contrite. But he had done no harm to the cause. Neither Vergennes, nor he, nor Deane could know that Dr. Bancroft was passing so much information on the clandestine shipments to London that, had Beaumarchais paraded a herd of elephants through the streets of Le Havre, it would have made little difference. The invoice of the ship *Amphitrite*, partially given above, is taken directly from the papers of William Eden, head of the British Secret Service. It was only by the greatest luck that the ship eventually evaded the frigates sent out to catch her and reached safe harbor in America after a most difficult voyage.

This example is only one of many. Despite the heartbreaking losses, enough ships like *Amphitrite* did get through to make the difference between victory and defeat for General Washington, but Deane was not to know that. His desperate letter to Jay already quoted ("If my Letters arrive safe they will give you some idea of my situation, without Intelligence, without Orders, and without Remittances, yet boldly plunging into Contracts, Engagements, and Negotiations . . .") was followed by other, similar cries of loneliness. Deane was a prolific letter writer.†

He was not ordinarily a self-pitying man. Ingenuous certainly, occasionally tactless, but by nature he was a cheerful soul who made friends easily. He had been one of the most popular men in the Congress. Waiting in Paris, without any official position, for the arrival of Benjamin Franklin and Arthur Lee was truly hard on him. When they joined him, a triumvirate of American commissioners was to be formed and, if things went well, they would establish themselves as a recognized American body. But it was a long six months between Deane's landing at Bordeaux in early summer and Franklin and Lee's appearance on the scene just before Christmas 1776.

Bancroft had been a devoted companion but, when he left for London, Deane was without one English-speaking friend. Caron de Beaumarchais did what he could to entertain him and "Dinner with Beaumarchais" is noted several times, apart from the innumerable occasions that they met to do business together, but it could not have been the easy relationship that it might have become out of office hours if the two men had spoken each other's language. It was embarrassing for Deane that Beaumarchais was carrying most of the burden of their common task, and he probably felt that the worldly playwright had other "fish to fry" in his spare time. What, after all, did a former Connecticut schoolmaster and merchant have in common with this mercurial man of the world who was his ally by pure chance?

It was up to Deane to discover Paris by himself in the intervals between his duties at the ports. Moving from the Hôtel du Grand-Villars on the rue St.-Guillaume to the Hôtel de Hambourg on the rue de l'Université, he was still in the heart of the Left Bank. A narrow street, running parallel to the Seine, on rainy days it seems monotonously gray, closed in, a passage to be hurried down. The sun brings a high blue sky under which the

† *This author counted the pages of a normal two-week period and from October 4 to 19, 1777, Deane wrote 151 pages in close longhand on large foolscap sheets. Boxes 6 and 7, Peter Force Papers, Silas Deane Correspondence, Manuscript Division, Library of Congress.*

gray magically becomes nacreous; the façades, transformed to honey and vivid white and soft beige, are as welcoming and beckoning as the little flags that decorate the cakes in the windows of the bakers' shops. In Deane's day there were no sidewalks and the traffic and the noise were infinitely more disagreeable than they are now. Occasionally the tall portals discreetly concealing a nobleman's house would be flung open for a coach to enter or leave the courtyard, enabling the passerby to catch a glimpse of the footmen standing on the steps of the great house beyond. The fine residences, islands of tranquillity, had gardens behind them. Mrs. Cradock, an English visitor, remarked sadly on the despairing regularity of it all. Pools with fountains, each with its statue in the middle, the straight lines of trees, the boxes and boxes of orange trees and lemon trees, the masses of potted flowers guarding the green lawns.

Silas Deane would have liked very much indeed to get into one of these splendid oases whose geometric regularity would have impressed him; but it was to be a year before we have his note: "Dined with the Duc de la Rochefoucauld." By then he knew Paris well, under the aegis of Benjamin Franklin, but his voluminous correspondence for the first six months of his stay gives no idea of his daily life off duty. There was a reason for this lack. In the instructions given him by the Committee of Secret Correspondence, it was clearly stated that he should not waste his time wandering about Paris sightseeing, as many foreign travelers were tempted to do in that city. Hence, it was natural that in his reports he should emphasize the responsibilities of his work with Beaumarchais and the arduous tasks that he was undertaking.

It would be a pity if we knew nothing of what Paris was like for our first envoy. Fortunately, the gap can be partly filled by accounts of other travelers, English and Russian, who stayed on the Left Bank in the late 1770's.‡³

‡ *The English travelers who gave the most details on conditions in France in the late eighteenth century were: Dr. Edward Rigby, who took a long voyage with his wife and two daughters; Arthur Young, whose observations are the*

On waking, Silas Deane would have had a cup of coffee brought to his bedroom by a valet whose job it also was to empty the chamber pot out the window.* The morning papers beside him, Deane could glance over such pieces of news as he could understand while he awaited the arrival at 8 A.M. of the hairdresser. Whether a gentleman wanted the services of this individual or not, it was mandatory to have him, for by 1776 the convenient, all-covering wig had gone out of fashion. Each morning six to eight thousand barbers rushed about the streets of Paris like so many Paul Reveres, curling irons at the ready, and their customers had to submit to the washing out of yesterday's pomade and powder and the application of today's, plus the curling of the long hair. It was much easier for the women, who could go for weeks without washing the complex edifices of real and false hair on their heads.

If the windows were open, the decibels rising from the rue de l'Université were already stupendous, for, besides the clip-clop of the horses and the racket of the iron wheels on the pavement, there was the noise of the crowds of street vendors, all shouting their wares. Anything could be bought from this huge population: old clothes, fresh milk from the country, sauce for tonight's dinner, porcelain, fruit, flowers, household articles of every kind. Cursing, the coachmen screamed at the vendors as they fought to avoid them in the heavy traffic. There were many accidents,† for it was considered stylish to drive very fast and,

---

most useful of all; Mrs. Cradock, who toured all France with her husband; and, of course, Horace Walpole, whose visits to France were more limited in range than those of the above-mentioned observers as his friends were purely of the political and social aristocracy. There were several Russian travelers whose works are worth a look: Von Vizine and the historian Karamsine, who lived around the corner from Deane. Both the latter are quoted in Charles Kunstler, La Vie Quotidienne sous Louis XVI.

* By 1780 a law was passed, and strictly enforced, to forbid this practice.

† "The carriages of the nobility clattered through at great speed, often causing loss of life and limb: there was actually a set tariff specifying the sum to be paid if you lost a leg, an arm, your life. J.-J. Rousseau himself was run over and gravely wounded. Finally, the noise was so unbearable that straw was used to cover the street whenever people were ill. Of course, it soon decomposed and added to the mud." Conversation with Olivier Bernier, 1979.

while ordinary rich men drove two or at the most four horses, the princes of the blood were entitled to six, the King to eight when he came to Paris. Besides the coaches, there were farm carts, ordinary cabs for hire, smart cabriolets driven at a gallop by young dandies who cared little on whom was splashed the mud from their high wheels. Much was written about *la boue de Paris*, the black, viscous filth that lay in the streets summer and winter. It was so acid from the contents of the open sewers and the chamber pots that a woman's skirt once soiled would rot away within a matter of hours. Even leather deteriorated unless immediately cleaned. This led to the existence of a very Parisian race, the *décrotteurs*, who appeared from nowhere on rainy days. "Clean your shoes, sir? Oh, sir, give me your silk stockings. I'll brush them off and have them good as new in a trice."

There were no dusty streets, as the mud was kept liquid even in dry weather, not only by the open drains but by blood from the animals who were killed directly outside the butchers' shops in every part of the city, for slaughterhouses did not exist. Accordingly, as there were no sidewalks, ladies never walked out. One evening, driving home after the theater along the rue St.-Honoré, one of the most fashionable streets in Paris, Voltaire and his mistress, Madame du Châtelet, got stuck in a traffic jam which held them up for so long that they became exasperated enough to leave their coach and take shelter for the night at a friend's house conveniently at hand. Madame du Châtelet's house was only a couple of hundred yards farther on, but it would have been unthinkable for her to walk this distance in her satin slippers and long dress.

The letter-writing travelers did not fail to note the squalor and coarseness of Louis XVI's Paris. The labyrinth of medieval streets in the quarters of Saint-Antoine and Saint-Marcel by which the English entered Paris shocked them, coming as they did from the well-kept thoroughfares of their own country. "The smells are horrible. These are not streets, but the ventilating pipes of sewers, filled with miserable people, their children half naked. The houses are too high to permit the air to circulate, and one drives along in a sort of twilight, as the day-light never reaches the lower floors."[4]

Curiously, there was very little of this kind of description after the first shock. Instead, the foreigners were astounded by the beauty of the new buildings. "You wouldn't know Paris," wrote Horace Walpole to Lady Ossory on September 9, 1775, "it has so much wonderful new architecture."[5] It was indeed an age of building. A hundred yards from the pestilential slums the visitor turned a corner to have his breath taken away by the beauty of the spectacle before him. And again and again the foreigners wrote of what the highly observant Arthur Young called the "good humor of the French." At any performance, a public concert in the Tuileries gardens or in a packed theater, the spectators would stand up, murmuring: "Sir, you are a foreigner, won't you take my place?"[6]

This cheerfulness and kindliness was to continue. One of the first American memoir writers of the period in Paris, young Elkanah Watson of Providence, Rhode Island, carrying dispatches to Franklin, landed near La Rochelle in 1779. "Our ears were constantly assailed by the cry of 'Voilà les braves Bostonés,' from the populace. The appellation of Bostonians is given generally, throughout France, to the American Insurgents. The insurrection having commenced in Boston, they confound the whole nation with that city."[7]

Watson was disturbed, like the other travelers, by the poverty that he observed in the towns on the way to Paris and in the capital itself. Then, like everyone else, he fell under the spell of the beauty and the gaiety. On a Sunday afternoon the Champs-Élysées was "thronged by the giddy population of Paris, embracing all ranks and conditions. Some were dancing in circles, indiscriminately mingled, to the music of the violin."[8] The violin was everywhere in the Paris of those days; the street singers competed with the cries of the street vendors. There never was a city so full of music.

When he wished to do so, Silas Deane could leave his hotel, cross the Seine, and, after pausing at one of the many restaurants on his path where for a modest sum he could enjoy a good meal, continue to the Palais Royal. It was said at the time that at the Palais Royal every pleasure in the world was assembled. Beautiful women, wearing bouquets of fresh flowers at their waists, strolled through the gardens and under the arcades, many of them ladies of easy virtue. The shops contained every object of luxury that could be invented, and it was a time when nothing was badly made, from a malacca cane to a pair of gloves scented with jasmine. There was gambling for those who wanted it and an orchestra played for those who wished to sit in a café and listen. The theaters were nearby, along the great boulevards which extended from the Madeleine to the Bastille, where it was fashionable for foreigners to chat, pointing out sights to each other. Four lines of splendid carriages formed a majestic flood; in them sat famous actresses, duchesses, members of the royal household. The background was as rich as the street scene, for some of the noblest residences in Paris were on the boulevards. And again there were always the street singers and the vendors, pretty girls selling gingerbread, charlatans selling magic elixirs to prolong life, and parrots and monkeys, the latter dressed in soldiers' uniforms, trained to take off their hats when someone cried, "Long live the King!"

However, the most colorful of scenes is little fun if there is no one with whom to share it. Deane far preferred his long days of hard work with Beaumarchais to his lonely existence at the Hôtel de Hambourg. His French was improving, but it wasn't good enough for making jokes, which is how friendships with foreigners can be made. It was a wonderful day when he at last received Dr. Franklin's letter from Auray, in Brittany, announcing his arrival in France.

The United States navy in its infancy had been hard-pressed to find a suitable ship to carry the seventy-year-old envoy and his two grandsons, but Captain Lambert Wickes, the twenty-four-year-old commander of the *Reprisal*, looked extremely smart as he welcomed the old man aboard. He wore a blue uniform with red lapels and red facing on his stand-up collar, slash cuffs over his wrists, and flat yellow buttons. His officers also wore bright new uniforms.[9] The navy did its best for the great Franklin and the voyage was as easy as Captain Wickes could make it. It was a reasonably swift winter crossing—October 26 to December 3—six to eight weeks was the average. But any crossing was exhausting for a septuagenarian suffering with gout and boils. He rested at Auray, so weak that he had to be helped up to bed. It meant everything to him to have the company of his beloved sixteen-year-old grandson, William Temple Franklin, known as Temple, who was to serve as his personal secretary. The seven-year-old Benjamin Franklin Bache, his special pet, had been brought along in order that he should acquire a French education.

Summoning his formidable reserves of fortitude and courage, Franklin and his little party took the road for Paris, arriving on December 22 at the Hôtel de Hambourg, where Silas Deane and Arthur Lee were waiting for them. Franklin already knew just how precarious was the American diplomatic position. The news of the reverses suffered by Washington's troops had reached Paris with grim regularity. Having been defeated on Long Island and having lost New York, they were forced to retreat to New Jersey. By December the forces had been reduced to 5,000 men. Some in their discouragement deserted, others left when their short terms of enlistment were up. Washington's fight to keep his army together was harder than his fight against the enemy. To the worried Vergennes at Versailles, the struggle sounded nearly hopeless.

Franklin held only one trump card in his appallingly weak hand: his own personal prestige. All Paris had been waiting for his arrival. Even blind old Madame du Deffand, who had no sympathy for the American cause, wrote to Horace Walpole on December 18, "Since three or four days people say in the morning that he has arrived and in the evening that he hasn't."[10] The excitement was so great that Parisians all over the city imagined they had seen him and gave eyewitness reports of encounters with him. Word had already come from Brittany of his appearance: the famous fur hat; the straggling, uncurled, unpowdered gray locks; the spectacles on the nose; and the plain costume that the French called Quakerish. Franklin was always thought to be a Quaker in Paris. There is no record that he ever said he wasn't; the Quakers were popular and he needed every ounce of popularity that came his way. Fashion-conscious Paris became enamored of his appearance.

On December 22, Madame du Deffand wrote to London again, giving the exact hour at which Franklin had arrived, 2 P.M. Although in her letters to Walpole, who was keenly pro-American and anti-Lord North's ministry, she said she wasn't in the least interested in knowing the new celebrity, she mentioned casually that she was expecting to meet him on the twenty-ninth. On the thirtieth she entertained him at an afternoon reception and, while she apparently wished to give Walpole the impression that this was an occasion of no importance at all, it is interesting to note the hour at which she summoned her secretary to dictate a letter describing the event: 6 A.M. the following morning.

It had been a great coup for a lady who at seventy-eight, totally blind, was still holding her own among the younger Paris hostesses. In the famous salon, hung in yellow silk, the tall curtains caught back at the windows by flame-colored grosgrain ribbons, Madame du Deffand sat by the fire in a barrel-backed armchair known as a *tonneau*. Franklin, wearing the fur bonnet and spectacles, sat beside her in a circle that included Silas Deane, the Duc de Choiseul, the Vicomte de Beaune, Monsieur Leroy, the Maréchale de Luxembourg, the Abbé Barthélemy. "The circle was completed by M. de Guines . . . everyone there was for America except M. de Guines and me."[11]

After the departure of the American commissioners, the conversation became highly political. Several people dropped in to hear about the party and to give news of freshly reported American disasters. Madame du Deffand had a supper engagement at her friend Madame de Mirepoix's at nine o'clock, so, on hearing the clock strike the hour, she slipped away, leaving her guests in hot debate around the fire.

While Franklin's effect on that monster of egotism, Madame du Deffand, was minimal, his effect on public opinion was enormous. No one has given more generous testimony to this than John Adams, although he grew to dislike and mistrust him when the two men worked together in Paris. Long after Franklin had died, he wrote: "His name was familiar to government and people, to kings, courtiers, nobility, clergy, and philosophers, as well as plebeians, to such a degree that there was scarcely a peasant or a citizen, a valet de chambre, coachman or footman, a lady's chambermaid or a scullion in the kitchen who was not familiar with it and who did not consider him a friend to human kind. . . . When they spoke of him, they seemed to think that he was to restore the golden age."[12] No tribute was ever better said.

Remarkably, Franklin never lost the affection with which he was greeted on his arrival. At the end of his mission, the feelings of the French were just as warm, and eight and a half years is a long time for any public figure to have retained a respect that amounted to veneration. In 1778 a lady who chanced to catch sight of him on the street burst into tears on hearing the crowd exclaim, "C'est Monsieur Franklin!" She cried unashamedly, not knowing quite why. "It had to do with Rousseau, with virtue, with Franklin. . . ."[13]

The first Christmas was spent settling down. Franklin and Deane were naturally compatible. Arthur Lee appeared nervous and edgy from the moment he arrived. Fortunately for everyone's peace of mind, the tactful, reassuring, and hard-working Dr. Bancroft had reappeared to join the mission. He had just entered into a written agreement with the British Secret Service granting him 500 pounds down and 400 pounds per annum in exchange for information on ships carrying contraband—their names, their captains' names, their invoices, and their sailing dates—on dealings and agreements between the American and

French governments, on all correspondence between the commissioners and the Congress, and on anything else that might be of interest to his employers.[14] The arrangement had been made for the drop on Tuesday evenings to be picked up by Lord Stormont's messenger.

It was a tall order, and even George III, who never liked him, was forced to admire his industry.

The British Ambassador, Lord Stormont, had received a full description of Madame du Deffand's reception for Dr. Franklin the next day and, on January 1, 1777, he wrote a dispatch to the Secretary of State in London, Lord Weymouth, that was remarkably cool in tone for a man who had reason to be very annoyed indeed.[15] Since the ambassador's arrival in Paris five years before, Madame du Deffand had consistently flattered him, been entertained by him, had urged him to bring the most famous English visitors to her salon, and had used him as her personal messenger when he crossed the Channel. Lord Stormont's luggage was always full of presents for Walpole—only last April there had been the fuss about a particular brand of cough drops that had to be added at the last moment because she had heard that her beloved English friend had a cold. Besides, her contempt for the American rebels was notorious.

What did this intimate little party for the arch-rebel signify? Admittedly, Madame du Deffand had been most annoyed when Stormont had married for the second time the year before. She had put it about that the bride was only fifteen years old and must have been a great heiress for him to have brought so awkward and ignorant a wife to the British Embassy. The old lady had been cold to his ravishing seventeen-year-old Louisa Cathcart, with whom he was much in love, but he had put this down to senile jealousy and the normal reaction of the hostess who prefers ambassadors to be extra men. They had seen much of each other since, and he had been sure that she was over her pique.

In any case, however much the treachery of Madame du Deffand had hurt him personally, the British Ambassador made nothing of it in his dispatch to Lord Weymouth and the emphasis of the report was on the Duc de Choiseul, who had been present to honor Franklin. While the meaning of his presence was not yet clear to Stormont, Choiseul and his supporters had but one aim: to bring down Maurepas and Vergennes. As for these two ministers, it was the ambassador's opinion "that they wished to wound but dared not strike."[16] In other words, the French government was not ready to risk war with England.

Stormont also enclosed the minutes of a secret meeting between Franklin and Gérard, Vergennes's deputy at Versailles, taken "by an informer hidden in the archives of the Foreign Office."[17] It was not an illuminating exchange. Moreover, it was too soon to make any assessment of Franklin. In the opinion of the ambassador, expressed on January 8,[18] nothing in France was more than a nine-day wonder, and the extraordinary popularity of the old man in the fur hat would fade as the British continued their military successes in America. Even so, Lord Stormont was a worried man. "In the difficult position in which I am placed, my lord, I am often obliged to take more upon myself than I would wish."[19]

It was indeed a difficult position, and Stormont deserves more attention than he has received from historians. Franklin made fun of him, inventing a new French verb, *stormonter,* meaning to lie, which at once became part of Parisian slang. Nothing is crueler than a joke like this one that sticks in the mind. It may explain in part why Lord Stormont invariably sounds slightly foolish in what has been written about him during the critical period of his Paris mission.

He was anything but foolish. Born David Murray, seventh Viscount Stormont, nephew and heir to the great Lord Chancellor, the first Earl of Mansfield, he was blessed with intelligence, charm, and taste. He had a distinguished diplomatic career, culminating in his appointment as Ambassador to Paris, the most important post in Europe, at the age of forty-five. A portrait in his family home in Scotland, Scone Palace, shows an arrestingly handsome young man with quizzical, amused brown eyes, emanating vitality. That he remained attractive is proven by a later picture of him as the "grand seigneur," wearing a red velvet ermine-lined cape casually flung over one arm. He is still dashing and without a trace of the pomposity that so often mars the portraits of Georgian aristocrats. Even unkind Madame du Deffand commented on his wit and sweetness.

Like many sons of the great Scottish houses, he had been sent to England for his education, accepting stoically the long, bumpy coach trips North for the holidays in anticipation of coming home to Scone, a pinkish sandstone pile standing above the Tay, one of the most famous salmon rivers in Scotland. He used to talk to his French friends about his love of the country, but they could never understand it, Louis XIV having bred out of the nobility their ties with the countryside. How could he have explained to someone who loathed going fifty kilometers out of Paris the utter happiness of waking up in the brisk Scottish air for a day spent whipping the fast-running Tay, whose black waters shone silver where the sun struck it? Or the fulfilling fatigue that flooded over one climbing home for supper up slopes of pine and larch?

He rejoiced in the rich soil of Perthshire and looked forward to retirement there. Madame du Deffand made a joke out of "Milord Stormont's" enthusiasm; it never would have occurred to her that one of the strengths of the United Kingdom was the attachment of its countrymen to their lands.

Anglomania is a disease endemic to the French; the fever chart goes up and down depending on circumstance, but the microbe is always latent, and, when Lord Stormont arrived in 1772, English ways had never been more fashionable. As very few people could read English, Shakespeare was beginning to be translated, and rich men had books that they had heard were worth reading translated at their own expense, as did the Duc de Choiseul when Madame du Deffand told him that Walpole had recommended a book by Edward Gibbon, *Decline and Fall of the Roman Empire*. Englishmen touring France were warmly received throughout the country. In Paris, the Palais Royal, where lived the King's cousin, the Duc d'Orléans, was the headquarters for enthusiasts of all things English from racehorses to philosophy. This passion was not in contradiction to the new craze for America and the Americans but paralleled it.

Throughout modern history, down to the present, a clever and attractive British Ambassador could focus pro-British sentiment in Paris and make his embassy a prestigious political and social center unrivaled by that of any other country. Stormont did precisely this. Making friends easily, speaking French perfectly, entertaining generously, he was the most popular foreigner of his day, admired at Versailles as he was in Paris. The King and Queen were charmed by him, and the pro-English Marie Antoinette received his pretty young wife kindly in 1776. His self-confidence is evident in his dispatches, which show an intimate knowledge of the intrigues and cabals of the Court; it was important for London to know who was up and who was down.

That such a shining sun of diplomacy could be eclipsed by a seventy-year-old colonial rebel would have seemed impossible, but, from the moment the *Reprisal* landed at Auray, Lord Stormont was, by his own admission, in a very difficult position. The battle was on during the year 1777, and when at the end of it Maurepas inquired if the British Ambassador had seen Franklin, he replied grimly that he had not but that he had seen his bust. He could hardly have avoided seeing not only a bust but also medallions and snuffboxes carrying Franklin's picture, and sketches and engravings of the new idol of Paris, for they were all over the city.

V

The Mission at Passy

THE FIRST MOVE ON THE diplomatic chessboard in 1777 was
made by the French with the granting of a second secret subsidy
to America of two million livres, to be repaid at an unnamed
date in the future. Emboldened by this success, Franklin came
back at once on January 5 with an audacious memorandum
signed by all three commissioners. In it he requested of France
eight ships of the line and a large quantity of munitions, adding
the optimistic proposition that, if England should declare war,
the "united forces of France, Spain and America" would bring
her to her knees.[1]

Once more Franklin was employing his tactic of bluffing with
a very weak hand. His stiff demands were coldly rejected by
Vergennes, whose reply was transmitted orally by Gérard because, as he wrote to the French Ambassador to Spain, "we
don't want to put a written document into the hands of the
Americans with which they might cause trouble."[2] Franklin,
who did not permit himself the indulgence of pride, refused to
be downcast by this crushing rejection of his proposal. He ended
the matter with a polite note thanking the French for their message. He never again brought up the subject.

For the next two months Franklin stayed in Paris, going
about a great deal. Then he moved the mission to the quiet village of Passy, just four kilometers from the Place de la Con-

corde, where he seemed to disappear. Vergennes wrote to the Marquis de Noailles in London: "I really do not know what Franklin has come to do here; at the beginning we thought he had all sorts of projects, but all of a sudden he has shut himself up in sanctuary with the philosophes. If he is pursuing any plans, it is not with the King's ministers but with those who oppose them. Apparently opposition is the element in which he thrives."

This comment showed a certain nervousness on the part of the Minister of Foreign Affairs. There were several sources of opposition to the government about which he had to worry. The King's disloyal brothers were forever scheming against him, as were the pro-English Orléans cousins at the Palais Royal. The Duc de Choiseul and his party lurked in the wings, ever hopeful of gaining power; and there were the younger philosophes, a large number of liberal, anti-monarchial thinkers and writers who were articulate heirs to the Encyclopédistes. Any one of these groups would have liked to persuade Franklin to join them in opposing the King and Vergennes.

Franklin would have been surprised had he read Vergennes's comment. Much as he delighted in the company of his intellectual friends, the national interest was his primary concern. It would have been very constructive to have seen more of the ministers. However, as he had not had one word of instruction from Congress, or any news of America in four months, he had nothing to talk to Vergennes about. For all he knew, General Washington was on the run and Lord Howe established as dictator. He could hardly ask for an appointment at Versailles in order to complain of his abandonment.

At last news and instructions came, in mid-March. In their relief, the three lonely commissioners must have read the dispatches again and again. Washington had lunged across the Delaware on Christmas Day, surprised and routed the Hessians at Trenton, and followed up his success at the Battle of Princeton a week later. The two actions were not great victories numerically, but psychologically they were overwhelming. The leader who had fumbled in Long Island and been driven into New Jersey like a stag at bay had displayed generalship of the highest order at a time of year when soldiers were not supposed to fight, and the remnants of his weary army had shown unexpected fortitude. "All our hopes," wrote the crestfallen British Secretary of State for the Colonies, Lord George Germain, "were blasted by the unhappy affair at Trenton."[3]

The instructions sent to the commissioners were euphoric and unrealistic. Congress proposed that France declare war against England, in return for which the United States would help her seize Canada, Newfoundland, the Floridas, the Bahamas, and the British sugar islands in the West Indies. The United States would supply two million dollars and six frigates. As for Spain, she was to be invited to join the war, and the United States would assist her in an attack on Portugal.[4] The dispatch ended with a disturbing little postscript hinting that without direct French intervention America might be obliged to ask England to make peace, granting independence to the former colonies.

Vergennes must have thought the Congress had gone mad when he read the proposal. He answered it politely, pointing out the gravity of the risks involved, and did his best to calm the Spanish Ambassador, the Conde de Aranda, who could hardly believe what he read when Franklin's message reached him. Proud Spain did not and would not recognize the United States, and had no wish for assistance from that miserable little country regarding Portugal or in any other way. Vergennes assured him that France's reply would be negative, as she had no desire to expand her territories, and asked the ambassador to understand and excuse the natural "enthusiasm" of so new and inexperienced a government.[5]

As for the postscript, the Minister of Foreign Affairs ignored it. Maurepas and he were haunted during this wearying period by the terrifying prospect of Great Britain, united with an independent United States, turning on France before she was ready for war, although they thought it unlikely Lord North would abandon his shortsighted policy which offered the colonies no alternative short of total surrender. The episode of the March instructions was soon forgotten.

Franklin went back to work with new hope, savoring the tidings of Trenton and Princeton, making it his policy to disturb Vergennes as seldom as possible. His sparing visits were one way of handling the minister; the British Ambassador had another. Morning, noon, and night he was at Versailles, protesting to Maurepas and Vergennes about the clandestine aid that neutral France was sending to America and especially the use of French harbors and port facilities by American armed ships. "Representations to the Ministers on the shelter and supplies to the privateers *Reprisal*,* *Lexington, Dolphin*," "the matter of the cutter *Greyhound*," "the fitting out of the *Eagle*," are samples of the subject matter in a list of the ambassador's visits to the ministers that cover two long columns of fine print.[6] Consider Stormont's dispatch to Lord Weymouth of August 6, 1777:

"On Monday night I received the honour of your Lordship's letter ⅍48. In the morning, when I went to Versailles, I wrote a note to Monsieur de Maurepas letting him know that I wished to see him for a moment, and that I would wait upon him as soon as I came from Court. I was immediately carried into his Closet. I began the conversation by saying that I was very sorry for the reason that I had for troubling him. The specific cause for the interview was the English desire to restrict American activity in French ports. The orders of the French ministry were being eluded. I was particularly talking about the affair of the *Greyhound*, a cutter at Dunkirk. . . ."

Then came three pages of complaint about the repairs being made to the cutter, followed by: "A great monarch has wise and just sentiments, that lead him to wish the continuance of the public tranquillity, and his ministers make similar professions. Yet their orders are no sooner given than they are eluded or openly overlooked. I must own to you, Sir, that I find myself in the most singular situation a foreign minister ever was placed in. I am naturally desirous to inform my Court of your real senti-

---

* *Stormont made a mistake.* Reprisal *was a naval vessel, not a privateer.*

ments and intentions, but I can form no opinion in regard to them that satisfies my own mind . . . your conduct is not reconcilable to any principles that I can conceive. Your conduct is neither peace nor war—if you really mean what you profess, if you really intend peace, it is astonishing that you suffer things to lead to the brink of the precipice, on the other hand, if France is resolved on war, it is astonishing that she should stoop so low as to use such an instrument to kindle the flame. You promised me in this very place that the *Greyhound* should not be permitted . . ."

This extract from a long dispatch gives an idea of Lord Stormont's style. This lecture was one of his gentler ones; on two other occasions he implicitly threatened war.[7]

Inevitably Maurepas or Vergennes (Stormont preferred his interviews with the former, who seemed the more embarrassed of the two) listened silently to what must have been a two-hour tirade and then, following professions of sympathy and of regret that the ambassador should have felt obliged to question the King's desire for peace, referred Lord Stormont to the department concerned with maritime matters. Monsieur de Sartine, Minister of the Navy, was just the man to talk to.

Why did Stormont press so hard? The French are a race which has always responded badly to scolding lectures from foreigners. While it may sound ill-advised for the ambassador of a great power to threaten, to hector, to try to intimidate the Chief Minister of the power to which he is accredited over the question of a tiny ship like the *Greyhound,* a strong case can be made for Lord Stormont's tactics. What he was seeking to do was to undermine the confidence of the King and the other ministers in the wisdom of Vergennes's policy. His instructions from London were clear: he was to object vehemently to the patent illegality of the flouting of the treaty of 1713 which bound France "not to receive into her harbors the prizes or privateers of Britain's enemies, except in stress of weather, shipwreck, or other real emergencies, nor to allow ships of war to be fitted out there."[8]

Nevertheless, American privateers were constantly entering French harbors to be fitted out for war, and harassing British ships to the point where insurance rates soared by 20 percent in 1777. The prizes were sold for good French gold livres to French buyers, and the Americans went merrily on their way unpunished. It was indeed proper cause for the strongest of protests.

Vergennes's position was not unassailable, and no one understood this better than Lord Stormont, who had observed him "narrowly," to use his own adverb, since 1774. He therefore adopted the deliberate policy of erosion of confidence suggested above, and it might well have succeeded.

Charles Gravier, Comte de Vergennes, had few friends at Court and no public support. The Parisians, totally unaware that the pro-insurgent articles in the papers in the autumn of 1776 were directly inspired by him, invented rude songs which they sang in the streets accusing him of cowardice. A more polite one started with the verse:

> *Querelleur il ne fut jamais;*
> *Toujours il aime la paix,*
> *Nous allons être à présent*
> *Battus, et jamais battants,*
> *Grâce à de Vergennes.†*

Throughout this period, in which attacks on famous personages reached the lowest levels, Vergennes was always the target if the government was the subject of abuse, just as Marie Antoinette, after her initial popularity, became the target of attacks on the Court. This did not make them allies—the Queen disliked him and regretted the loss of Choiseul.

It is ironic that Vergennes, who had the courage and patience to pursue the only pro-American policy in Europe, should have been accused of prudence. Spain, after her first clandestine loan, backed off from giving America support and persisted in her refusal to admit the independence of the new republic. The other

---

† *"Fighter he never was, All he liked was peace, Now we will be beaten and never the winner, Thanks to Vergennes."*

powers feared the wrath of Britain, and Frederick the Great of Prussia, "that great liberal" as the philosophes called him, behaved typically when he told his ministers "not to treat with the American envoy but 'mit Complimenten abweisen' [put him off with compliments]."[9] One of Benjamin Franklin's problems in Paris was to know what to do with the unemployed American emissaries who had been assigned to European courts by the optimistic Congress in Philadelphia and then turned back by the countries to which they had been posted.

Vergennes's private life was a happy one. As a young diplomat he had been rash and passionate. He was dismissed from his post as Ambassador to Turkey for marrying his mistress, by whom he had had two sons. The courtiers at Versailles put it about that he had bought a slave in Constantinople at the bazaar, but this was only malicious gossip; he had fallen in love with Madame Anne Testa, a widow of Franco-Greek origin. They retired to Vergennes's small estates in Burgundy with their sons until such time as he was forgiven and sent to Sweden as ambassador. There he spent several lonely years, as his wife was considered by the Foreign Office too lowborn to accompany him. Reunited when he was named Minister of Foreign Affairs in 1774, he rejoined his family with delight and, as his wife had not yet been received at Court, he bought her a lovely house, "La Solitude," in the town of Versailles.

He himself settled down in the southern apartments of the Ministry of Foreign Affairs, which were in the wing of the palace communicating directly, as did Maurepas's, with the King by means of an inner staircase. From these rooms he wrote to his wife, when the pressure of work prevented his coming home, some charming love letters. One of the first of them showed his state of mind. He thanked her for a bouquet of flowers that she had sent him, for they made him feel less apart from her (they were ten minutes away from each other), and then he burst out: "I have tasted the delights of power that are claimed to give such pleasure. But I feel on the contrary that I am like a ship tossed about in the seas by storms. It would be far easier to navigate my way back to port, but surely it would be premature to take refuge? Forgive the outburst that I am giving you, but between us we can say anything to each other. As for the Court, I am entirely out of my element."[10]

This letter was written in August 1774. The tone soon changed, while the ship steadied. Never again was there a suggestion that Vergennes might not stay the course. The more he studied the character of his master, the more devoted he became to the King and the less inclined to leave his service.

While the people of France still loved Louis XVI in 1777, fashionable society in Paris, composed of men and women who were liberal, pagan, and as dissolute in their morals as they were elegant in their demeanor, felt little loyalty toward the young man who tried so hard to do his best as a Christian monarch. It was easy to make fun of the figure who was very awkward and so shortsighted that he recognized people by the sound of their voices. (The King could not wear glasses, as it was considered beneath his dignity.) But Vergennes never made fun of him. Instead, when he heard from his office overlooking the courtyard of the palace of Versailles the sound of the trumpets announcing the return of the King from hunting, he would rise from his desk and watch from the window, smiling, as the guards sprang to attention and the tired King emerged from his carriage.‡

Beaumarchais was the other younger man to whom Vergennes was devoted, and it was he who suggested the argument most likely to stiffen the resolve of the King and his other ministers should Lord Stormont's thunder cause it to weaken. If England should achieve reconciliation with her former colonies, what was to prevent her seizing the valuable French sugar islands in the West Indies? On the other hand, should the insurgents, with French aid, win their struggle, what a splendid prospect France had of taking over all the lucrative trade with America which had so far been an English monopoly. Ver-

‡ *It was often said that Louis XVI was drunk because he lurched out of his carriage on his return from the hunt. This accusation was false; he was overcome, not by alcohol, but by physical exhaustion at the end of the day because he played as hard as he worked.*

gennes himself was far less interested in trade than he was in balance-of-power politics, but it was a time to use every weapon at his command and he employed the commercial one with considerable effect.

To placate Lord Stormont, he would order American privateers conspicuously seized, only to quietly release them a few weeks later. However, by the end of July such evasive tactics were wearing thin indeed under the British Ambassador's pressure, and on July 23, Vergennes presented to the King a memorandum born of sheer desperation. In it he said that the time had come for France "either to abandon America or to aid her courageously and effectively. Secret assistance was no longer sufficient . . ."[11] He hoped that the King's uncle, the Spanish King, would join France in a defensive and offensive alliance with the United States, and he stated that, in case of a British ultimatum, the joint French and Spanish navies were, if combined, now sufficiently strong to meet the demands of war.*

The King accepted the proposal, on condition that Spain agreed, and Vergennes dispatched the memorandum to Madrid. To French dismay, it was turned down by the new Spanish Foreign Minister, the Conde de Floridablanca. Then came the first news of the American war since Washington's success at Trenton had reached Paris in March. This time the news was bad: General Burgoyne had defeated the Americans at Ticonderoga.

It was a miserable autumn for Franklin at Passy. Vergennes marked time while Lord Stormont renewed his remonstrances. It would still have been possible to adopt the first alternative he had given the King in the July memorandum, i.e., "to abandon America," and a weaker man would have done so. If that had happened, Lord Stormont would have been acclaimed a great ambassador, Franklin an aged failure, and the United States would have lost the War of Independence.

During these months when their cause seemed doomed, each

---

* *Vergennes reckoned that the Spanish contempt for the United States would be outweighed by the terms of the "Pacte de famille" under which France and Spain were bound to support each other.*

of the American commissioners behaved according to his fashion. Solid Silas Deane lived with Franklin and also had rooms in Paris at the corner of the rue Royale and the Place de la Concorde, where he conducted his business. He was responsible for procuring matériel for the American army. Among the major suppliers was Leray de Chaumont, in whose stately château, Chaumont, on the Loire, uniforms were being woven. There were many French merchants to write to, and Deane tried to slip words of encouragement into his letters to them. "The taking of Philadelphia is nothing of any consequence," he remarked breezily in the last paragraph of an order addressed to: "Monsieur Lange, Merchant, at Bordeaux."[12] And then there were the sea captains, with whom his correspondence was voluminous. The privateers which caused Lord Stormont such distress were far more numerous and more important than the ships of the small American navy. It was they that bore the brunt of the war at sea, which has been described as "the splendid madness of challenging the Royal Navy."[13]

Congress had called on the privateers early in the struggle, and any vessel, old or new, that could possibly be converted into a ship of war was prepared for service, armed with a few hastily mounted guns, and sent off to sea. A privateer might be anything from a converted schooner to a small open boat, a ship of the merchant marine or a brig. Privately owned and armed, she bore a letter of marque, or commission, from the government permitting her to prey on the enemy's commerce. While the owners realized the lion's share from the sale of prizes and their cargoes, the rest was divided between officers and crew. At the end of a long cruise, it was not unusual for a common sailor to receive on top of his wages an additional $1,000, an enormous sum for those days. Although eagerly sought, the prizes were incidental. The primary job of the privateers was the transport of supplies.

According to Deane's lists, saltpeter was the most important article the privateers carried. In 1776 there had not been enough gunpowder to stop the third British charge at Bunker

Hill, and when Washington arrived to take over the army he had asked for a stocktaking. It was said that when he saw the figures he was so appalled that he did not speak for half an hour. More than 90 percent of the powder used during the first three years of war had to be imported, and it was the privateers that were the army's lifeline. The little ships were commanded by young men in their twenties who, judging by their letters, were poorly educated, sometimes nearly illiterate, but marvelously brave. They met and engaged both the King's ships and big, heavily armed British privateers. A typical attack was one launched by Captain Haraden of the *General Pickering*, who, with a crew of 45 men and boys and 14 six-pound guns, seized the *Achilles*, a British privateer out of London carrying 150 men and 40 guns.

Deane knew all the captains and wrote them reams of careful advice. Captain Fogg was advised to try for a safe port in New England, traveling under the convoy of Captain Nicholson, and, should he fall behind, to make for the first safe port in North Carolina. It would be kind of Captain Nicholson to deliver a packet of letters with his own hand to Colonel Harrison of Virginia, "if not send it by some safe person." Captain Courter was entrusted with letters and dispatches for the Congress—"on no account will you let them go out of your possession until you deliver them up to the Honourable Committee for Foreign Affairs. On your embarking secure them in a proper manner for being sunk in case of actually being taken by the enemy. We give you one hundred Louis D'Ors for your expenses." It was the nightmare of the commissioners that their dispatches would be lost or seized, as they so often were, and a red-letter day when, after months of waiting for news, Deane could write, "Captain Young, of the sloop *Independence*, arrived at Passy with despatches from Congress."

The attrition was fearful. Arthur Lee wrote a correspondent in Congress on November 30, 1777: "Possibly none of our letters have reached you, or your answers have miscarried; the interceptions of our correspondence have been very considerable.

Adams, by whom we wrote early in the summer, was taken on this coast, having sunk his despatches. We hear that Hammond suffered the same fate on your coast. Johnson, by whom we wrote in September, was taken going out of the channel; and poor Capt. Lambert Wickes, who sailed at the same time and had duplicates, we just now hear has foundered near Newfoundland, every man perishing but the cook. This loss is extremely to be lamented; as he was a gallant officer and a very worthy man. Your despatches which were coming on a small sloop from Morris' River, and by the ——————— Packet, were both sunk on the vessels being boarded by English men-of-war."

Congress did not receive a single one of Franklin's dispatches during his first year abroad. This was disturbing enough, but much more serious was the loss of the ships carrying the precious tools of war to General Washington. It will never be known for how many interceptions the spy Bancroft was directly responsible. He had every opportunity, living as he did with Franklin at Passy, a bosom member of the little official family.

Arthur Lee did not live with Franklin, Deane, Bancroft, and the grandsons. This curious man had not been the original choice of the Congress, for it had been hoped that Thomas Jefferson would be the third commissioner. When Jefferson found himself unable to leave his affairs in America, Lee appeared to be a suitable replacement. Born into one of the most famous families of Virginia, Arthur Lee at thirty-six had all the qualifications needed for the job save one. He was well educated: a graduate of Eton College and the University of Edinburgh, where he had taken a law degree. He had traveled widely in Europe before taking Franklin's position as Colonial Agent for Massachusetts in London in 1775; he was fluent in French and other tongues and was a true patriot, dedicated to the cause of independence. It was an exemplary dossier.

Unfortunately he completely lacked the ability to get along with his fellow men. This is a serious defect in any calling, but in a small diplomatic mission under wartime strains, it can be dangerous. Beaumarchais, who had worked with him in London, spoke of him as "the bilious Arthur Lee, with his yellow skin, green eyes, yellow teeth, and hair always in disorder." Vergennes wrote: *"Je crains* [I fear] *Monsieur Arthur Lee,"* meaning not that he was physically afraid of him, but that he dreaded his visits. The usually patient Franklin wrote to Joseph Reed in Philadelphia on Lee's departure: "I caution you to beware of him; for in sowing suspicions and jealousies, in creating misunderstandings and quarrels, in malice, subtility, and indefatigable industry, he has I think no equal."[14]

It was Lee's suspiciousness that made Franklin in another instance write that he had a sick mind. Having misunderstood the sense of Beaumarchais's supply contract with Deane, Lee became persuaded that the two men had combined to steal the public monies. Franklin he thought "was concerned in the plunder, and in time we shall collect proofs."[15] Franklin's grandnephew, Jonathan Williams, American shipping agent at Nantes, was surely in on the dishonest game. Then there were the spies—Arthur Lee saw spies everywhere, and while there were indeed a great many British agents in Paris in 1777, Lee missed one who was right under his nose, Major John Thornton, his own secretary.

Jealous of Silas Deane, whom he accused of having assumed responsibilities that should have been his, resentful of Franklin's eminence and the veneration with which he was regarded in Paris, Arthur Lee eagerly seized the opportunities two missions gave him, one to Spain and the other to Berlin. Both were unsuccessful and Berlin was positively ludicrous. Already frustrated at being snubbed by Baron Schulenburg, the Prime Minister, who told him that he could only remain in Prussia as a private citizen, he was further maddened by discovering on returning to his hotel one June day that all his papers had been stolen. Certain that the British were guilty, Lee raised such a fuss that the King ordered an examination of the case and the papers were returned as mysteriously as they had disappeared. For once the paranoid Lee was quite correct in his suspicions, and Hugh Elliot, the British Minister in Berlin, received from his government an official reprimand and, less officially, a reward of 1,000 pounds in cash.

In Paris, Arthur Lee had two companions, both as unhappy as he himself. One was his brother William, who had been appointed to Berlin and Vienna by the Congress but was received by neither Court. The other was Ralph Izard, a well-to-do South Carolinian who had been appointed to Tuscany. He too had been turned away. With nothing to do, the two unemployed diplomats hung around Franklin's neck like millstones and, when not engaged in cadging a meal at Passy, employed themselves in criticizing Franklin and Deane and egging on Arthur Lee in his campaign of backbiting and intrigue.

The autumn brought news of the loss of Philadelphia to Lord Howe, following the fall of Ticonderoga and ominous rumors of further engagements in upper New York State, where General Gates and General Arnold were facing General Burgoyne. Franklin's unruffled composure was heroic. "To the French, he still showed the calm, smiling face which reassured and charmed them."[16] It did not improve the morale of the mission to receive letters from Congress announcing that the country could not survive without alliances and further loans. It was, in Thomas Paine's famous phrase spoken earlier that year, "a time to try men's souls."

While Silas Deane plodded on, drafting letter after earnest letter to the merchants and the sea captains, Arthur Lee too was writing letters. His were of another kind. To his two brothers in America, both members of Congress from Virginia, and to his friend Samuel Adams, also in Congress, went page after page attacking Deane for misappropriation of public funds. The vindictive attack paid off, and Deane was recalled the following March to account for himself.

Arthur Lee was also busy on his own behalf. On October 4, he wrote two letters, one to Sam Adams in which he stated that after having visited several of the courts of Europe he had found that "this of France is the great wheel that moves them all. . . .

If there should ever be a question in Congress about my destination I should be much obliged to you if you would remember that I should prefer being at the court of France." To Richard Henry Lee he wrote, "My idea, therefore, of adapting characters and places is this: Dr. Franklin to Vienna . . . respectable and quiet; Deane to Holland, the Alderman [William Lee] to Berlin."

There is only one reason that this poisonous, egocentric, arrogant intriguer should be remembered in American history and that is for recording a conversation with Franklin on October 25 in which the latter recounted the story of the revolution as he had seen it while Lee was in England. It was the kind of talk that leaders ordinarily engage in when the battle is over and they have time to reminisce about the past. Only a man of Franklin's greatness could have detached himself from his present gloom and ordered his thoughts into the noble words that come clearly to us through the unlikely hand of Arthur Lee:

> He told me the manner in which the whole of this business had been conducted was such a miracle in human affairs, that had he not been in the midst of it, and seen all the movements, he could not have comprehended how it was effected. To comprehend it we must view a whole people for some months without any laws or government at all. In this state their civil governments were to be formed, an army and navy were to be provided by those who had neither a ship of war, a company of soldiers, nor magazines, arms, artillery or ammunition. Alliances were to be formed, for they had none. All this was to be done, not at leisure nor in a time of tranquility and communication with other nations, but in the face of a most formidable invasion, by the most powerful nation, fully provided with armies, fleets, and all the instruments of destruction, powerfully allied and aided, the commerce with other nations in a great measure stopped up, and every power from whom they could expect to procure arms, artillery, and ammunition, having by the influence of their enemies forbade their subjects to supply them on any pre-

tence whatever. Nor was this all; they had internal opposition to encounter, which alone would seem sufficient to have frustrated all their efforts. The Scotch, who in many places were numerous, were secret or open foes as opportunity offered. The Quakers, a powerful body in Pennsylvania, gave every opposition their art, abilities and influence could suggest. To these were added all those whom contrariety of opinion, tory principles, personal animosities, fear of so dreadful and dubious an undertaking, joined with the artful promises and threats of the enemy rendered open or concealed opposers, or timid neutrals, or lukewarm friends to the proposed revolution. It was, however, formed and established in despite of all these obstacles, with an expedition, energy, wisdom, and success of which most certainly the whole history of human affairs has not, hitherto, given an example. To account for it we must remember that the revolution was not directed by the leaders of faction, but by the opinion and voice of the majority of the people; that the grounds and principles upon which it was formed were known, weighed and approved by every individual of that majority. It was not a tumultuous resolution, but a deliberate system. Consequently, the feebleness, irresolution, and inaction which generally, nay, almost invariably attends and frustrates hasty popular proceedings, did not influence this. On the contrary, every man gave his assistance to execute what he had soberly determined, and the sense of the magnitude and danger of the undertaking served only to quicken their activity, rouse their resources, and animate their exertions. Those who acted in council bestowed their whole thoughts upon the public; those who took the field did, with what weapons, ammunition and accommodation they could procure. In commerce, such profits were offered as tempted the individuals of almost all nations, to break through the prohibition of their governments, and furnish arms and ammunition, for which they received from a people ready to sacrifice every thing to the common cause, a thousand fold. The effects of anarchy were prevented by the influence of public shame, pursuing the man who offered to take a dis-

honest advantage of the want of law. So little was the
effects of this situation felt, that a gentleman, who thought
their deliberations on the establishment of a form of gov-
ernment too slow, gave it as his opinion that the people
were likely to find out that laws were not necessary, and
might therefore be disposed to reject what they proposed,
if it were delayed. Dr. Franklin assured me that upon an
average he gave twelve hours in the twenty-four to public
business. One may conceive what progress must be made
from such exertions of such an understanding, aided by
the cooperation of a multitude of others upon such busi-
ness, not of inferior abilities. The consequence was, that in
a few months, the governments were established; codes of
law were formed, which, for wisdom and justice, are the
admiration of all the wise and thinking men in Europe.
Ships of war were built, a multitude of cruisers were fitted
out, which have done more injury to the British commerce
than it ever suffered before. Armies of offence and defence
were formed, and kept the field, through all the rigours of
winter, in the most rigorous climate. Repeated losses, inevi-
table in a defensive war, as it soon became, served only to
renew exertions that quickly repaired them. The enemy
was every where resisted, repulsed, or besieged. On the
ocean, in the channel, in their very ports, their ships were
taken, and their commerce obstructed. The greatest revolu-
tion the world ever saw, is likely to be effected in a few
years; and the power that has for centuries made all
Europe tremble, assisted by 20,000 German mercenaries,
and favoured by the universal concurrence of Europe to
prohibit the sale of warlike stores, the sale of prizes, or the
admission of the armed vessels of America, will be effec-
tually humbled by those whom she insulted and injured,
because she conceived they had neither spirit nor power to
resist or revenge it.[17]

If Franklin's words made any impression on Arthur Lee he
did not record the fact. His next diary entry is typically self-pitying, full of the persecutions he suffered from Deane.

November was a terrible month. The mists from the river

enveloped the village of Passy, and the inhabitants of the Hôtel de Valentinois felt that the cold was penetrating their very bones. Deane worried about his little son Jesse, whom he adored and from whom he had no news, although the boy was due to arrive in France to join him and receive the advantages of a European education in the same school as Franklin's grandson Benny Bache.† The tension between Lee and Deane grew so great that while working in the same house they communicated by correspondence in the third person:

"Mr. Deane's compliments to Mr. Lee, and once for all distinctly insists that when he has complaints to make he makes them to the right person . . ."[18]

Dr. Bancroft did his best to keep up the spirits of the mission while they waited for news of the engagements they knew to have taken place the preceding month at home. Twice there were rumors of victories—twice the sources turned out to be unreliable.

It was on December 4, just before noon, that Jonathan Loring Austin of Boston jumped out of his carriage and ran up the steps, all but shouting his great tidings. Burgoyne's entire army had surrendered at Saratoga!

Beaumarchais, who happened to be on hand that morning, raced off to Paris at such reckless speed (he was probably eager to speculate as a result of the news) that his cabriolet overturned, and he injured his arm badly.[19] That other great speculator, Dr. Bancroft, left hurriedly for London. Franklin calmly prepared the following announcement, to be circulated all over Paris that same historic day:

> *Mail arrived from Philadelphia at Dr. Franklin's house in Passy after 34 days.*
> *On October 14th General Burgoyne was forced to lay down his arms, 9200 men killed or taken prisoner.*
> *Besides the General, 4 members of the English Parliament were among the prisoners.*

† *Jesse eventually arrived in April, in charge of John Adams, and Franklin undertook the responsibilities of his education.*

General Howe is in Philadelphia, where he is imprisoned. All communication with his fleet is cut off. Seventeen of his ships which wished to approach were destroyed or captured.

General Washington with his army, other generals with detached forces and militia are surrounding the city. General Gates and his victorious army are coming to join them.[20]

❧ VI ❧

Danger and Triumph

FRANKLIN HAD BEEN WARNED by a friend soon after his arrival in Paris that he must beware of the spies who were surely all around him. He replied on January 19, 1777, in a letter over which he must have taken careful pains, for it is full of crossings out and corrections:

"As it is impossible to discover in every case the falsity of pretended friends who would know our affairs; and more so to prevent being watched by spies when interested people may think proper to place them for that purpose; I have long observed one rule which prevents any inconvenience from such practices. It is simply this: to be concerned in no affairs that I should blush to have made publick, and to do nothing but what spies may see and welcome. Where man's actions are just and honorable, the more they are known, the more his reputation is increased and established. If I was sure, therefore, that my valet de place was a spy, as he probably is, I think I should not discharge him for that, if in other respects, I liked him. . . ."

The former Director of the Central Intelligence Agency, Mr. Richard Helms, kindly gave the author an up-to-date opinion on Franklin's letter: "There is a substantial difference between living an official and personal life which is beyond reproach (or embarrassment) and having state or military secrets spied out by a foreign agent. One's personal misbehavior may lead to blackmail but in and of itself seldom loses wars. The information Dr. Bancroft acquired might have done just that. Franklin may have been naïve in these matters (Americans are to this day, I can assure you), or he may have been afflicted with that strange conviction which appears to derive from the Christian religion: if one is pure of heart and upright in conduct, God will somehow protect one from evil, harm, and maybe even spies."

The remarkable naïveté of Franklin's thinking can only be explained by the view just cited.

The hierarchy of the British Secret Service in 1777 went as follows: William Eden, the chief, bearing the nominal title of Undersecretary of the Foreign Office, reported to the two Secretaries of State for Foreign Affairs, the Lords Weymouth and Suffolk. All important communications went to the King and Lord North. Deputy to Eden and in charge of superintending the continental agents was Paul Wentworth.

Wentworth, a relative of a close friend of John Adams, Governor John Wentworth of New Hampshire, was a Tory gentleman with excellent manners. He owned land in New Hampshire and also a plantation in Surinam, where he had met Edward Bancroft before the war. A cosmopolitan figure, he had spent the last ten years in and out of Paris. There he kept a mistress, Mademoiselle Desmaillis, in whose house he gave lavish parties for his many French friends. Beaumarchais, who knew him well, told Vergennes that he spoke French perfectly, "as well as you do, and better than I."[1]

Wentworth's Paris acquaintances were mainly bankers and merchants, with the odd exception of the philosopher Abbé Raynal, whose best-selling book on America had made him famous. His friends knew him as a heavy speculator in international markets, and while his stock-jobbing was not always successful he was admired for the irreproachable honesty of his dealings. At the beginning of the colonial struggle, he favored the patriot cause and assumed the position of Colonial Agent for the Province of New Hampshire, just as Franklin was the Agent for Massachusetts. But he resigned before hostilities began, having already entered the Secret Service of His Majesty's government.[2]

At a time when corruption was rife and venality common-place, Wentworth was unusual in that he was never mercenary. He refused to take more for his services than his agreed salary of 500 pounds a year. Lord North wrote of Wentworth: "As he refuses all indemnification and indeed every sort of emolument except a place, I really am distressed when I propose to him the trouble and expense of these expeditions."[3] The reward he desired, and which was half promised to him, was a seat in Parliament, a baronetcy, and a respected position in what would now be called the "British Establishment."

Unscrupulous except in money matters, Wentworth was an intelligence agent of unusual natural ability. His audacity and competence made him invaluable to Eden. He kept twenty addresses and went under as many different aliases as he organized an intricate continental network of spies. Beaumarchais, who feared him, was among his greatest admirers and regarded him as one of the cleverest men in England.[4] It was Paul Wentworth who turned Bancroft the summer that the latter met Deane in Paris. He negotiated his salary, trained him, taught him what information he was expected to extract from the American mission and how to convey it. The dangerous expedient of the drop in the hollow tree in the Tuileries gardens was a typical Wentworth touch.

The techniques used to transmit secret messages during the Revolutionary period would seem crude today. Aside from invisible ink, there were ciphers, of which the most frequently employed by both British and Americans was the Dictionary code.* Eden favored the Walpole code but Wentworth seldom used any of them, preferring instead to trust his couriers and write longhand reports in which he substituted numbers for proper names. (Vergennes was #201, Franklin #72, and so on.)

Despising Bancroft as a man because of his endless demands for money, Wentworth had the highest regard for him profes-

---

* "The use of a dictionary paged backwards, supplemented by the use of a transposed alphabet. . . . A 'transposed alphabet' is apparently a subsitution system in which the cipher alphabet is a reversed standard alphabet." Wayne G. Barker, ed., History of Codes and Ciphers (Aegean Press, 1978).

sionally. The double-dealing doctor was as reliable as he was hard-working. But should he fail in his duty to report the innermost secrets of the American commissioners to Eden, should he omit to provide Lord Stormont with further evidence of French violations of neutrality, a backup agent was in place as Arthur Lee's secretary. He was John Thornton, an able young man. The "third man" in the American mission was William Carmichael.

The case of William Carmichael has been before the diplomatic historians for two hundred years, but the verdict is not yet in. What is certain is that "he went to the verge, if not over the edge, of treason."[5]

An agreeable young Marylander of independent means, Carmichael had come over from London to offer his services to Silas Deane before Franklin's arrival. The hard-pressed Deane took him on as secretary. During his stay in London he had lived much in the company of American sea captains and their mistresses, and his natural taste for low company made him useful when the time came for the commissioners to recruit the men who would be commanding the munition ships and privateers fitting out in France. Deane kept a regular table at his old home, the Hôtel de Hambourg, where Carmichael could play host to "such of his Countrymen as are engaged in the service of the Congress."[6]

These countrymen were a rough crowd, sailors on leave—brave men trying to forget the dangers ahead of them on future voyages in the brief oblivion provided by women and drink, courtesy of their sophisticated friend, William Carmichael. One of Wentworth's agents, Colonel Edward Smith, kept a close eye on the roistering group at the Hôtel de Hambourg with the intention of winning over Carmichael, who, as Silas Deane's confidential secretary, would have been a useful prize. Smith entrusted the task of subverting Carmichael to one of the sea captains, Captain Hynson from the Eastern Shore of Maryland. Hynson was a natural choice, as the two men had been cronies in London, where their mistresses lived together. A miserable, venal young man who wholly lacked the patriotism of his fellow seamen, he was willing enough to sell out to the British, but it is doubtful that he accomplished his task. He boasted to his superior that his friend and fellow Marylander had promised him the opportunity to embezzle state papers from Deane's office, he intimated that he had all but brought Carmichael "into the system," he raised Smith's hopes to such a point that he wrote an optimistic report to Eden on the case. But did he really bring Carmichael over the edge of treason? The evidence is flimsy.

There almost seemed to be two William Carmichaels. One was the boon companion of the hard-drinking sea captains who wrote a note to Hynson in June from the apartment he had taken in the Palais Royal, where he was entertaining Dr. Bancroft as a temporary guest. Deane was up in Normandy, working on a shipment with Beaumarchais. In full holiday mood, he told Hynson: "Bancroft and I keep a decent house. We see none but Ladies of the first Quality. I have not seen a strumpet for three weeks." It would be interesting to know more about the Carmichael-Bancroft friendship. The insignificant traitor Hynson disappeared from the scene soon after the failure of one of Eden's more unsuccessful plots and returned to America in disgrace.

The other William Carmichael was the serious young diplomat who addressed an earnest appeal to Vergennes:

"At this very instant, I am performing a duty to my fellow-citizens," he wrote. "It is in the interests of France not to allow the ardour of the American people to cool, which it might as certain Members of Congress are Repenting their Decision to take up arms and declare Independence. Wearied by a ruinous war the Americans may listen to an Accommodation and then France would lose forever the Opportunity of Humiliating England and of acquiring for herself an immense Commerce, becoming the Factor and also the Mart of Europe."

The minister himself could not have better stated his own chief concern. To add to his worries, the early spring of 1777 had brought a mass of rumors to the effect that the British government was engaging in a peace offensive. This was a ploy on the part of Eden, and a very effective gambit in the war of nerves of which Lord Stormont's exhausting visits to Versailles were a part. Then there were Beaumarchais's letters to Vergennes couched in the author's dramatic style:

> *Sunday, March 8*
> *Monsieur le Comte:*
> *Another letter, you will say—the man never stops. Well! How can I stop, Monsieur le Comte, when every moment new subjects arouse my vigilance? You had better know everything. Lord Germain's private secretary has arrived via Le Havre, on a secret mission to see Mr. Deane and Dr. Franklin. He is carrying peace proposals and has been offered a superb reward if he succeeds. The offers are such that they can be sent to Philadelphia without the slightest discredit to the honor of the envoys.*[7]

> *Monday, March 9*
> *Monsieur le Comte,*
> *The peace offers are magnificent, perfectly acceptable . . . please inform Monsieur de Maurepas and give me your orders for Versailles. . . .*

> *Undated*
> *Monsieur le Comte,*
> *We now think, in fact we are pretty sure that Mr. Schmitz, secretary to the Lord, is right here in Paris at Lord Stormont's where he is carrying out his master's secret orders relating to the accommodation with America.*
> *He is disguised in a chaplain's wig while little Matly, the real chaplain, is pretending to have renounced the church and to have given up his place to a new incumbent. I am on the track of the rest of the story and it will not escape me.*

Beaumarchais had every reason to sound feverish. While he was genuinely devoted to the American cause, there was also the question of the personal fortune he had invested in Roderigue Hortalez.

This particular rumor turned out to be false, but another disturbing development had been brought to the attention of Vergennes by Silas Deane. The very heading of the report, addressed to Gérard, is out of a detective story:

"Report from Monsieur Gérard received from Mr. Deane concerning the nocturnal conference held near the statue in the Place Vendôme between Mr. Carmichael and an 'Unknown.' "8

Deane wished to inform Gérard of the negotiations which a person not named had broached with William Carmichael, the first part of which Franklin and he had already given Vergennes. The minister had advised that the meetings should be continued in order to clarify the intentions of the "Unknown." These were now made painfully clear.

The latest interview, like the others, had taken place late at night. The stranger warned that it was the ambition of France to weaken England and her colonies, the one by means of the other, in order to humiliate the one and to conquer the other. He set himself to approach the Americans with their error and their blindness. "Judge," he said to Carmichael, "the intentions of France and Spain by their conduct. What could be more feeble and insignificant than the assistance which is given to you? It is certain they will never go to war with England. . . . Why not deal with England? The English government is resolved to treat with you on satisfactory conditions. The dignity of the Crown and that of Parliament will not yet allow them to make the first advances, but they only desire to have a basis of some kind, and overtures from you of some kind."9

Vergennes evidently took the story very seriously, for he informed the King and Maurepas immediately, and wrote a long report to the Court of Spain in his own hand describing it. At the last moment he held back this report, which was never sent. Why? One wonders. Could he have doubted Carmichael's veracity?

People who did not wish to be seen together in eighteenth-century Paris met at a variety of places, such as the public baths on the Seine, which were popular with those seeking a discreet rendezvous for love or business. The attendant left his clients alone after opening with his key the little cabin containing two chairs, a couch, towels, and the bath. Franklin himself once chose the Bains Poitevin for a business meeting. Then there were dusky groves in the parks; there were small hotels that specialized in letting rooms by the hour, no questions asked. By comparison with these, the Place Vendôme in the dead of night was a lunatic choice for an assignation. The beautiful, vast square was lonely after dark, its great houses shuttered, unless the owners were entertaining. Any passing policeman or ministerial spy would have been electrified at the sight of two men huddled together under the equestrian statue that then stood in the center of the square. And what prompted Carmichael to go the Place Vendôme in the first instance? It was a risky thing to meet a man alone in the dark who wouldn't give his name. And who was the English interlocutor? Obviously one of Eden's agents. He wouldn't have trusted one of his minor operatives with this assignment. It could have been Paul Wentworth, or at the very least Colonel Smith, both of whom were known to the American.

What is certain in the mysterious story is that Vergennes distrusted Carmichael so much that Franklin and Deane, despite their faith in him, were obliged to send him home a few months later on the excuse of carrying dispatches. He became a member of Congress from Maryland for a year, but diplomacy still attracted him. He joined John Jay's mission to Spain in 1779, serving as secretary of legation. Jay grew to distrust him intensely, and beautiful Sarah Jay, who was a stranger to malice, wrote the one venomous letter of her life on the subject of William Carmichael.

The Battle of Saratoga awoke the English to the real danger of the situation. Until then it hadn't seemed possible that they could lose the American colonies—to many members of Parliament it had all been a bad dream invented by the Whig opposition. To the worried Cabinet it became obvious that they must send their best man to sound out the Americans at Passy as to what offers of reconciliation they would now accept. Paul Wentworth, Eden's most brilliant agent, was their choice. As North wrote to the King, "he is the truest and most important informer we have."

Unfortunately, George III, who had read all Wentworth's reports, greatly disliked the bad news they contained and dismissed the warnings as he had those of Bancroft since 1776. Diverting his attention from the ill tidings to their bearer, he announced that reliance could not be placed on the word of a speculator. In fact, no power had ever been better informed of the secrets of its adversaries than was England by its Secret Service. But the King's horror of gambling, combined with his distaste for adverse reports, caused him to reject the truth. And so the olive branch that could have divided opinion in America two years earlier was offered too late.

Late as it was, Paul Wentworth did his best in Paris that December. On arrival, he had written to Silas Deane to say that "a gentleman who already had some acquaintance with him wished to improve this; but fearing objections to an unexpected visit asked the favor of a private interview." He announced that he would wait for him in his coach on the following morning near the Barrier leading to Passy. After this he would attend the exhibition at the Luxembourg Gallery, and in the evening would go to the Poitevin Bathing Machine (public baths) on the river, leaving a note with the number of the room engaged.[10] Deane replied crisply that he would be in his office on the rue Royale in the morning, where he would be delighted to see anyone who had business with him.

The two men's meeting was a long one, continued over a roast at dinner. Wentworth described the plan of conciliation, under which the colonies were to be self-governing in their own affairs and Parliament was to intervene only in external matters. Then he offered the Connecticut merchant the richest of bribes, dangling before him a Christmas garland of honors. Privy Seals, Great Seals, baronies, knighthoods, and governor-generalships would be awaiting any American who helped to bring about a settlement, and with these fine administrative positions would come great wealth.

Deane rejected the propositions outright, and when Franklin at last received Wentworth two weeks later, it was on the express understanding that no bribes would be offered. They had known each other since the days in London when each had represented his own province, and Wentworth was astonished by the change in his former friend. Having made it clear that America would never consent to peace without independence and that he had no power to treat, Franklin then wandered on in a manner that the spy considered "eccentric." "Nobody says less, generally, and keeps a point more closely in view, but he was diffuse and unmethodical today."

Nothing could have been further from Franklin's mind than to have an efficient business conversation. He had nothing to say to Wentworth, but for the sake of Vergennes's police agent who was surely pacing the street outside the house at Passy, eye on watch, it was imperative to give the appearance of a long, important interview. He meandered, reminiscing about the past, then, turning to the barbarities of the British during the war, "he lost breath in relating the burnings of towns, the neglect or ill-treatment of prisoners . . ."

After a good two hours of this Deane came in, and Franklin invited Wentworth to stay and dine with them and Bancroft. The conversation was cheerful but completely inconsequential. Wentworth went home the next day. His visit, by increasing French anxiety over a possible Anglo-American rapprochment, had greatly assisted the Americans. Vergennes was worried by his spy's report of the long interview—the friendly luncheon.

Upon receipt of the news of an American victory at Saratoga, he had sent his congratulations to Franklin. A few days later he followed up this formal overture by a secret meeting with the Americans. He spoke of his desire to conclude the alliance for which they had been asking for over a year, contingent, of course, on the agreement of Spain. It would take three weeks for his courier to go to Madrid and return with the answer. But only five days later Gérard announced that the government had decided for the alliance and that France would go ahead alone. For the sake of courtesy to their Spanish ally, they would not conclude the negotiations until the courier returned.

Wentworth's appearance had precipitated events. His arrival had been picked up at once by the police, and it was known that he was in close touch with Lord Stormont, who did not hide his visits. But what exactly had he come to propose to the envoys at Passy? While Vergennes had perfect faith in Franklin's integrity, there existed the familiar nightmare possibility: the British might have offered terms that no ambassador could turn down.

The threat was useful in convincing Louis XVI and those ministers who remained recalcitrant. Despite the echoes of Turgot's warnings of the year before and without the approval of Spain, whose negative reply was received on New Year's Eve, the whole council voted affirmatively on January 7, the day after Franklin's interview with Wentworth. Maurepas had been laid up with a crippling attack of gout during the three weeks of the crisis, and the King, accompanied by Vergennes and his closest assistants, had climbed the stairs up to the low-ceilinged room under the roofs of Versailles day after day to consult with the bedridden Chief Minister. The sick old man, the unprepossessing King, and the "prudent" Minister of Foreign Affairs were together responsible for the bold decision. To them it must have seemed an eternity since the days when they were poring over the reports of Bonvouloir and Beaumarchais, but it had taken less than two years to change the course of world history.

It was nearly a month before the Treaty of Amity and Commerce was signed. The delay was caused by the French hope that the Spanish would change their minds and come in. During this interim period, the British should have made a preemptive strike, for, as the Secret Service and the navy had managed to keep Congress completely in the dark about Franklin's progress toward an alliance with the French, a generous offer of reconciliation from the English might have been gratefully received in America. Washington was forced to spend that grim winter immobilized in Valley Forge, and despite the victory at Saratoga the preceding October, many members of Congress rightly foresaw a long, exhausting struggle ahead. Fortunately for the United States, the cherished British habit of a long parliamentary Christmas recess was ineluctably engrained. Consequently, the British government remained at a standstill until mid-February.

North and Eden had been watching the European situation closely, and when the Elector of Bavaria died without an heir on December 30, 1777, they observed with delight Vergennes's dangerous position. Joseph II of Austria, the older brother of Marie Antoinette, prepared to add the rich country to his empire. Frederick the Great of Prussia could hardly sit by while the Hapsburgs picked off this rich plum. He mobilized for war. Joseph II at once asked for 20,000 French troops should the Prussians attack. At the same moment, Frederick II asked for help from Louis XVI. It looked very like the start of a general European war.

However, Vergennes had made his decision long ago. Writing to the Marquis de Noailles, his ambassador in London, on January 17, he said:

"The death of the Elector of Bavaria is a regrettable event, but, thank God, it will not force us to be distracted from our true interests. I have no difficulty imagining the pleasure it would cause London to see us engulfed in German affairs. We have too often made wars for interests that are not our own, but I do not believe that this time we will fall into temptation."[11]

In another note to Noailles, he ordered the ambassador to encourage the English in their hope that France would be drawn into a major continental war and to imply that Versailles was in a state of deep disquiet. For Noailles's own information, he added that there was no fear of the government being diverted from "our first enemy, England."

It had by no means been as easy as Vergennes made it sound. Marie Antoinette, who could be aroused to political passion when the affairs of Austria were in question, was up in arms against the passivity of the Minister of Foreign Affairs, and the Cabinet was uncertain as to what course should be adopted. The resolute Vergennes stuck to his policy of non-intervention. He eventually arbitrated a European settlement that was known as the Peace of Teschen.

On February 6, 1778, a little group of French and Americans gathered in Silas Deane's rooms on the corner of the rue Royale and the Place de la Concorde, in that noble house known as the Hôtel de Coislin. Gérard signed the treaty† for France, followed by Franklin, Deane, and Lee. Franklin had abandoned his usual brown coat for a blue velvet one, and the others wore their best clothes. Dr. Bancroft, urbane as usual, was on hand and managed to get a copy of the treaty to London in forty-two hours, the receipt of which precipitated a dramatic race across the Atlantic.

The British Parliament was at last roused to action. On February 17, Lord North introduced his bill of conciliation with the colonies. Before the measures had even gone through Parliament, the draft was rushed off on the warship *Andromeda,* which reached New York on April 14. The preceding day, the French ship *Sensible,* carrying the Franco-American agreement, had landed at Casco Bay, having gone north to avoid the British cruisers lying in wait along the coast from Philadelphia to Boston. Silas Deane's brother Simeon carried the treaty overland to Congress in York, Pennsylvania.[12]

It was a close race. The British terms assured home rule for the colonies, reform of the taxation laws, a truce to be followed by a general pardon. All the objectionable acts passed since 1763

† *The substance of the treaty was: "France was to help the United States achieve its independence. The United States was to make common cause with France if war should break out between France and Great Britain. Neither should conclude peace with England without the consent of the other, and they mutually agreed not to lay down their arms till American independence should have been assured by treaty. In the matter of commerce, France and the United States were to be most-favored nations to each other, with certain stipulations, and their ports freely open to trade in general." Carl Van Doren,* Benjamin Franklin, *p. 595.*

were to be suspended. Peace commissioners would soon arrive to enter into talks about the details of the agreements. The offer was tempting. Knowing nothing of the negotiations in Paris and concerned over the cost of the war, some members of Congress initiated a movement to accept the Bills of Conciliation. May 2 brought the amazing text of the French alliance with a letter of explanation from Franklin. When the British peace commissioners arrived, they found the alliance ratified by a revitalized Congress, united in its aim of achieving complete independence.

In Paris, hostilities seemed imminent by March and Lord Stormont was recalled. He left Paris on March 20, the very day that Franklin and his fellow commissioners were received by Louis XVI.

The courtyard of the Palace of Versailles was a scene of intense activity on ordinary days: merchants displaying and selling their wares, tourists from Paris and the rest of France who had come to see the Palace and Court, officious porters who rented ceremonial swords to those visitors who did not have them, for it was forbidden to enter the Palace without one. There were people coming on business to the ministers' wing, where Vergennes toiled, there were flocks of sedan chairs for ladies, bearing the King's arms, and carriages belonging to the privileged few who had the right to drive in: dukes and peers, ambassadors, cardinals, foreign grandees. It was crowded, messy, and very noisy. The public privies were in one corner directly beneath Voltaire's apartment, which was one small, smelly room.

On the day of Franklin's visit the word that he was coming had got about, and the crowds had been waiting patiently all day on the Avenue de Paris to see him arrive. The coaches entered the gilded gates to shouts of *"Vive Franklin!" "Vive l'Amérique!"* as the people surged forward, attempting to push their way over the cobblestones to where the little cortège had stopped at the entrance to the Salle des Ambassadeurs.

In the background, filling the Cour de Marbre, stood the troops of the King's Household, an elite corps of royal bodyguards with enormous dash and style. The Gardes Françaises wore long, sky-blue coats, red vests, and red stockings. Next to them were the Gardes Suisses in red coats, blue vests, and stockings. White plumes soared from the officers' multicolored tricorn hats, and the regimental flags, great silken squares of every hue, rippled in the light breeze.

It was a festive, gala day, yet dignified in its joy and celebration. The sonorous drums sounded their deep, martial beat as the American envoys entered the palace and mounted the Escalier de la Reine between two stiffly erect rows of honor guards. Led by an official whose title was "introducer of ambassadors," they passed through a large room known as the Salle des Gardes. Here the bodyguards ate and slept; today their camp beds had been thrust behind screens, and their rough tables and chairs were arranged in orderly fashion against the leather-covered walls.

Then came an antechamber paneled in gold and white which led into the "Oeil-de-Boeuf," the long, richly ornamented room where the courtiers congregated at Versailles. Between the King's and Queen's state apartments, just off the Galérie des Glaces, it was always full of huddled groups discussing the latest news, a wary eye on the door of the King's room. Here were heard the first rumors of scandal, the first hints of changes of appointments, the first whisper of the latest intrigue or cabal.

The Oeil-de-Boeuf was crowded as the Americans entered. A hush fell over the courtiers as they craned their necks to see. Four of the diplomats, Silas Deane, Ralph Izard, Arthur Lee, and his brother William, were wearing court dress as etiquette demanded. Franklin had had too much success playing the simple Quaker philosopher to abandon the role now. He made the concession of exchanging his fur hat for a white one, but he wore a plain brown velvet suit with his white stockings and buckled shoes.

The Duc de Croÿ, an elderly aristocrat who managed always to be at the center of events at Versailles, stepped forward to greet Franklin. He had just been telling a friend how strange it was to have Lord Stormont gone, and he wrote in his diary:

"What an idea to substitute a rebel for the British Ambassador on the very day of his departure!" In spite of his resentment, the old courtier could not resist a gesture of respect for the philosopher-scientist. Famous for his bons mots, he now pulled off one that sped all over the Court within hours: "It is now the fate of you who discovered electricity, to electrify two continents." Franklin bowed, the sea of milling spectators parted, and the usher scratched on the King's door.‡

The party entered the state bedroom just as noon struck to find the King awaiting them after his *lever*. He was sitting in an armchair, his back to the marble chimney. At the window that gave onto a balcony overlooking the courtyard stood a group of his gentlemen. Eel-like in his agility, the Duc de Croÿ managed to slip in just behind the envoys and was able to hear every word of the brief conversation. The King, with what the Duc found to be unusual grace and warmth, said to Franklin: "Please assure the Congress of my friendship. I hope that this will be for the good of both nations. I should also like to say that I am very satisfied with your own conduct in particular since you arrived in my kingdom." Franklin replied, "Your Majesty can count on the gratitude of the Congress and on the fidelity with which its engagements will be carried out."[13]

The audience at an end, the Americans retraced their steps and crossed the courtyard to Vergennes's apartments through a dense crowd of cheering, shouting people. After a splendid banquet given by Vergennes, the party was taken to meet the Queen informally. She was playing cards, surrounded by her ladies. Marie Antoinette politely asked Franklin to stand beside her. The Duc de Croÿ thought her very gracious in the words she addressed to him considering that her sentiments were known to be pro-English.

It was Franklin's great day, and as he drove into Paris that evening further crowds along the way applauded his triumph. He deserved it.

‡ *At Versailles one scratched rather than knocked on the doors of royalty.*

❧ VII ❧

Life in the Hôtel de Valentinois

As a result of Arthur Lee's vicious attacks on his probity, Silas Deane was recalled by Congress. He returned to America just eleven days after the reception at Versailles, carrying a diamond-encrusted gold snuffbox as a testimonial from Vergennes and a ringing letter of appreciation for his services that Franklin had written on his behalf to James Lovell, a leading member of the Committee for Foreign Affairs. To the great annoyance of Arthur Lee, the French government paid him the honor of permitting him to sail home in the Comte d'Estaing's fleet with Monsieur Conrad Alexandre Gérard, the newly appointed Minister to the United States.

Lee, who still resented being left out, wrote Franklin a bitter letter on April 2. Franklin answered:

"It is true I have omitted answering some of your letters. I do not like to answer angry letters. I am old, cannot have long to live, have much to do and no time for altercation. If I have often received and borne your magisterial snubbings and rebukes without reply, ascribe it to the right causes: my concern for the honour and success of our mission which would be hurt by our quarreling, my love of peace, my respect for your good qualities, and my pity of your sick mind. . . ."[1]

Franklin must have felt abandoned. Deane had managed most of the accounts of the mission and, with only the impossible Arthur Lee, Dr. Bancroft, and the feckless young Temple to count on, he was overwhelmed with work. One major concern since his arrival had been the French and other European officers who wished to join the American army. Silas Deane, in his enthusiasm, had agreed to recommend a great many volunteers in the early days who had proved worse than useless to Washington. They maddened the American generals by demanding high rank and high pay, without possessing the qualifications to receive either. What Washington needed and eventually got were able specialists like General Duportail, who became his chief of engineers.*

The most exceptional foreign officers to serve in the first part of the war were the young Marquis de Lafayette and the Prussian Baron von Steuben, the latter a superb drillmaster who turned the untrained American militia into a force as disciplined as the English. There were later many other valuable volunteers, but the flood of requests for recommendation was a heavy drain on Franklin's time and energy.

"Not a day passes in which I have not a number of soliciting visits, besides letters. . . . You cannot imagine how I am harassed. All my friends are sought out and teased to tease me. Great officers of all ranks, in all departments; ladies, great and small, besides professed solicitors worry me from morning to night. The sound of every coach now that enters my court terrifies me. I am afraid to accept an invitation to dine abroad, being almost sure of meeting with some officer or some officer's friend who, as soon as I am put in a good humour with a glass of champagne, begins his attack on me."[2]

If the above sounds ungenerous, even fractious, it must be remembered that, while many of the petitions to Franklin were from young men genuinely imbued with the ideals of the American cause, the majority were motivated by boredom and a thirst

* Duportail remarked after a long march through the South: "This war is certainly more popular in the cafés of Paris than it is here."

for adventure. They expected to have their equipment supplied, their travel paid for.

Franklin's patience wore thin from time to time. Here is a fragment from a journal written during this year describing some of the problems that beset him.

Passy, Sunday, December 13, 1778. A.M.

A man came to tell me he has invented a Machine, which would go of itself, without the help of a Spring, Weight, Air, Water, or any of the Elements, or the Labour of Man or Beast; and with force sufficient to work four Machines for cutting Tobacco; that he had experienc'd it, would shew it me if I would come to his House, and would sell the Secret of it for Two hundred Louis. I doubted it, but promis'd to go to him in order to see it.

A Monsieur Coder came with a Proposition in Writing, to levy 600 Men to be employ'd in landing on the Coast of England and Scotland, to burn and ransom Towns and Villages, in order to put a stop to the English proceeding in that Way in America. I thanked him, and told him I could not approve it, nor had I any Money at Command for such Purposes. Moreover that it would not be permitted by the Government here.

A Man came with a Request that I would patronize and recommend to Government an Invention he had, whereby a Hussar might so conceal his arms and habiliments with Provision for 24 Hours, as to appear a common Traveller, by which Means a considerable Body might be admitted into a Town, one at a time unsuspected and afterwards assembling, surprize it. I told him I was not a Military Man, of course no Judge of such Matters, and advised him to apply to the Bureau de la Guerre. He said he had no Friends and, so could procure no Attention. The number of wild Schemes propos'd to me is so great and they have heretofore taken so much of my time, that I begin to reject all, tho' possibly some of them may be worth Notice.

Received a parcel from an unknown Philosopher who submits to my Consideration a Memoir on the Subject of

Elementary fire, containing Experiments in a dark Chamber. It seems to be well written, and is in English with a little Tincture of French Idiom. I wish to see the Experiments, without which I cannot well judge of it.[3]

It was Franklin's energy that saved him, that and his love of life. A close French friend, Dr. Pierre-Georges Cabanis, analyzed him well: "Franklin's most original trait, the one that would have made him unique no matter in what century he lived, was his art of living in the best fashion for himself and for others, making the most effective use of all the tools nature has placed at the disposal of man. . . . He would eat, sleep, work whenever he saw fit, according to his needs, so that there never was a more leisurely man, though he certainly handled a tremendous amount of business. No matter when one asked for him, he was always available. His house in Passy, where he had chosen to live because he loved the country and fresh air, was always open for all visitors; he always had an hour for you."[4]

The loan of a part of the Hôtel de Valentinois at Passy had been a lifesaver. The owner was Jacques Donatien Leray de Chaumont, the wealthy shipping magnate who also held several important Crown sinecures. He had come to the Hôtel de Hambourg immediately after Franklin's arrival to offer his help and had been introduced by Silas Deane, who already knew him as a generous supplier of credit, munitions, and uniforms. Vergennes, a close friend of Chaumont's, had probably suggested the arrangement. It suited the government to have the Americans just outside Paris, away from Stormont's spies (they could not have known that the master spy was a member of the mission) and easily available for discreet visits from French officials. Passy lay on the road to Versailles.

Franklin may have had misgivings about accepting the generosity of Chaumont. John Adams, when he arrived, was horrified by the grandeur of the establishment and did his best to find out what vast sum was being expended on it. Later, when Franklin became minister plenipotentiary, he did pay rent, but in the first years he was only too grateful to accede to Chaumont's genuine desire to contribute to the American cause.

The great house towered over its gardens on flat terrain; below it down a steep hillside flowed the Seine. The view across the river stretched for miles across the Plaine de Grenelle, and on clear days the Château de Meudon was visible down the valley. In winter the village had few residents, but spring brought a mass of fashionable pleasure seekers to the secluded villas surrounded by the trees that were typical of Passy: beech, acacia, and chestnut. The mineral waters owned by Franklin's friend and neighbor, Monsieur Le Veillard, were famous. The spa adjoining the springs contained an elegant casino. Passy was a merry place on Sundays. Family parties and an occasional pair of lovers wandered among the fountains and gardens as music from the band at the casino below floated up to them. For those who wished to stray further afield, the Royal Forest of Rouvray (today known as the Bois de Boulogne) adjoined the village.

It is not surprising that Adams was staggered by the magnificence of the residence. Chaumont had bought the rich furnishings and pictures of the Valentinois family with the house. The Valentinois, collectors in their own right, were connected by marriage with the ruling family of Monaco and the combined riches were enormous. In one salon known as the Lantern Room there were forty-one pictures on the walls, and the catalogue lists the names of Rembrandt, Rubens, Brueghel the Elder, and Holbein.[5]

Over the eight-year period of their stay, the Americans moved several times to different parts of the vast establishment. At first they lived in a series of lovely low buildings known as the *basse cour,* while the Chaumonts occupied the main house, a five-minute walk through the gardens. Madame de Chaumont was a pleasant, witty woman with whom Franklin made great friends. It had always been his way to get on with his landladies and their families. One of the three daughters took over his housekeeping and supplied the food for Franklin's dinners. He provided the wine. The description of his cellar is impressive: "1,040 bottles in 1779, 1,203 bottles in 1782, with a prevalence of red and white Bordeaux, no less than five varieties of champagne, and a goodly supply of Spanish wines (Xeres) for which he had a predilection."[6]

Although the Duc de Croÿ, who came to admire Franklin, found the food at the Hôtel de Valentinois sparse by his standards, the dinner menus sound to us very generous. Rather than the fashionable dinner hour of three o'clock, Franklin preferred 1 or 2 P.M. as the time to gather the mission and its guests together for the main meal of the day. It consisted of a joint of beef or veal or mutton, followed by fowl or game, with two vegetables, pastry, hors d'oeuvres, butter, pickles, radishes, two fruits in winter, four in summer, two compotes, cheese, biscuits, bonbons, and ices twice a week in summer and once in winter.[7]

Among the lilacs and the lindens of his first spring in Passy, a glass of his good Bordeaux in his hand and the sun warm on his septuagenarian back, Franklin fell in love. Anne-Louise d'Hardancourt Brillon de Jouy was a beauty in her thirties, married to a businessman twenty-four years her senior. On the surface she had everything that she could have desired: riches, a husband who spoiled her, two healthy daughters, a fine house in Passy in which she could indulge her very real talent for music. The harpsichord was her favorite instrument and her reputation was that of a first-class amateur. Her indulgent husband had just given her several models of the piano, a new instrument which she played with brilliance.

Under the smooth surface she was an earlier Madame Bovary. Devoid of humor, immensely self-centered, and tiresomely prone to complain, she led the infatuated Franklin a pretty dance. Flattered by the attentions of a great man, bored with her husband and the limitations of her Passy life, she flirted and teased and talked of her virtue. Music was the bond, for Franklin loved romantic Scottish airs and ballads and was rightly proud of his own invention, a perfected form of the German harmonica.

Dependent all his life on the society of women, but too old

for a physical affair, Benjamin Franklin had a romance with Madame Brillon of the sort the French call an *amitié amoureuse*. Sitting on his lap, she called him Papa, and kissed him as she played with his straight gray hair. She was arch and coy and teasing: it was just like her to sit in a bath while her husband and Franklin played a long game of chess in the same room. As eighteenth-century bathtubs were covered, there was nothing indecent about the scene, but Franklin was sufficiently aroused to feel that he had to write a letter of apology when he got home. Her innumerable letters make tedious reading, but there was no harm in the silly woman and in one way she was extremely useful. From the moment he arrived Franklin had never stopped trying to improve his French, and she was an editor of his style. By the time he left for America, his written French was excellent; he had taken infinite pains to please Madame Brillon and, of his poems and "Bagatelles," the most famous and amusing was written to her:

DIALOGUE BETWEEN THE GOUT AND MR. FRANKLIN

GOUT: *You know Monsieur Brillon's gardens and what fine walks they contain; you know the handsome flight of one hundred steps, which lead from the terrace above to the lawn below. It has been your custom to visit this amiable family twice a week, after dinner, and it is a maxim of your own, that "a man may take as much exercise in walking a mile, up and down stairs, as in ten on level ground." What an opportunity for you to have had exercise in both ways! Did you embrace it, and how often?*

FRANKLIN: *I cannot answer that question offhand.*

GOUT: *I will do it for you; not once.*

FRANKLIN: *Not once?*

GOUT: *Not once. During this glorious summer, you went there at six o'clock. You found that charming lady, with her lovely children and friends, eager to walk with you and entertain you with their agreeable conversation. And what did you do? You sat on the terrace, you praised the beautiful view, contemplated the beauty of the gardens below; but you did not take a single step toward going*

*down and walking through them. On the contrary, you
called for tea and the chessboard. And there you were,
glued to your seat, until nine o'clock. All this, after you
had already played some two hours at the house where you
dined. Then, instead of walking home, which might bestir
you a little, you step into your carriage. . . . You philosophers are wise men in your maxims and fools in your conduct.*

FRANKLIN: *But do you regard as one of my crimes that I
return by carriage from Madame Brillon's?*

GOUT: *Yes, indeed. For you, who have been sitting all
day long, cannot say that you are tired from the work of
the day; therefore, you cannot need the relief of the carriage.*

FRANKLIN: *What then would you have me do with my
carriage?*

GOUT: *Burn it, if you wish; for once, at least, you would
get some heat out of it.*[8]

Franklin wrote this charming piece during the autumn and
winter of 1780–81 when he was wracked with gout and deeply
concerned over political affairs. It conveys as nothing else does
the fun that he found in his friendship with Madame Brillon. It
was a lighthearted relationship, and she only hurt him once.

He was devoted to both his grandsons. Little Benny Bache,
who had been sent to school in Geneva to acquire a solid Swiss
education, gave Franklin little cause for worry. Temple, on the
other hand, was a pleasure-loving fop, and his adoring grandfather conceived the idea that marriage to a nice, sensible French
girl might be the cure for his frivolity. Madame Brillon's daughter Cunégonde was the bride he had in mind. He put his heart
into the letters he wrote to her parents attempting to overcome
the problem of the religious difference between the two young
people, that being Madame Brillon's avowed reason for opposing
the marriage.

It was not her real reason, however. She was a snob, a bourgeoise of limited vision who desired for her daughter a rich

Frenchman with a secure position. It was useless for Franklin to suggest that Temple might well become his own successor, and that he, to make sure of his grandson's safe establishment, would remain in France to the end of his days. Madame Brillon was adamant. Having lost the battle, Franklin never brought up the subject again. One of his greatest strengths was his refusal to permit himself hurt feelings. Another facet of his happy nature was a capability to be devoted to several women at the same time. Anne-Louise Brillon de Jouy was not to be the great love of his Paris career.

Franklin was more fairly judged by his friend Dr. Cabanis, quoted above, than he was by Arthur Lee, who complained to Temple that Franklin went out so much that he could only work slowly. Considering the immense amount of correspondence and the number of demands on his time that his fame and popularity brought him, it is amazing that he accomplished as much as he did. Besides the pleasant interludes with his personal friends like Madame Brillon, there were the time-consuming obligations that fell on him as an accredited representative of his country.

From the time that he had been received at Court in 1778 until the end of his mission in 1785, it was his duty to join the other foreign ambassadors in the ritual of driving to Versailles every Tuesday to be received in audience by the King and Queen. His acquaintance with the monarchs never went beyond these very formal calls. The Queen, sensitive as she was to fashion, was never attracted by intellectual currents of opinion and could not understand how members of her Court found Franklin charming. What she enjoyed was playing games and laughing with young men and women of the upper class, the handsomer the better. It seemed absurd to her that pretty Comtesse Diane de Polignac, for instance, should go mooning about Versailles carrying a terra-cotta medallion of an old colonial rebel wearing a fur hat. The King, although he had accepted the American alliance for reasons of state, agreed with his wife that the Franklin mania was ridiculous. To tease Diane de Polignac, he sent her a Sèvres chamber pot in the bottom of which the King had placed a picture of Franklin.

As well as his regular weekly visits to Versailles, there were special occasions which also required Franklin's presence: When the Court went into mourning, it was obligatory for the foreign ambassadors to follow suit. On December 26, 1780, Franklin wrote:

"Went to Versailles to assist at the ceremony of condolence on the death of the Empress Queen" (Maria Theresa, the mother of Marie Antoinette). "All the foreign ministers in deep mourning—flopped hats and crape, long black cloaks, etc. The Nuncio pronounced the compliments to the king and afterwards to the queen in her apartments. Much fatigued by the going up and down the palace stairs, from the tenderness of my feet and weakness of my knees; therefore did not go the rounds."[9]

Versailles was dreadfully cold in winter and the distances almost beyond the strength of an old man who suffered agonies from gout. Franklin did his duty, climbing the stairs to call on Maurepas in his third-floor eyrie, dragging himself across the cobblestones of the vast courtyard to talk business with Vergennes, mounting the long Escalier de la Reine to congratulate the Queen on the births of the royal children.

The first child was a princess known as Madame Royale. Her coming seemed a miracle, for the parents had been married eight years. To Louis XVI, suffering under the mingled ridicule and pity of his subjects for what was considered his hopeless impotence, the visit of Joseph II of Austria in 1777 had been a godsend. The Queen both looked forward to and dreaded the arrival of her august older brother. Perhaps he would advise her how best to defend herself against the avalanche of filthy pamphlets which had begun to circulate in Paris. "How many times," wrote one author in A Reprimand to the Queen, "have you left the nuptial bed and the caresses of your husband to abandon yourself to bacchantes or satyrs and to become one with them through their brutal pleasures?" She could never get used to the horror of it. Sometimes she was accused of lesbianism; another broadsheet held that she pursued butchers in the street, forcing them to sleep with her; and that she preferred two butchers in bed to one alone. There was no escaping the torrent of abuse. Just before Joseph's visit a whole collection of vile songs about the Queen had been flung into the Oeil-de-Boeuf, and when she brushed the episode aside, attempting to jest, he had reproved her from Vienna.

Joseph II, Emperor of Austria, was a highly eccentric man. An unpublished document in the Vienna archives recounts that he amused himself by firing from his window at the dogs passing along the ramparts, and that he would "drive away with blows from his whip the girls bringing petitions. His greatest enjoyment was to go and watch the women in labor at the public hospital in the city or to spend hours at a tower overlooking a courtyard full of screaming madmen."[10]

In family matters this autocratic sadist was a font of practical common sense. In a quiet talk with his unhappy brother-in-law, he discovered what was wrong and what could be done about it. It appeared that poor Louis XVI was not impotent at all, he was simply psychologically frozen. Fully capable of erection, he would enter the Queen "and lie there for ten minutes without the instinct of knowing how to proceed."† Joseph didn't hesitate for a moment. Abandoning delicacy for clinical counsel, he told Louis XVI exactly what he should do and then stamped off to tell the Queen what part she must play. Having lectured her on being a wife, he then lectured her on being a queen, taking her over the coals for her extravagances.

It had been a long time since Marie Antoinette had been properly scolded. She respected her brother as head of the family and listened to him gratefully when he gave his advice. Re-

† Letter of Joseph II to his brother, the Grand Duke of Tuscany. It was thought for a long time that Joseph persuaded Louis XVI to undergo an operation, but more recent research has established that during the relevant period the King never canceled a day of hunting. Even such a minor operation of the kind would have in those days necessitated ten days or so in bed. Olivier Bernier, 1979.

garding her follies in dress, jewels, and gambling, her promises to reform were ephemeral, but that she was kinder and more tactful with her awkward husband is proved by the birth of their baby, the little girl born on December 19, 1778. It would be nice to write that Marie Antoinette at last found happiness in the marriage bed and fulfillment in her life as mistress of the greatest palace in Europe. Unhappily she found neither.

Much has been written about the squalor of Versailles under the ancien régime, with the courtiers and visitors relieving themselves in state rooms and on the staircases. The "sewer smell" permeating everywhere has been effectively described by nineteenth-century anti-Bourbon historians again and again, but this is a wild exaggeration. In the reign of Louis XVI, the inhabitants of the palace did their best to keep it and themselves clean. There were 230 bathrooms, of which the King and Queen had seven, and exquisite little rooms they were, with their paneled walls among the prettiest in the palace. They were furnished with delicate sofas and chairs and mirrors. The fastidious Marie Antoinette took at least one bath a day, and both she and the King had flush toilets. Everyone else had *chaises percées* in their apartments. Visitors who asked permission to use one of them were charged a fixed price of four francs a visit. The servants probably did use the inner courtyards, but it would have been unthinkable for a courtier to have done so except in the most dire emergency.

No, it was not the sanitary conditions that made life at Versailles seem unbearable to Marie Antoinette. It was the crowds and the ruthless etiquette that she longed to escape. There were ten thousand persons living permanently in the palace, besides which any one who possessed a hat and a sword or cared to hire them from the porter at the gate could enter the palace at will. The noise was indescribable as the public surged through, just as it is today. While the King placidly ate his way through gigantic meals before the gaze of crowds of people, the Queen sat rigid, toying with a cup of broth and never removing her gloves.

Hating the ironclad routine that bound her, as time went on she increasingly retreated from her role as a public figure.

Fleeing from her official apartments, she took to a labyrinth of small rooms which lay behind them, each a masterpiece of decorative art. The little blue-paneled "Méridienne" was her favorite, even though it looked out on a dark inner courtyard, as did all her private rooms. She was far happier playing in the lovely park of the Petit Trianon with a group of favorites, etiquette dismissed. Best of all was escape to Paris to dine with friends or to attend a masked ball at the Opéra, or on one famous occasion to sit with her ladies on a bench in the Tuileries gardens, eating strawberries and cream on their laps as might any petites bourgeoises on a summer afternoon.‡

The King was indulgent. The Queen did not wish to receive that dull ambassador who asked permission to come on Wednesday as he had been unable to attend the regular Tuesday reception of diplomats. Why should she bother with him? He had been at Versailles only a week ago. It bored her to take supper again with the hideous Italian wives of the King's two disloyal brothers, Provence and Artois. There was no love lost there, and the Queen might as well go to Paris, escaping thereby another of the hated *grands couverts* which put her on show before the crowd watching their monarchs at table.

Versailles diminished as a center of attraction as the reign went on. The *noblesse de cour* (aristocrats who lived at and for the Court) started to stay in their houses in Paris, going out to perform their duties on their days of "service." The Marquise de La Tour du Pin, a shrewd observer, wrote that it had become fashionable to complain of the tedium of going to Court. "The ladies-in-waiting couldn't bear not to come into Paris for supper two or three times during the week of their duty at Versailles. It was considered stylish to complain of service at Court, while all

‡ *Every move she made was the subject of public comment. The Tuileries episode was considered shocking by her enemies, but one passerby, who had observed the little picnic party, cried with the sheer beauty of it—"an outing à la Rousseau."*

the same making the most of the privileges that went with the honor of being part of the Queen's household."

It is hard to blame the ladies-in-waiting. In winter the drafts whistled down the corridors, and in the summer the little attic rooms in which many of them slept were like ovens. There was nowhere to lay their tired heads during the interminable days of hanging about the state rooms, nor would they have dared to lie down could they have done so, for fear of disarranging their coiffures. Madame de La Tour du Pin, like all the most fashionable young women of her time, had her hair done by Léonard, and once this supreme artist had achieved the edifice on her head she never left a standing position or a stiff chair until the evening ceremonies were ended, which could mean eight or ten hours.

To reach her attic room at midnight or later, a weary lady-in-waiting coming off duty had to climb flight after flight of narrow, unlit, winding stairs, her giant "pannier" skirt, twenty-one feet around, brushing the dusty plaster walls. Candle in hand, she felt her way into a room so low that only the smallest woman would be able to stand upright in it. There was just space enough for a bed and a chair. Light and ventilation came from a single window looking into the blackness of an inner courtyard far below. Heaven knows what she did with her clothes—no closet or wardrobe for them—and, above all, with her headdress. At the very least her coiffure would have been a foot and a half high and might well have carried a full-rigged ship, or a garden of fresh flowers emerging from little crystal vases filled with water, the whole shaky creation embedded in her hair.*

There was another reason besides the Queen's frequent absences that made Versailles a duller court during the 1780's than it had been in the preceding reign. In the days of Louis XV, the *noblesse de cour* could hope for titles, appointments,

---

* It is a curious sensation today to climb up to one of the attic rooms left unrestored. This author was accompanied on a sunny October morning by a kind young curator, his flashlight and his strong right arm at the ready, but it was a tiring experience. What could it have been like in a "pannier"?

money, simply by standing around the King long enough. It was said that when he became familiar with your face he would ask you to supper, and if you said a few funny things that amused him anything might happen—you could be awarded a pension, be made a marshal of France, or a duke. It had, therefore, been very important to be constantly available and at your best. With Louis XVI it was useless to stand around. Agonizingly shy, so conscientious that he disapproved of handing out honors without good reason, he was indulgent only to the requests of the Queen and Maurepas. To them he nearly always gave in, and there were few favors left over.

Now and then, great ceremonies brought luster to the dimming stage, but whereas in Lord Stormont's early days it had still been vitally necessary for a foreign envoy to be at Court as often as possible to hear the gossip, for Franklin the central interest of Versailles was that it remained the place where government business was conducted. With the exception of the Ministry of Finance, all government departments were established there. While it was, therefore, the hub of the great wheel of administration, to hear the news the ambassadors went out in Paris.

It would be impossible to exaggerate the importance of the political salons where society congregated during the reign of Louis XVI. Franklin had understood this at once, and when John Adams arrived to replace Silas Deane in April, he attempted to explain to him that the houses to which he would be introduced were news centers, not unlike the forums and bazaars of the ancient world.

Adams and his ten-year-old son John Quincy had suffered the usual hard and dangerous winter crossing. From the moment the ship left the shores of Massachusetts, his diary entries were full of self-pity. In wartime any important official who was unlucky enough to fall into enemy hands on the high seas was destined by British law to be taken and incarcerated in the Tower of London as a state prisoner. Somehow, Adams felt, he would not be so fortunate. It would be just his luck to end up in horrible Newgate Prison as a common felon. After all, as he was to write again and again, he was a "man of no consequence." He spent the voyage grimly studying the French language.

They landed at Bordeaux, and proceeded to Paris, where, after being turned away from several hotels that were full, they at last found lodgings at the Hôtel de Valois on the rue de Richelieu. Adams was proud of John Quincy: "My little Son had sustained this long journey of nearly five hundred miles, at the rate of a hundred miles a day, with the utmost firmness, as he did our fatiguing and dangerous Voyage."

Like all newly arrived travelers, they found the noise of hurly-burly Paris appalling. They woke to the crash of the iron rims on the wheels of fast-driven carriages on the cobblestones below, the shouts of the drivers, the shrill, incomprehensible cries of the milkmaids and street vendors making their early-morning rounds. As soon as possible they drove out to Passy, where Franklin welcomed them with delight. He insisted that they should leave their noisy hotel at once and join his Passy household. What could be easier or more natural? John Quincy could enter the excellent boarding school of Monsieur Le Coeur right there in the village, joining his father on weekends. As for Mr. Adams, he was launched into Parisian society that very night at a dinner he attended with Franklin given by Monsieur Turgot, the eminent economist and philosopher who had been Comptroller of Finances. On hearing of the arrival of the new commissioner, Turgot had sent a most pressing invitation urging Adams to accompany Franklin to the party.

There was just time to move the Adamses into the comfortable rooms in which Silas Deane had lived—John Adams found them much more luxurious and elegant than he would have liked—before setting off for the three o'clock dinner at Turgot's. Franklin was happier than he had been for months. The two men had served together in Congress and had always agreed on public affairs; he had the highest respect for Adams' ability and integrity and could now look forward not only to sharing his responsibilities with a first-class partner, but also to the congenial

companionship he had badly needed since the acrimony between Deane and Lee had poisoned the atmosphere in the house. Although the shy Adams had been worried about his clothes, he need not have been concerned. Turgot was the best of bachelor hosts, and the twenty guests he had assembled were easygoing aristocrats who were thoroughly accustomed to receiving strangers in their midst. Moreover, the freshly arrived Adams was lionized as a welcome novelty. It was the custom of the day to have general conversation, and the company plied him with questions about the latest news from America. In his own opinion he came off very adequately in his answers, translated by Franklin.

Adams was impressed by the famous Turgot, but he was especially struck with the wisdom and distinction of his neighbor at table, the Duchesse d'Anville. This great lady and her son, the Duc de la Rochefoucauld d'Anville, had been among the first people in Paris to take up Franklin. The Duchesse, who read English but could not speak it, had a good political mind and unlimited intellectual curiosity. Widowed when she was still young, she had since kept open house for all her son's clever liberal friends. Both mother and son had been attracted early on to the American cause, and in the Duchesse's house Franklin had met the most interesting people in Paris. Rochefoucauld,† unlike his mother, spoke English easily and was a scholar who was admired for his translations of the documents of the American Revolution. Besides the constitutions of the thirteen states, he had boldly undertaken the translation of the Declaration of Independence, the publication of which had been instantly banned by the French government in 1776. Turgot was an intimate friend, and d'Alembert and Condorcet were in and out of the house.

It was said that the Duchesse had such influence with the Royal Academy of Science that she could make members at

---

† *The Duc de la Rochefoucauld d'Anville (often spelled Enville), philosopher and lover of liberty, was stoned to death by a mob in Paris in 1792 before the eyes of his mother.*

pleasure. With all this, she was still an attractive woman whose portrait shows a gentle face of great charm, smiling under the brim of a big straw hat whose crown is encircled with a blue taffeta ribbon. She carries a bouquet of daisies and cornflowers and wears a simple white muslin dress. It is exactly the costume she would have chosen for Turgot's dinner party. Ladies of her class and kind rose late and, after taking a cup of chocolate and attending to their correspondence, were apt to ride briskly for an hour or so in the Forest of Rouvray. On returning, they put on a morning dress and hat to go out to dinner—the real ceremony of dressing occurred later in the day. The men, however, dressed for dinner, never in uniform but in full dress and sword, which costume they wore throughout the evening.

The young Rhode Islander Elkanah Watson wrote in his memoirs of his delight and astonishment at the informality of French entertainments in contrast to what he had expected. Adams was later to comment, with less delight, on the same phenomenon, but that first night he was too bemused by the magnificence of the house and the grandeur of the company to be critical. He could not have guessed that Turgot probably had no idea how many people would actually sit down at his table. He would have asked certain people to come to meet Franklin and Adams, but in any big house dinner was an elastic meal to which intimate friends were welcome whenever they chose to turn up. They might sit down twelve, or forty, strong. Miraculously, the household always provided enough food.

Once the host decided that the guests were assembled—Turgot would not have waited after three o'clock had struck—the maître d'hôtel announced that the meal was ready and the guests trooped into the dining room, sitting wherever they chose. A pretty woman was likely to sit between two men, but often men sat together. Astonishingly, in that era of privilege and inequality, there was no fuss about being seated by rank. The eighteenth-century French host considered that anyone who had the honor to sit at his table was equal to his fellow guests, so took no trouble over who sat where. Occasionally, in

Caron de Beaumarchais

who liked to be called "l' Américain"

Paris theater scene—the crown.

Voltaire, "the unique man"

Meeting in the Bois de Boulogne

The Appointment

Precautions

Perfect Harmony

Bedtime

the case of a foreign ambassador or some other distinguished personage, the host or hostess might conceivably say, "Do come and sit by me," but it was all immensely casual. The food was not passed, but was placed on the table in front of the guests, the wine on a buffet behind them. The tempo of rapid general conversation—Franklin complained that four or five people sometimes spoke at once, interrupting each other—was undisturbed by the need to move to reach for the next course or another glass of wine, as each guest was expected to bring his own manservant who would stand behind his chair. If he had omitted to bring his own man, the house provided a footman to whom the guest had only to turn, saying, "A glass of champagne," "Some roast beef, please," and the servant immediately filled the order. The meals, therefore, went much more rapidly than they do today, and two hours was considered a long time to be at table, even when the menu went something like this, as it would have at Turgot's house on the occasion of the dinner attended by Franklin and Adams in 1778:

It started with a *grande entrée*, roast beef. Then came two soups, one of cucumber and the other of green pea with croutons. Oysters on the half shell, little melons and small pâtés, cold fish in mayonnaise (a new and fashionable delicacy) were followed by a boiled leg of mutton, roast venison, veal marinated in a cream sauce *piquante*, roast squab, several of the earliest spring vegetables, and two green salads. Dessert brought lemon sherbet, four kinds of stewed fruits (plum, apple, prune, peach), apricot tarts, and small pastries containing scrambled eggs. (A strange addition to the dessert course, but it was often on the menu.) Such fresh fruits as were in season ended the meal. All varieties of wine were provided, though Burgundies were then more in favor than Bordeaux. The service was directed by a maître d'hôtel, a sort of superior butler who wore full dress, just as the male guests did, and even carried a sword.

It is hard to believe the quantity of decorative objects that covered those huge dining-room tables, already laden with food. There were fresh flowers in vases of crystal and gold, there were candelabra holding six to eight candles, although it was after-noon. On the tablecloth might be layers of colored sand, green, purple, pink, in which patterns had been drawn, garlands or harps or geometric designs. Even more elaborate were the land-scapes built of starch with an overlay of "frost"; there were houses surrounded by gardens of real flowers, grottoes and rocks, hills encircled by rivers. As the heat of candles melted the "frost," the "frozen" rivers flowed; the flowers thawed, revealing their bright colors; the hills became verdant and the roofs of the houses red. These artistic innovations were the pride of the ser-vants who spent hours designing them in every fashionable house.

When the candles had burned down and the meal was over, no one bothered to return to the drawing room. Saying goodbye was not the time-consuming ritual it is today. The guests simply walked out, shouting something over their shoulders to their hosts, who muttered a phrase of farewell in return. It was then time for the ladies to go home to dress for the evening, as the opera and the theaters started at six-thirty or seven o'clock. The men wandered off to pay their calls—this was the hour at which the political hostesses received. Supper, a more intimate meal than dinner, could be at any time from nine on, and unless there was a ball people stayed talking with undiminished enthu-siasm until very late. Madame du Deffand seldom went to bed before two or three in the morning. Society was inexhaustible, but it must be remembered that no one worked and that the aristocrats left the care of their country estates to managers whom they rarely saw. Nor did they bother about the details of running their Paris establishments. It never occurred to anyone to question the price of food or to look at the household books, although food was expensive in the 1770's and 1780's.

Occasionally some nobleman would go spectacularly bank-rupt, as was the case with the Prince de Guéménée, who found himself 30 million livres in debt in a year when the whole na-tional budget of France was 250 million. This scandal did shake Paris and the Court, but the memoirs rarely mention money worries. Ambassadors lived very well. Although Franklin and Adams filled pages of their correspondence with their concerns about expense, there were already nine servants at Passy before Adams brought two of his own. Their meals, as has been said, were comparatively generous; however, on the evening of Turgot's feast they went home to sup alone on cheese and beer at nine o'clock.

Franklin must have looked forward to this quiet evening in which he could pour his heart out to someone he could trust. He described the disputes that had taken place between Deane and Lee. He spoke of Lee's intolerable temper. He told of the interference of Ralph Izard and William Lee, who hung about the fringe of the mission making nuisances of themselves. Adams' response was both sanctimonious and selfish, and his long entry describing the conversation shows not one trace of sympathy for Franklin.

However, with his son happily established at school, Adams attacked the affairs of the mission and worked hard and well. He sorted out the accounts, corresponded with the merchants and sea captains as Silas Deane had done, and wrote spirited letters to his friends in the Congress describing the atmosphere of Paris:

"In this Kingdom, I have the pleasure to assure you, that I have found a universal favour to America. . . . I have never seen a French Tory. They tell me, it is the first Time the French Nation ever saw a Prospect of War, with Pleasure."[11]

When his work was done, he dined out with Franklin and his friends or studiously toured the sights of the city. It should have been the beginning of the happiest of diplomatic assignments, but instead it was to be a wretched time for this great, but oversensitive man.

❧ VIII ❧

"Douceur de Vie"

ABIGAIL ADAMS, who had already been left behind in Massachusetts while John Adams served his country during the congressional years, found her husband's absence in France almost more than she could bear. The fitful mails brought little news from him, and his letters, when they did come, seemed to her inadequate. In October 1778, six months after his arrival in Paris, she burst out:

"In the very few lines I have received from you, not the least mention is made that you have ever received a line from me. . . . But I cannot take my pen with my Heart overflowing and not give utterance to some of the abundance which is in it. Could you after a thousand fears and anxieties, long expectation and painfull suspences be satisfied with my telling you that I was well, that I wished you were with me, that my daughter sent her duty, that I had ordered some articles for you which I hoped would arrive &c. &c. — By Heaven if you could you have changed Hearts with some frozen Laplander or made a voyage to a region that has chilled every Drop of your Blood. — But I will restrain a pen already I fear too rash, nor shall it tell you how much I have suffered from this appearance of—inattention."[1]

In December—the winter of 1778-79—Abigail wrote John: "How lonely are my days? How solitary are my nights? Secluded from all Society but my two Little Boys, and my domesticks, by the Mountains of snow which surround me I could almost fancy myself in Greenland."

It had been Mrs. Adams' eager desire to accompany her husband to Paris instead of remaining at home to care for the younger children and the farm. She had begged to come, pleading that the dangers of the ocean voyage were indifferent to her provided that she shared them with him. But Adams was adamant; the North Atlantic was no place for a woman in wartime, with the risk of capture by the enemy added to the natural perils of the winter sea. It was very hard on this brave and intelligent woman to be left behind, and if the few letters she received were anything like his diary entries the list of his glamorous engagements must have driven her mad:

"Dine with the Duchesse d'Anville, at the Hotel de Rochefoucaullt with a large Company of Dukes, Abbes and Men of Science and Learning among whom was Mr. Condorcet, a Philosopher with a face as white as a Sheet of paper, I suppose from hard Study . . ."[2]

"Dr. Franklin, Mr. Lee and myself went to Versailles, were introduced to the Levee of Mr. de Sartine. . . . We were soon conducted down to dinner, which appeared to me as splendid as any I had seen, all Elegance and Magnificence. . . . During the dinner many other Gentlemen came in who I suppose had dined elsewhere, walked the room, leaned over the chairs of the Ladies and Gentlemen at Table, and conversed with them."[3]

Dinner at Madame Brillon's, dinner at the Maréchal de Mouchy's, at Madame Helvétius', at the Duc d'Ayen's. Or, for a change of scene: "This evening Mr. Chaumont took me in his carriage to the Concert Spirituel in the Royal Garden of the Tuilleries. A vast number of Instruments were performing to an immense Crowd of Company. There were Men Singers and Women Singers. The Gardens of the Tuilleries were full of Company of both Sexes walking."*[4]

_____

* Adams did not mention the hundreds of prostitutes who assembled in the Tuileries gardens every day at the time of the fashionable afternoon parade which took place between five and seven. They stood on the iron chairs to at-

While poor Mrs. Adams undoubtedly pictured her husband relishing every moment of his gay Paris existence, the only occasion that he really enjoyed was the dinner at the charming Madame d'Anville's, and that was only pleasant because she was the hostess. He had been profoundly shocked at Madame Brillon's to discover that among the guests at table was the host's mistress, a young governess who lived in the house. As for Madame Helvétius, the widow of a famous philosopher, his suspicions could hardly have been darker:

"That She might not be alone, however, entirely without the Society of Gentlemen, there were three or four handsome Abby's who daily visited the House and one at least resided there. These Ecclesiasticks, one or more of whom reside in allmost every Family of Distinction, I suppose have as much power to Pardon a Sin as they have to commit one, or to assist in committing one. Oh Mores! said I to myself. What Absurdities, Inconsistencies, Distractions and Horrors would these Manners introduce into our Republican Governments in America: No kind of Republican Government can ever exist with such national manners as these. Cavete Americani."[5]

Had Abigail Adams only known it, her husband was far too distressed by the frivolity of French ways to enjoy the lovely houses to which he was invited.

"Every fashionable House had compleat setts of Accomodations for Play, A Billiard Table, a Bacgammon Table, a Chesboard, a Chequer Board, Cards, and twenty other Sorts of Games, that I have forgotten. I often asked myself how this rage for Amusements of every kind, and this disinclination to serious Business, would answer in our republican Governments in America. It seemed to me that every Thing must run to ruin."[6]

If John Adams had been able to speak the language, he might have been less harsh. The French were very polite to foreigners

---

tract customers, lifting their skirts to show off their wares. Curiously, nobody objected although the gardens were full of decorous family parties and well-brought-up young girls with their attendants. The eighteenth century was a mixture of crude bawdiness and elegant refinement.

in the eighteenth century, but few of them had bothered to learn English, and nothing is more dispiriting than to hear a language spoken rapidly around you which you cannot understand. Adams felt an oaf, and his sense of inferiority was not improved when he learned enough French to appreciate the fact that Benjamin Franklin's use of the language was anything but accurate or correct. The unselfconscious old man generally preferred to remain silent in company and to listen while the others talked, but when he did speak, his French, while fluent, was full of mistakes. He didn't mind and neither did his admiring friends, but Adams was too inhibited to emulate him.

He struggled to learn. It occurred to him to take up the theater, where he carefully followed the dialogue with a book of the play in his hand. He consulted learned men who advised him to study the works of the great seventeenth-century churchman Bossuet. Reading Bossuet in the reign of Louis XVI was about as useful as it would be for a diplomat today to try to learn French by reading the works of General de Gaulle, but Adams was persistent.

"Although my Ignorance of the Language was very inconvenient and humiliating to me . . ."[7] This sad phrase is enough to make the heart of every non-French-speaking American who has lived in Paris ache for the shy Adams. Conversation in the circles in which he moved was on a high level. It was not enough to be familiar with the writers and philosophers of France, for the wave of Anglomania in the eighteenth century had introduced every educated Frenchman to the works in translation of the English philosophers of the seventeenth and eighteenth centuries. Hobbes, Locke, Hume, and Shaftesbury were frequently quoted. Adams possessed an excellent classical background, but he had had little chance to study the modern thinkers.

Arriving for dinner at the Prince de Tingry's splendid house, as he did on an April day, to find the host standing before his drawing-room fireplace "harranguing upon Tolleration and Liberty of Conscience"[8] must have been most intimidating for

Adams. The more intellectual salons were full of brilliant men standing up and haranguing upon heavy subjects. The bigwigs always hogged the place of honor before the fireplace in those chilly, high-ceilinged rooms. It was said of Diderot that he would have lectured on philosophy to a platoon of guardsmen. Once, at Madame Geoffrin's, he spoke without drawing breath for an hour and a half on "The General Will."

Madame Geoffrin was the hated rival of Madame du Deffand. Without birth, without talents, without much money, she collected around her all the most remarkable men in literature and the arts and the most interesting foreign visitors. The Scottish philosopher David Hume was an intimate; Horace Walpole was another; the eight-year-old Mozart had played the clavichord in her drawing room; and Franklin had been brought to see her in the year of his arrival.[9] Wearing a plain gray woolen dress and the soberest of black bonnets, she drew people to her by her shrewd mind and lack of pretension.

There were many competing political salons. The house of the rich banker Jacques Necker and his wife was an important pro-American center. Necker held high office as Turgot's successor. While he conspicuously lacked brilliance, he tried to make up for it with vague, pontifical pronouncements which sounded impressive to those guests at his table who were not financial or economic experts. The well-meaning but humorless Suzanne Necker was the daughter of a Swiss pastor. As a young girl in Lausanne she had been wooed by Edward Gibbon, but, when he returned to England, his father announced that he would cut him off without a penny if he contracted so humble an alliance. He gave in rather easily, making the famous comment, "I sighed as a lover, I obeyed as a son."[10]

Suzanne Necker came to Paris without friends, but, thanks to an education far superior to that of the aristocratic ladies with whom she associated there, she had the brains to take good advice. Within two or three years, she had established her liberal political salon on Fridays, having been warned that it would be fatal to attempt to compete with Madame Geoffrin's Mondays and Wednesdays, with Madame Helvétius' Tuesdays, or with the philosopher Baron Holbach's Thursdays and Sundays. Fridays, said the malicious intellectuals who thronged her hospitable house on the rue de Cléry, suited her admirably as it was theoretically a Catholic fast day and so she could conceal the ignominy of having the worst cook in all Paris.[11] In spite of the plain-living, high-thinking atmosphere of the rue de Cléry, clever and important men assembled in Madame Necker's bluestocking salon. There were few women. While the great ladies accepted her as the wife of an important official, they never became her close friends.†

The Comtesse d'Houdetot was another pro-American hostess. She was nearly fifty by the time she met Franklin and embraced his cause and his friendship, but Sophie d'Houdetot was ageless in her enthusiasms. She was extremely plain; even Jean-Jacques Rousseau, who wrote his novel *La Nouvelle Héloïse* for her during a summer of blinding passion under the acacias at her house in Eaubonne, admitted: "The Comtesse d'Houdetot was nearly thirty years old and not in the least beautiful; her skin was badly marked with the traces of smallpox, her color was indifferent, she was shortsighted and her eyes were crossed, but with all this she still looked young. . . . she had a forest of thick black hair which came down to her knees, her figure was adorable and her movements were a mixture of gaucherie and grace, both at the same time. She was a natural spirit whose gaiety, giddiness, and naïveté combined harmoniously; she was always bursting out with charming sallies which were perfectly spontaneous. . . . her character was that of an angel, combining every virtue except those of prudence and strength."[12]

This description is hardly rhapsodical, coming as it does from the greatest romantic writer of his day, but Rousseau may have been in a jaundiced mood when he wrote it. His summer passion had been unrequited, and, on the return of Madame

† *The Neckers had an only child, Germaine, who, as the famous Madame de Staël, eclipsed her mother's position in Paris society, but, as a good daughter, attracted many illustrious persons to the Necker salon.*

d'Houdetot's lifelong lover, the Chevalier de Saint-Lambert, the episode was over. However, Rousseau never forgot the evenings under the acacia tree; thirty years later the posthumously published second part of his *Confessions* told the story of his unfulfilled love. Besides being immortalized by Rousseau and befriended by Franklin, Madame d'Houdetot was regarded as the kindest of women by all who knew her. The critic and writer Sainte-Beuve, who could be cruel, said of her: "Madame d'Houdetot is one of those souls one can paint in a word: she has gone through life seeing only the good."[13]

On a lovely April day in 1781, this earnest, energetic woman gave a *fête champêtre* for Franklin at her country place in Sannois, ten miles or so from Passy. It must have been a terribly tiring occasion for a man with bad legs. The guests ran out to meet his carriage and escorted him on foot through the fields, singing, to the banquet where they toasted him, freedom, the United States, and the lightning rod. An orchestra played—Franklin planted a Virginia locust in the garden—there was dancing and more toasting. At the end, as Franklin was getting into his carriage, Madame d'Houdetot recited a sentimental verse in his honor. If he was exhausted when he got home, it was worth it, for she was a loyal supporter and good friend to America throughout Franklin's years in Paris.†

There were hostesses who were neither as intense as Madame d'Houdetot nor as bluestocking as Madame Necker. The Maréchale de Luxembourg, a widow only ten years younger than her best friend, Madame du Deffand, lived for fun despite her age and failing health. One night, sitting by the Duc de Choiseul, she complained that society had grown intolerably boring since women had become so serious and political. What was more, one no longer drank champagne at supper. The Duc

---

‡ *The best description of Madame d'Houdetot is in Claude-Anne Lopez's brilliant study of Franklin and his women friends in Paris,* Mon Cher Papa. *Mrs. Lopez remarks: "In another age, the Countess would undoubtedly have been president of some organization for Franco-American friendship, and it is as such that Franklin always treated her."*

laughed and suggested that he should give a supper at which there would be only one woman, Madame de Luxembourg, and a group of the most charming men in Paris. She approved the idea but insisted that it should be she who gave the party. A date was agreed upon, and the supper took place. The food was sublime, the champagne flowed, and the occasion had all the gaiety for which the hostess had longed. There were eight men, all glamorous and none of them interested in philosophical discussion. "MM. de Choiseul, de Gontaut, de Guines, de Laval, de Besenval, d'Estrehan, de Mun, and Donnezan were their names."[14] At the end of the merry meal, the hostess opened a little package which had been handed to her and brought out rhymed couplets addressed to each guest "as a surprise." She sang them out loud, and someone thought them so amusing that they have been preserved.

No one would have been surprised for a moment by Madame de Luxembourg's performance. Rhyming was an established tradition in such houses. Sometimes Madame du Deffand used to ask Voltaire or her gifted friend the Chevalier de Boufflers to write the verses for a special occasion, but she and Madame de Luxembourg were accustomed to turning them out themselves, often quite spontaneously as they sat down to table.[15] Totally unselfconscious in their enjoyment of pleasure, these people would have been bewildered by the modern term "identity crisis." They knew exactly who they were, and, as every day seemed to have twenty-five hours in it, there was always plenty of time for fun. They loved dressing up to do plays that took weeks of rehearsal. The portraitist Madame Vigée-Lebrun described a hilarious performance of *The Marriage of Figaro* by the guests of the Comte de Vaudreuil, a rich and fashionable courtier who had a private theater in his house just outside Paris, Beaumarchais had come out to watch. As the author of the play, he was offended when the elaborately dressed audience interrupted the flow of the performance by asking for an interval to open the windows in view of the summer heat. In a second he was at the windows, cane in hand, breaking them all. Fresh air filled the little theater, to the delight of the audience, and the play went on.

Madame Vigée-Lebrun is a good example of what Talleyrand meant when he wrote in his memoirs, *"Tous les rangs sont confondus* [Social distinctions are all mixed up]." In earlier reigns it would have been inconceivable for an artist to have attained her position in society. Young, lovely, and very talented, she too had a salon. Even the King heard of one supper she gave on the spur of the moment at which she dressed the guests as Greek gods and goddesses in the draperies and laurel crowns she and her laughing guests found in her studio. As it happened, she had just been working on the portrait of a nobleman who wished to be painted as a classical hero in the manner of Poussin, so the props were at hand. A neighbor who collected antiquities came to the rescue with ancient vases and statues to furnish the dining room; the cook produced vine leaves to garnish the crisp skin of a freshly roasted chicken; someone brought a bottle of "ancient Cyprus wine," which the young daughter of the house served in a long-necked Grecian vase. The Marquis de Cubières, a late arrival, gave one look at the party and rushed home to fetch his guitar, managing somehow to mount it as a golden lyre and return before the candles were half burned down on the festive table. Madame Vigée-Lebrun wrote delightedly that it was the best party she had ever given.[16]

What fun young people had! It was an eager, idealistic generation—the men who were to fight under Rochambeau and call themselves *"les Américains"* and the women they loved were united in the certainty that reforms would ensure France a future under cloudless skies. Talleyrand wrote, looking back on that era: "All young men considered themselves fitted to rule the country. They criticized all the measures adopted by the ministers. The personal acts of the King and Queen were brought under discussion, and nearly always incurred the disapprobation of the salons of Paris. Young women spoke pertinently about all branches of the administration."[17] He added: "The power of what in France they call *society* was prodigious during the years which preceded the Revolution."[18]

Then there were the times when they forgot politics. A moonlit night would tempt them into larking down the river to Passy by ferry in order to play at Monsieur Le Veillard's casino. By daylight, the Moulin Joli was the favorite place to picnic; from all accounts, it was a magical spot. An island in the Seine covered with woods and orchards, it could only be approached by a bridge out of a fairy tale made of moored boats, each boat half smothered in baskets of flowers. Once there, one ate one's meal lying on the grass in the shade of poplars and willows. Madame Vigée-Lebrun never forgot one particular willow which formed a wide arch. Lying beneath it, she found the reflection of the flower-decked bridge in the water mesmerizing —she felt lulled into a delicious forgetfulness of time and responsibilities. There must have been a little orchestra playing somewhere, for all the memoirs speak of the sound of violins. It was not only the young who loved the Moulin Joli. The famous diplomatist the Prince de Ligne mentioned the wide-arched willow in his old age, and Benjamin Franklin and Madame Brillon spent their happiest hours on the romantic island.

The vitality of the young was never-ending. While it would have been considered unthinkably tedious to spend long summers on parental estates in the remote provinces, nearly everyone seemed to possess a relative living in the country just outside of Paris whom they were more than happy to visit. Madame du Vigean, the mother of two pretty and popular girls, gave a party at her estate near Montmorency one June night in 1778: "They walked through the shady park to discover at the end of an allée twenty-four lutes and violins, their sweet strings vibrating from a flowered grotto. . . . a sort of joyous madness overtook the insouciant band of young companions; they whirled, they pirouetted, they soared into the air as they danced on the fresh green grass. Finally they returned to Paris by the light of flaming torches, the violins followed them beside the carriages, playing the tunes that were in fashion that summer."[19]

Return to Paris would not have meant the end of that intoxicating evening for the young men of the party. In an era when even old ladies like Madame du Deffand seldom went to bed before two in the morning because there was so much to talk about, they too would have sat up to talk and talk. There was the current ministry to tear apart and remake, new gossip about the latest iniquity of the reactionary Parlement de Paris, and plans to draw up to redress the injustices of the outmoded legal system. As the world of the arts was as close to them as the political world, the relative merits of the two leading composers of the time, Gluck and Piccini, were discussed with a passion that sometimes went from heated argument to café fisticuffs. Talk of Gluck would lead to the Opéra and the stars that he had formed, Madame Sophie Arnould and her companions, the demoiselles Laguerre and Levasseur. It was a great age for opera and theater—the Comédie-Francaise and the Comédie-Italienne each sold more than 200,000 seats in the year 1778, a figure that sounds incredible as the population of Paris was not much over 700,000. However, as these two great companies were subsidized by the state, tickets sold at 20 sous normally and were free on certain holidays and feast days, so the theater was not a pleasure limited to the rich.

Many small things contributed to the *douceur de vie** which Talleyrand said no one could ever know who had not lived in France before the Revolution. Accustomed to luxury all around them, the golden young people probably took for granted the beauty of everyday objects. A doorknob, a lock on a desk drawer, the very identification plates carried by cab drivers and porters in the market were objects of the chiselers' art. The Prince de Condé *was* considered a touch eccentric to have silk curtains in the windows of his horses' stalls at Chantilly, but it was taken for granted that the ordinary wicker hamper into which dirty clothes were flung should be lined in silk taffeta, lilac or blue, or

* Douceur de vie *literally means "sweetness of life," but I prefer "pleasure of life," which is the translation given by Duff Cooper in his classic biography,* Talleyrand.

pale green like the Queen's. It was hard to find a common object that was not lovely.

The Marquise de La Tour du Pin wrote, "We went marching to the precipice, laughing and dancing. Serious people talked about the disappearance of abuses. France, they said, was going to be regenerated. The word Revolution was never pronounced—anyone who had dared to say it would have been considered out of their minds. Among the people of my society a false security seduced the wisest spirits, for everyone was so anxious to see an end to all the abuses."[20]

This charming and perceptive woman had earlier criticized many facets of the fashionable world in which she had been brought up. In exile, remembering, she saw it as nostalgically as did her friend and contemporary Talleyrand, and she wrote:

"I rather doubt whether there exists in social relations today the ease, the harmony, the good style, the absence of all pretension which reigned in those days in the great houses of Paris."[21]

"Absence of pretension" is the key phrase. Madame Necker, who was pretentious, was laughed at by Madame de La Tour du Pin and her friends. Madame Geoffrin was the hostess they admired, for she possessed to an extraordinary degree the ease and good style of which Madame de La Tour du Pin spoke.

It was a pity that John Adams felt no joy in his first spring in Paris. Occasionally, through the narrow tunnel of his gray northern blinkers, he would catch a glimpse of beauty that pleased him. The pavilions of royal Marly impressed him so much that he wrote several pages in praise of the architecture.†
In another passage he all but rhapsodized over Dr. Barbeu Dubourg's collection of pictures. There are hints that he was excited by things foreign and exotic, then down comes the shutter with a hard snap. It was as if there was another man inside him, a romantic trying to get out of the compact, rotund body of the John Adams we know. Had he guessed that the ancien régime was to be swept away forever within ten years, would he have

† *"Noble and laughing Marly, embowered in its jasmine," was Madame Vigée-Lebrun's description. John Adams' was longer, but less romantic.*

been less censorious? That he had no premonition of the coming of the French Revolution is proved by a line in his autobiography written years later: "To be sure it had never yet entered my thoughts, that any rational Being would ever think of demolishing the Monarchy and creating a Republick in France."[22]

Much of Adams' discontent was caused by his mistrust of Franklin. Here is his cruel indictment, dated less than two months after his arrival in Paris:

> *May 27th. Wednesday. I must now, in order to explain and justify my own Conduct give an Account of that of my Colleague Dr. Franklin. It is and always has been with great reluctance, that [I] have felt myself under the Necessity of stating any facts which may diminish the Reputation of this extraordinary Man, but the Truth is more sacred than any Character, and there is no reason that the Character of Mr. Lee and Mr. Izzard not to mention my own, should be sacrificed in unjust tenderness to that of their Ennemy. . . .*
>
> *I found that the Business of our Commission would never be done, unless I did it. My two Colleagues would agree in nothing. The Life of Dr. Franklin was a Scene of continual dissipation. I could never obtain the favour of his Company in a Morning before Breakfast which would have been the most convenient time to read over the Letters and papers, deliberate on their contents, and decide upon the Substance of the Answers. It was late when he breakfasted, and as soon as Breakfast was over, a crowd of Carriages came to his Levee or if you like the term better to his Lodgings, with all Sorts of People; some Phylosophers, Accademicians and Economists; some of his small tribe of humble friends in the litterary Way whom he employed to translate some of his ancient Compositions, such as his Bonhomme Richard and for what I know his Polly Baker &c.; but by far the greater part were Women and Children, come to have the honour to see the great Franklin, and to have the pleasure of telling Stories about his Simplicity, his bald head and scattering strait hairs,*

*among their Acquaintances. These Visitors occupied all
the time, commonly, till it was time to dress to go to Dinner. He was invited to dine abroad every day and never
declined unless when We had invited Company to dine
with Us. I was always invited with him, till I found it necessary to send Apologies, that I might have some time to
study the french Language and do the Business of the mission. Mr. Franklin kept a horn book always in his Pockett
in which he minuted all his invitations to dinner, and Mr.
Lee said it was the only thing in which he was punctual.
It was the Custom in France to dine between one and two
O Clock: so that when the time came to dress, it was time
for the Voiture to be ready to carry him to dinner. Mr. Lee
came daily to my Appartment to attend to Business, but
we could rarely obtain the Company of Dr. Franklin for a
few minutes, and often when I had drawn the Papers and
had them fairly copied for Signature, and Mr. Lee and I
had signed them, I was frequently obliged to wait several
days, before I could procure the Signature of Dr. Franklin
to them. He went according to his Invitation to his Dinner
and after that went sometimes to the Play, sometimes to
the Philosophers but most commonly to visit those Ladies
who were complaisant enough to depart from the custom
of France so far as to procure Setts of Tea Geer as it is
called and make Tea for him. Some of these Ladies I
knew as Madam Hellvetius, Madam Brillon, Madam
Chaumont, Madam Le Roy &c. and others whom I never
knew and never enquired for. After Tea the Evening was
spent, in hearing the Ladies sing and play upon their
Piano Fortes and other instruments of Musick, and in various Games as Cards, Chess, Backgammon, &c. Mr. Franklin I believe however never play'd at any Thing but
Chess or Checquers. In these Agreable and important Oc-
cupations and Amusements, The Afternoon and Evening
was spent, and he came home at all hours from Nine to
twelve O Clock at night. This Course of Life contributed
to his Pleasure and I believe to his health and Longevity.
He was now between Seventy and Eighty and I had so
much respect and compassion for his Age, that I should*

*have been happy to have done all the Business or rather
all the Drudgery, if I could have been favoured with a few
moments in a day to receive his Advice concerning the
manner in which it ought to be done. But this condescen-
tion was not attainable. All that could be had was his Signature, after it was done, and this it is true he very rarely
refused though he sometimes delayed.*

*From the 26 I remained at home, declining all invita-
tions abroad, arranging the public affairs, and reading
french Litterature.*[23]

It would be natural to suppose that, if John Adams felt as bitterly as is suggested in the above *cri de coeur,* he then remained
sulking in his rooms at Passy, barely speaking to Franklin and
declining all invitations to dine and wine among the dissipated
French. Instead, his diary shows him dining out two days later,
May 29, and again on June 2—the latter a rather grand party
given by the Minister of the Navy, Monsieur de Sartine, at
Marly, where the Court was in residence. After dinner he accompanied Madame de Sartine to the residence of the Spanish
Ambassador, the Conde de Aranda, for coffee, ice cream, and
cakes. Adams' bark was always worse than his bite, and he probably relieved his rancor by expressing it on paper.

July found him cooperating closely with Franklin in a melo-
dramatic episode involving a spy whose pseudonym was Charles
de Weissenstein. One day the porter at Passy picked up an envelope addressed to Franklin—marked "secret and confidential"
—that had been thrown through the iron bars of the front gate.
In it was a long letter in which the writer, signing himself
Weissenstein, proposed himself as an intermediary with King
George III. He was an Englishman, he said, who was sure that
America would be betrayed by France, and, while he felt that
the North ministry had made foolish mistakes in their dealings
with the former colonists, it was not too late to achieve reconciliation if the King himself was approached. There would be
rewards for "Messrs. Adams, Hancock, Washington, etc., etc.,
etc.," and, as well as financial emoluments, they would also re-

ceive peerages. Franklin must come to the Cathedral of Notre
Dame between twelve and one on either July 6 (Monday) or
the following Thursday. There, in the right-hand aisle as he entered, he would see a man sketching or taking notes. He would
be wearing a rose in his buttonhole. Franklin was to leave his
answer where the man could pick it up.

Franklin, whose innocence in regard to spies has already been
demonstrated in the case of Dr. Bancroft, was for some reason
convinced that this message was from the King of England himself. He wrote an indignant answer, described by Adams as "a
Dose that will make them sick."[24] After consulting together, the
two men decided to put the whole thing into the competent
hands of Vergennes. The Paris police reported that "at the Day,
Hour and place appointed a Gentleman appeared and finding
nobody wandered about the Church gazing at the Statues and
Pictures and other Curiosities of that magnificent Cathedral,
never losing Sight however of the Spot appointed and often returning to it, looking earnestly about at times as if he expected
Somebody. . . . He remained two Hours in the Church, and
then went out, was followed through every Street and all his
motions watched to the Hotel where he lodged. We were told
the day he arrived there, the Name he assumed, which was
Colonel Fitz— something, an Irish name that I have forgotten."[25]

Nothing more came of the "King's offer," and Franklin and
Adams decided that it was too unimportant to merit a report to
Congress, but it amused Adams to speculate on what titles
would have been suggested to his colleagues and how many
would have received them. In his virtuous indignation at the
very idea of creating a House of Lords in a republic, he scorned
the vision of himself as Duke of Braintree and his daughter as
the Lady Abigail Adams, but it diverted him to joke with
Franklin about who among them would have been most highly
honored by the King.

The second anniversary of the Declaration of Independence
was celebrated on the Fourth of July by a dinner for fifty Ameri-

cans and French at the Hôtel de Valentinois. In spite of the "handsome posies" laid beside each person's plate and the display of the American flag and the Cap of Liberty, the occasion was marred by the bad manners of Mr. Ralph Izard. The rich South Carolinian had so annoyed Franklin by his unwarranted interference in the affairs of the mission that he had refused to invite him but, on the insistence of Adams, permitted an invitation to be sent out in the name of Adams only. Izard came and behaved well enough at the dinner, but afterwards he infuriated his hosts by saying it was a pity they had not asked "some Gentlemen of that Country. He would not allow those we had to be Gentlemen. . . ."[26] As the French guests had all been close friends—Passy neighbors and supporters of the American cause, plus a sprinkling of Foreign Office officials with whom the commissioners had worked closely—Adams was outraged at Izard's snobbishness. Did he care only about dukes and princes?

There was never to be harmony within the first American diplomatic mission, and it was with real relief that John Adams learned on September 14 that Congress had revoked the joint commission and had elected Franklin as sole American Minister Plenipotentiary to the Court of France. For months he had been saying that one man could do the job more satisfactorily than three, and he generously approved of Congress's decision to recall him. It was not so with Arthur Lee, who, it will be remembered, had been plotting for over a year to take Franklin's place himself. Lee stamped and sulked and lingered in France as long as he could, but Gérard, the French Minister in Philadelphia, had made it clear to Congress that Lee would be unacceptable to France—perhaps he quoted Vergennes's *"Je crains Monsieur Arthur Lee"* to one or two members of the Committee for Foreign Affairs. "No soul regrets their departure," wrote Franklin after Arthur Lee, his brother William, and Ralph Izard had all been recalled and were on their way home.[27]

As the Adamses, father and son, waited at the port of Brest for the ship on which they were to sail for America, eleven-year-old John Quincy exchanged warm letters of farewell with

Franklin. Addressing him as "Dear Friend," instead of "Honoured Sir" as was customary, he enclosed letters to be distributed among his friends in Passy. His last letter ended: "but as the boat is just now a-going I cannot write any more and so conclude myself your affectionate friend, John Q. Adams."[28] Franklin wrote back that he would see to "Dear Master Johnny's" errands and wished him a good voyage and a happy reunion with his mother in Massachusetts. It was like Franklin, overworked as he was, to find time to answer the letters of a boy.

❧ IX ❧

Death of a Diplomat

THE VENOMOUS LETTERS THAT Arthur Lee addressed to
Congress on the subject of Silas Deane had their effect. When
Deane returned from France in the late spring of 1778, he
found that his personal feud with his fellow commissioner had
become a national issue tearing the Congress apart. The powerful Lee faction, which had enlisted Samuel Adams as their
spokesman, demanded to know why Congress should be expected to repay the French for the supplies that had been sent
to America. Arthur Lee had been promised them as a free gift
by Beaumarchais in 1776, they said; therefore the contract that
Deane had made with the firm Roderigue Hortalez had been
merely a clever cover behind which Beaumarchais and he were
planning to line their own pockets at the expense of the hard-
pressed Americans.

Even now the documents are not available to show exactly
what had happened between Arthur Lee and Beaumarchais in
London before Deane's arrival.[1] Possibly Lee was right. In his
enthusiasm, Beaumarchais may have planned to convince the
King and Vergennes that French support should be extended
without question of reimbursement and told Lee to take it as a
fait accompli. But when Silas Deane appeared, vested with authority to *purchase* goods on terms of easy credit, to be repaid in
American produce, it was obvious to Beaumarchais that Deane,

not Lee, was the agent with whom the French must deal. Why, after all, should the French force free supplies on a people who had offered to pay for them? Both Vergennes and Beaumarchais had seen Deane's instructions from Congress, which were perfectly clear.

Silas Deane had friends who were as powerful as the Lee faction in the dispute which was "Prosecuted with a degree of acrimony that make the later breach between Jefferson and Hamilton seem like a decorous spat at a vicarage tea party."[2] Robert Morris, John Jay, and John Dickinson were not likely to forget that it was to Deane that the country owed the shipments of supplies which had turned the tide at Saratoga. Tragically, Deane's own defense of his case was hopelessly disappointing to his supporters. He had responded so immediately to the demand for his recall that before he left France he had not been able to secure proper vouchers covering his transactions. In any case, as John Adams discovered, he had left the accounts of the Paris mission in a muddle.

Congress kept Deane cooling his heels for months. While he waited for a hearing, the Lee party attacked with every kind of discreditable rumor. Although most of the charges were pure slander, one of them was true: in association with a Philadelphia merchant, Samuel Wharton, and Dr. Edward Bancroft, he had leaked news of the treaties of alliance with France in order to promote their mutual interests on the London Stock Exchange.[3] This venal action cannot be excused, but it must be remembered that the concept of conflict of interest was a very different thing during the late eighteenth century than it is today. It was accepted that patriots as highly regarded as Robert Morris and Nathanael Greene* should represent public and private interests at the same time. "Government officials engaged in procurement, commissary, and quarter-master matters, intermingling the government's business with their own, bought

* Morris was the financier of the Revolution; Greene was Washington's quartermaster general. The war could hardly have been won without the services of these two able men.

ships in the public service or public ships for private business. Robert Morris, who became the virtual manager of foreign procurement, once remarked to a protégé, 'I shall continue to discharge my duty faithfully to the public and pursue my private fortune by all such honorable and fair means as the time will admit of, and I dare say you will do the same.' "[4]

As for the virtuous Lees, William, the brother of Arthur who had been hanging about Paris while he futilely waited for a diplomatic assignment, had also attempted to capitalize on his inside knowledge of the French alliance.[5] Arthur Lee filled an entire Continental frigate with his own merchandise on his return to America in 1779. Public officials during the American Revolution showed little self-restraint.

That Silas Deane gambled heavily is unquestionable. However, during his Paris years, he never betrayed a public trust. Reading in an English newspaper "a most infamous Libel asserting that I had made a Fortune of thirty, or forty thousand pounds . . . by purchasing Arms at three Livres, and charging Congress a Louis d'or for them,"[6] Deane asked for help from Franklin to refute the charge. Franklin responded with a strongly phrased affidavit over his signature as American Minister to France. Having declared that the statements in question were, according to his best knowledge and belief, "entirely false," he then added: "I have never known or suspected any cause to charge . . . Silas Deane with any want of probity, in any purchase, or bargain, whatever, made by him for the use or account of the United States."[7]

When William Lee read this certificate in the London *Courant* in 1783, he said that Franklin had already been charged in America with being "as deep in the mud as Mr. Silas Deane is in the mire, about the same magazine of old rusty iron."[8] The Lees had done their best to bring down Franklin on the rumor of some ill-advised land speculations in Ohio, known as Vandalia, and another of their attacks was directed at the employment of his grandnephew, Jonathan Williams, to handle supplies for Deane at Le Havre. The barbed shafts glanced off the stout oak of which the old man was made. Poor Silas Deane was made of weaker stuff. He should have risen above the ugly storm and, by keeping silent, ridden it out. It was easy enough to prove that the vast fortune he had garnered, according to his enemies, was a figment of their imagination. He was very hard up, having contributed much of his private wealth to the American cause during his service in France from 1776 to 1778.† But it was not in the nature of this naïve, tactless man to remain silent. In December 1778, Deane exploded with a poorly written public defense of his own conduct and a violent attack on Arthur Lee. This outburst was answered by a highly indiscreet letter from Tom Paine to a newspaper exposing the whole story of France's clandestine aid to America before the alliance. Paine was the secretary of the Committee for Foreign Affairs, and his public admission made nonsense out of the protestations of neutrality that Maurepas and Vergennes had given Lord Stormont in 1776–77. Gérard, the French Minister, rushed to Congress, howling about the honor of France. When his report reached Versailles, Vergennes was a very angry man. An embarrassed Congress dismissed Paine from his position, and the investigation dragged wearily on. Deane's accusers were permitted to state their charges, but he was only allowed to defend himself in writing.[9]

In March 1779, a congressional committee brought in its report on the imbroglio. Deane was neither convicted nor cleared, but one tangible result of the investigation was that Congress was convinced that the joint commissioner system could only lead to "suspicions and animosities . . . highly prejudicial to the honor and interests of the United States."[10] From now on only one minister would be appointed for each foreign Court, and he must be of a quality counted on "to put the public good above private gain or personal rancor."[11]

Deane was free, but the rest of his life was lived under a cloud of suspicion that destroyed him. After a year and a half,

† *Congress eventually repaid his heirs $37,000 in 1842, thus recognizing the justice of Deane's financial claims against the United States.*

he went back to Paris in a pathetic effort to have his accounts audited, and, having failed in the attempt, he became a lonely, embittered drifter. For a time he lived in Flanders because it was cheap; then, after the peace treaty was signed, he moved to London.

In the year 1781, Deane did a terrible thing which changed his position overnight from that of a man who might have been a cheat to that of a traitor to his country. He opened negotiations with the British government on March 3, 1781. George III wrote of him to Lord North as one "whose services had been offered."[12] In May and June, in a series of letters to old friends in America, he advocated reconciliation with England without independence. Ironically, just as he was sitting down to write these epistles, Washington and Rochambeau were meeting in his former home at Wethersfield, Connecticut, to plan the Yorktown campaign. The letters, thanks to the ever-efficient British Secret Service, were published in New York just as the whole country was celebrating the victory at Yorktown.

Deane's behavior is inexplicable. The kindest thing to say is that, unable to support the strain of the congressional investigation, he suffered a nervous breakdown. John Jay thought that "mortifications had poisoned his heart and turned his brain." Robert Morris was as horrified as the rest of Deane's friends. A letter written in 1783 by the wretched man is an example of the self-pity that revolted his supporters.

"Publicly Stigmatized both in America, and in France, as a Defaulter and Traytor, I did not think it prudent to withstand the general Torrent, and therefore retired into exile, as obscure, and low as the circumstances to which I was reduced. I passed near Eighteen Months at Ghent in narrow cheap lodgings most of the time without a servant, and dining at a Table d'hote or ordinary, saw no one, that I could avoid seeing, and corresponded with scarce a person out of Flanders."[13]

In all the years of his rejection he never stopped calling himself an American or accepted guilt for anything more than a mistaken political judgment. "Have I exceeded the bounds ever allowed to free citizens, in writing or speaking on political subjects? Have we, in our contest for liberty, forfeited the rights of private judgment and of freedom of speech?"[14]

Losing the friendship of John Jay must have hurt him badly. It was Jay, then serving on the Committee of Secret Correspondence, who had sent him off to France with a supply of Sir James Jay's invisible ink, retaining himself the chemical solvent with which to read Deane's reports. It had been John Jay to whom he had addressed those long, eager letters from Paris in 1776, and it was Jay who had championed his cause during the nightmare of the investigation of his conduct in Philadelphia in 1778. In 1780, the bedraggled Deane was in Passy, staying in his old rooms in Franklin's house while he attempted to sort out his tangled accounts. Jay was in Madrid, having been appointed American Minister to Spain. Their correspondence began in October with Deane writing six letters to one of Jay's.[15] At first Deane's letters were cheerful, chatty, and full of news that he thought might have reached Paris before Madrid and so would interest Jay and his wife. They must have been unnerving letters to receive as, in between the items concerning the health and welfare of common friends written in plain English, Deane would sometimes insert a most alarming and important piece of news written in cipher. This example is from his letter of October 16:

"The Affair of Mr. Laurens, you are acquainted with by the public papers, for which it is a fruitful, and seasonable Subject as that of Electioneering is exhausted in England. His Son sailed Ten Days before him for Europe but has not been heard of. OUR FORCES IN SOUTH CAROLINA under GATES HAVE BEEN DEFEATED, OUR LOSS IS GREAT. Baron de Kalb‡ killed and ABOUT 2500 KILLED AND PRISONERS. . . ."* The letter concludes with a touching paragraph: "But Adieu to Politics. I promise to meddle

‡ *General the Baron de Kalb was a German volunteer, a middle-aged soldier of fortune who proved to be a first-class commander.*
* *The parts of Deane's letters printed in small capitals were in code which has been deciphered by Professor Richard B. Morris. The quote is from Morris'* John Jay: The Winning of the Peace.

no more with them in our future correspondence but to follow the Example you have set me in your Letters and write only on indifferent Subjects. Your happiness and prosperity can never be of this kind with me, and from that motive I wish to know at least the Outlines of your Situation. But perhaps you think me Gloomy if not disaffected. . . ."

This communication had crossed a short letter from Jay in which he sounded like the competent New York lawyer that he had been before the war, full of brisk advice to Deane to collect facts and evidence with which to confound the sea of enemies he felt were all around him. Evidently, on reading the above he was moved with pity for his old friend, for he answered immediately, opening with a beautiful line:

"How happens it that you do not know me? Time and opportunity have not been wanting. I suspect that you sometimes see double. . . .

"If my Regard for my Friends be measured by the Length of Letters I write them, I confess they often have reason to complain. . . . Could I transport myself for a few Hours to Passy we should soon find ourselves in a Situation similar to those we were in at Mrs. House's in 1775.† . . . These are not times to bid adieu to politics. While you can be useful in them don't restrain your Pen from those Subjects. . . ."

It was a warm, affectionate letter—the last of its kind. By June 16, 1781, Jay was writing "Dear Sir" instead of "Dear Deane" and his tone was cold and impersonal. He must have heard the first of the rumors of treachery. The close correspondence broke off, but a later letter has often been quoted by historians. In it Jay said that friendship had ended when Deane "advised Americans to desert that independence which they had pledged to each other their lives, their fortunes, and their *sacred honour* to support."[16] This censure was strong, but even more crushing was Jay's answer to an unsuccessful effort by Deane to see him in 1784:

† *Mrs. House had kept the boardinghouse at Fish and Market streets in which both Jay and Deane stayed while in Philadelphia in 1775.*

". . . I love my country and my honour better than my friends, and even my family, and am ready to part with them all whenever it would be improper to retain them. You are either exceedingly injured, or you are no friend to America, and while doubts remain on that point, all connection between us must be suspended. I wished to hear what you might have to say on that head, and should have named a time and place for an interview, had not an insurmountable obstacle intervened to prevent it. I was told by more than one, on whose information I thought I could rely, that you received visits from, and was on terms of familiarity with General Arnold. Every American who gives his hand to that man, in my opinion pollutes it."

These hard words must have been written in the white heat of anger. Jay was the last man to turn his back on a friend. However, the thought of Deane fraternizing with Benedict Arnold in London was too much for him or any other American patriot to stomach. Arnold's betrayal of Washington had shocked opinion more than any other single incident of the war.

Who did remain loyal to Silas Deane in his last years? It would seem that his one support was Dr. Bancroft. It was Bancroft who pulled him through countless illnesses, rescued him when he was down and out, drunken, and living in low lodging houses. He lent him money, sympathized with his woes, and wrote his obituary when, on the point of sailing home to America in 1789, he suddenly died.

Dr. Bancroft had grown ever more popular and more successful during the years since he had joined the American mission in Paris. Besides retaining his post there, from where he successfully speculated on the London Stock Exchange with his generous salary from William Eden, he had from time to time been commissioned to undertake special missions by distinguished personages. Although the Court of Versailles continued to spy on all Americans attached to Franklin's mission, there was never the faintest suspicion of Bancroft's activities as "Edward Edwards," his Secret Service code name. Vergennes, who had the greatest confidence in him, sent him to Northern Ireland in

1779 to investigate the chances of fomenting an uprising there. It was thought that the Irish grievances were not unlike those of the American colonies in earlier years, and that the fertile ground could best be exploited by an American. It was Lafayette who had suggested Bancroft, on the grounds of his courage, and Vergennes persuaded Franklin to lend him to the French. Bancroft accomplished the job with his usual competence, spending some time in Ulster disguised as an English merchant. He reported that the Irish indeed longed for independence, but were too divided among themselves to attain it.

Vergennes was grateful to Bancroft for having undertaken what he considered a dangerous mission and accepted the negative conclusions of his findings. How it must have amused Eden and Wentworth to have their spy influence the foreign policy of France! They may well have written the report themselves; in any case they would have taken good care of Bancroft in Ireland. What the French government paid him for "the dangerous mission" is not recorded, but, as Eden had earlier raised his salary to 1,000 pounds a year as long as he remained in Paris, it is not surprising that Deane, on his return from America, found Bancroft "agreeably situated and most esteemed in the world of politics, science and letters in which he moved."[17]

In 1783, after the conclusion of peace, Bancroft went to America on a private mission to try to recover some money that had been lent by the Prince of Luxembourg to the state of South Carolina. It had been many years since the boy from Westfield, Massachusetts, had left his home to seek his fortune in the West Indies as an apprentice physician. Now he returned as a very important person, Dr. Edward Bancroft, a fellow of the Royal Society whose scientific investigations on the theory of colors and dyes had given him a most dignified position among his colleagues in London. He came also as a friend of Lafayette, who introduced him to Washington as "a sensible and a warm friend to our cause."[18] Having met everyone of consequence in Philadelphia, where he had landed, he proceeded to Liberty Hall, the home of Governor William Livingston of New Jersey, father-in-law of John Jay. After a stay with the hospitable Livingstons, he went on to New York, where he spent almost a week in Washington's entourage, "feasting, visiting, dancing &. . . ."[19] Never neglectful of his duty, he found time to give news to the British Cabinet of American conditions and politics as he saw them.

On returning to England in 1784, he found that the new government, only too anxious to forget the American war, had no further use for him as an agent. He, therefore, retired from government service on his pension and sent the new Foreign Secretary, the Marquess of Carmarthen, the already-mentioned memorandum recounting his staggering activities in Paris during the preceding eight years. He ended succinctly:

> *One years Salary was due to me at midsummer last, which I request the payment of: what it shall be, must depend on the Kings pleasure, and that of his Ministers: I make no Claim beyond the permanent pension of £500 pr an. for which the Faith of Government has been often pledged; and for which, I have sacrificed near eight years of my Life, and my pursuits in it; always avoiding any Kind of appointment, or emolument from, as well as any sort of Engagement to, any Government in the United States; in the full determination, of remaining to the end of my Life, a faithful Subject to my natural, and most Gracious Sovereign.*
>
> St. James's 16th Sept'r 1784[20]

Bancroft had always kept a home for his wife and children in London, occasionally employing the services of Mrs. Bancroft as a courier. In Paris he had had a mistress, darkly referred to by John Adams, who never met her, as "The Woman" in the one critical sentence he ever wrote about Bancroft. She was never mentioned again in any contemporary correspondence. After his retirement, the eminent member of the Royal Society lived to a ripe old age, engaged in putting his theory of colors to commercial use for the printing of calicoes.

That should be the end of the Bancroft-Deane story, but it

cannot be closed, for we owe to a great American historian, the late Dr. Julian P. Boyd, a version very different from the one recounted above. His description of events is as compelling reading as a good detective story. The provocative title is "Silas Deane: Death by a Kindly Teacher of Treason?"

It will be recalled that Silas Deane had been the teacher of Edward Bancroft during his early days as a New England schoolmaster. Before going to England to study medicine, Bancroft had already practiced it as an apprentice, first in Barbados and then in Surinam, where he lived on Paul Wentworth's plantation and became an expert on dyes and poisons. The use of curare, Professor Boyd tells us, was one of his specialties. From now on the story is his:

During the summer of 1776, soon after Dr. Bancroft joined Deane in Paris on Franklin's orders, their relationship became that of teacher to pupil; this time Bancroft was the teacher and the lesson taught that of treason. It took very little time for the stronger man to turn the weaker one into his accomplice as a spy. ". . . Lacking both discretion and integrity, he [Deane] promptly betrayed the confidence of the minister [Vergennes] and the honor of his country."[21]

"It is incredible to suppose that the two men did not come to a prompt understanding. . . . Within a very short time the two friends, their indissoluble partnership in infamy launched on a sea of claret, were involved in vast schemes for gaining wealth from trade, fitting out privateers, purchasing supplies for Congress, land speculation, stock jobbing, manipulation of news, and *spying and double dealing.*"‡[22]

Bancroft's value to his English masters was immensely enhanced by bringing in Deane; no other member of the Secret Service had an American commissioner in his pocket. Paul Wentworth, Bancroft's old patron from the Surinam days, was justly proud of him. Wentworth came to Paris to interview Deane personally in December 1777, and before leaving "he

‡ *Author's emphasis.*

had evidently concluded some sort of understanding with Deane."[23]

It was about then that the British spy George Lupton, alias Jacobus Van Zandt, slipped into Deane's office and found there letters addressed to Deane under his cover name "Benson." "George III, eternally suspicious of his own spies, had at last found in the camp of the enemy one he was willing to trust. Deane seems not to have required anything more than talk about rewards."[24]

Dr. Bancroft kept very close to Deane during his years of disgrace and exile, not entirely from unselfish motives, although he was genuinely attached to the wretched puppet whose strings he had manipulated for so many years. In 1789, however, the situation changed dramatically. Six years had passed since the end of the war, and the bitterness against Deane in America had softened. He was invited to go home. Friends and family offered security and a new start; there was to be a house provided by his brother Barnabas, and his brother-in-law, Winthrop Saltonstall, wrote that "no one will be happier in embracing you in this part of the world than I shall. When at New London I shall be happy in receiving you into my family, and though not with that elegance you have been used to, you can no where receive a more sincere and hearty welcome."[25]

Silas Deane's hopes rekindled. He was only fifty-two, and his health had greatly improved during his last year in London. A generous friend bought him a passage with Captain Edward Davis of the *Boston Packet,* and Deane embarked from Gravesend about the middle of September. Due to bad weather, the ship was obliged to anchor off the Downs. On the twenty-second, Deane was walking the quarterdeck with Captain Davis when he was overcome with dizziness "and an oppression of the stomach."[26] He was at once put to bed. Twice he attempted to speak to the people around him, but no one could understand his inarticulate sounds. "A drowsiness and insensibility continually incroached upon his faculties."[27] He was dead four hours after the onset of the illness. The body was buried at Deal, just inland from the ship's anchorage. An entry in the parish register for September 26, 1789, recorded the fact that "Silas Deane, Esq. Minister Plenipotentiary from the United States of America to the Court of France in 1777 and 1778 [sic] died in the Downs on his passage from London to America."[28]

Within a few days the rumor was all over London that Deane, in a last fit of despondency, had taken his own life with a self-administered overdose of laudanum. "But if, as the rumor asserted, Deane died from a dose of opium—or some other poison—*was* his death 'voluntary and self-administered'?"[29] The source of the rumor was Bancroft. His only possible motive could have been self-protection. The captain's letter describing the actual circumstances of death has been lost, but Professor Boyd speculates that, at any time after his return to America, Deane could have revealed certain secrets in Dr. Bancroft's past that would have had a disastrous effect on the doctor's secure position in London and might even have lost him his valued pension. A few drunken babblings, picked up and reported to the British government, or merely published in the newspapers, could have spelled disaster for the happy Bancroft family. So, reluctantly, the good doctor resorted to the only means by which he could close Deane's mouth once and for all. Bancroft was the one who had organized his stores for the voyage. "As a medical man he could have supplied the tincture of opium if Deane required it—and he could also have employed this or some of the sea stores as a vehicle for conveying to the unsuspecting Deane a toxic substance added by himself. It is conceivable that Deane was a laudanum addict, and that Bancroft, knowing this, took advantage of the fact."[30]

Dr. Boyd is careful to state that the story of the crime is his own hypothesis, unproved and perhaps unprovable. If it was only the tale of Silas Deane's death that was at issue, it would be absurd to quibble with the three monographs that comprise his series. However, in building up the story for the last dramatic act of the play, Dr. Boyd makes a very serious charge indeed. This is that Deane turned traitor under Bancroft's influence soon after he arrived in Paris. Yet he gives no facts to prove his statements that Deane "betrayed the honor of his country" before 1781 and that he engaged in "spying and double dealing" as American commissioner.[31]

In justice to Silas Deane, it must be said that the scaffolding on which Dr. Boyd erects his stage for the murder scene is flimsy. Consider the supposed deal with Paul Wentworth. At the eleventh hour, when the British government woke up to the fact that the French were on the point of signing a treaty of alliance with the American colonies, Wentworth was sent to Paris in the hopes of converting Franklin and Deane to a reconciliation. The results of the mission were not merely negative, they were disastrous from the British point of view. Vergennes, whose enthusiasm for the alliance had been diminished by the threat of a general European war following the death of the Elector of Bavaria a few weeks before, was marking time when Franklin arranged for the news to be leaked to him of the pressing offers conveyed by Paul Wentworth. The danger that the Americans might agree to an accommodation seemed to him so great that he and Maurepas encouraged the King and Cabinet into an acceleration of the negotiations which led to the treaties.*

Lord North had never made a more stupid move. Had it resulted in the conclusion of an understanding with Deane, as Professor Boyd states it did, the mission might have been considered a partial success. But, when Paul Wentworth offered his tempting bait of rewards to Deane, the fish refused to bite, according to Wentworth's reports to Eden.

Immediately after the "understanding with Wentworth," Dr. Boyd tells us, George III had at last found in Deane a spy that he could trust. The evidence here is the aforementioned letters

---

* The story of the failure of the mission is well recorded: Wentworth to Eden, Paris, Dec. 11, 1777, Auckland MSS (SF 225); Wentworth to Eden, Paris, Dec. 17, 1777, Auckland MSS (SF 231); Wentworth to Eden, Paris, Jan. 7, 1778, Auckland MSS (SF 489); Wentworth to Eden, Paris, Jan. 10, 1778, Auckland MSS (SF 235).

found by the spy George Lupton. As the contents of the letters are not disclosed, this is hardly proof of treason. Deane, who also used the cover name "J. Jones" in private correspondence, may have been dealing with his stockbroker concerning a speculation he preferred to keep secret, or, for that matter, a woman. Lupton was the weakest link in the Eden-Wentworth Paris network, a miserable creature who was subsequently dismissed from the Secret Service in 1778 for incompetence.[32]

If Silas Deane was a traitor during his two years of public service in France, it is extraordinary that William Eden's papers[33] contain no hint of the fact. The work of the Secret Service during the American war is meticulously documented, volume after volume. For example, three agents were on the William Carmichael case, and their attempts to turn him are described in minute detail and endless length. If it was so important to subvert a young man holding the relatively minor position of Deane's secretary, how much more of a triumph it would have been to have persuaded the commissioner himself to spy for England. Yet the first mention of treasonable correspondence by Deane with Paul Wentworth and other spies comes in January, February, and March 1782, four years after Deane had left public service.[34]

The secret that Dr. Bancroft was so desperately eager to conceal—so eager that it led him to murder Deane, according to Boyd—was the long-ago story of George Aitken, more commonly known as John the Painter.† John the Painter, a young Scotsman, came to see Deane in Paris in 1776 soon after his arrival from America. He proposed to sabotage the royal dockyards in England by the use of an incendiary device of his own invention.[35] Deane, ever enthusiastic, procured a passport for him from Vergennes, and in late November Aitken terrified the whole of England by burning up the rope house at the Portsmouth dockyard and later by destroying two warehouses at Bristol. This was the only mission of sabotage attempted in Eng-

† *His nickname came from the fact that his profession was that of a house painter.*

land during the Revolutionary War. Aitken was caught, tried, and sent to the gallows at Portsmouth on March 10, 1777.

Somehow, it was known to the British police that the usually cautious Bancroft had met Aitken at a coffeehouse, and, although he managed to extricate himself from complicity in the plot, he felt himself for a time to be in grave danger. It seems very odd that Bancroft should ever have become involved, but Dr. Boyd suggests that Deane and he may have "employed the affair of John the Painter as an elaborate cover for their own private game—a cover that, if successful, would not only keep the game going but make an American hero of Deane and guarantee American confidence in Bancroft."[36]

By the year 1789, when Deane was about to sail for America, the case of John the Painter was hardly fresh in the public mind. The Scotsman had long been considered a pyromaniac—certainly an unbalanced personality. Discovery of the part Bancroft had played in the story, which was at worst only a fringe role, would hardly seem sufficient cause for the British government to punish him severely at this late date. And how could he have been proved guilty, with the testimony against him coming from that discredited figure, Silas Deane?

We may never know how Deane died, although a heart attack seems a more plausible cause of death than the fine hand of Dr. Bancroft. What is certain is that, during his two years in Paris, Deane fulfilled the hope he had expressed to his wife in the spring of 1776 of acquitting himself well.‡

‡ *It was with the greatest reluctance that I found myself disagreeing with the distinguished historian Julian P. Boyd. His trilogy "Silas Deane: Death by a Kindly Teacher of Treason?" written in 1959 fascinated me, but a study of the documents persuaded me that he had been misled. I should have let the subject rest, had not his hypothesis become incorporated in the works of the modern historians who have quoted Professor Boyd verbatim, without reference to the original souces.*

On entering the hall of the American Embassy in Paris one's eye is immediately caught by a marble plaque giving the list of names of the men who have represented our country in France. It began, when I last saw it, with Benjamin Franklin. Perhaps Silas Deane deserves to be added, for he was our first diplomat abroad.

❧ X ❧

A Letter of Resignation

ON MARCH 12, 1781, FRANKLIN WROTE a long letter to Samuel Huntington, President of the Congress, offering his resignation.

"I have passed my seventy-fifth year, and I find that the long and severe attack of the gout which I had the last winter has shaken me exceedingly, and I am far from having recovered the bodily strength I before enjoyed. I do not know that my mental faculties are impaired; perhaps I shall be the last to discover that; but I am sensible of great diminution in my activity, a quality I think particularly necessary in your minister for this Court. I am afraid, therefore, that your affairs may sometime or other suffer by my deficiency."[1]

All that he asked was that Congress would take his grandson Temple under their protection. While still too young to qualify for an important diplomatic post, Temple had learned much during his apprenticeship in Paris. Perhaps he would someday be useful as secretary to an American Minister in Europe? In the meantime, feeling himself too weak to risk another Atlantic crossing, Franklin looked forward to remaining in Europe and, after taking a tour of Italy and Germany with Temple, to settling down there in "philosophic leisure."

Congress refused to consider the very idea of letting Franklin retire, and by August he was writing briskly that his health and spirits had improved and that he must buckle down to business once more. It is a wonder he had hung on so long without submitting his resignation, for he was now into the sixth year of his mission without respite. It would have given him immense pleasure to have seen Italy and Germany, above all in the company of his beloved Temple, but he was never to leave Paris until he returned to America.

When the day finally came, it must have seemed a long time since the euphoric spring of 1778—the French alliance consummated and the praise of all France ringing in his ears. That spring he had taken young Temple to meet the dying Voltaire. The great writer had blessed the young man, murmuring, "*Dieu, liberté.*" The audience had caught the low-spoken words and burst into tears as one man, so touched were they by the tender spectacle as "the apostle of tolerance and the liberator of the New World embraced."*[2]

This meeting was perhaps the sentimental zenith of the Franco-American alliance of 1778, but the rest of the spring too had been a time of hope and promise. Admiral d'Estaing had sailed with his fine fleet—20 ships of the line and 13 frigates carrying 4,000 soldiers. He was handed sealed orders, and it was only when he was well at sea that he learned the identity of his passenger, Monsieur Gérard, and knew that he was carrying the first French diplomat to America.

---

* *John Adams, who was on the scene, was deeply embarrassed by the embrace of the two old men, and wrote a cruel description: "After dinner We went to the Academy of Sciences. . . . Voltaire and Franklin were both present, and there presently arose a general Cry that Monsieur Voltaire and Monsieur Franklin should be introduced to each other. This was done and they bowed and spoke to each other. This was no Satisfaction. There must be something more. Neither of our Philosophers seemed to divine what was wished or expected. They however took each other by the hand. . . . But this was not enough. The Clamour continued, untill the explanation came out. 'Il faut s'embrasser, à la francoise.' The two Aged Actors upon this great Theatre of Philosopy and frivolity then embraced each other by hugging one another in their Arms and kissing each others cheeks, and then the tumult subsided. And the Cry immediately spread through the whole Kingdom and I suppose over all Europe Qu'il etoit charmant. Oh! il etoit enchantant, de voir Solon and Sophocles embrassans. How charming it was! Oh, it was enchanting to see Solon and Sophocles embracing!"[3]*

At Versailles they waited for news. It was a burning summer
—the hottest France had known for years. For reasons of economy, the King announced, the Court would stay at Versailles instead of moving from palace to palace as it usually did. The
Queen, expecting her first child, strolled in the shady woods of
the park of Trianon with her ladies—the courtiers on duty at
the palace fanned themselves as they walked on the gravelly surface of the baking-hot terrace. All the trees near the palace had
been razed a few years before during a reforestation program, so
Versailles was hotter and less beautiful than it had been in the
preceding reign, or as it is today. It was pleasanter to remain in-
doors, lounging in the high-ceilinged rooms out of the glare of
the merciless sun.

On the twenty-second of June the Oeil-de-Boeuf was full of
lethargic courtiers, desultorily exchanging gossip. In their ar-
caded offices a quarter of a mile away, the clerks in the Archives
of the Ministry of Foreign Affairs bent over black lacquered
desks, their quill pens traveling evenly across the paper in front
of them. They would hardly have looked up at the sound of a
galloping horse pounding up the Avenue de Paris, for breathless
couriers were always clattering into the courtyard at all hours of
day and night. Then the news flashed through Versailles with
electric speed and a cry went up, passing from salon to salon,
echoing through the vast mirrored gallery, shouted from stable
to office to scullery, "GUERRE! GUERRE!"

The French frigate La Belle Poule had been attacked by an
English frigate off the coast of Brittany and the battle had lasted
for five hours. In the end the British ship had disengaged and
tacked off, out of action, without replying to the last fifty shots
fired by the French at her retreating stern. Although La Belle
Poule was in shambles, shot through and through and with half
her crew dead or wounded, Captain de la Clochetterie had
brought her back to the Brittany shore. This first action in the
war had been a creditable one for France.

On the same eventful day, good news arrived of the Comte
d'Estaing's fleet. It had passed the 34th latitude on May 20 and

was approaching America without incident. Sartine, Minister of the Navy, was bursting with pride as he informed the King. It was a night for celebration. In the general excitement, a hero of the occasion was Léonard, the most fashionable hairdresser in Paris. Within hours this artist had designed a new coiffure, and within days it was being worn by every great lady in Paris and Versailles. The name, of course, was *"à la Belle Poule,"* and it involved carrying the model of a full-rigged ship, masts, sails, and all, on top of one's head embedded in what was known as a pouf—a sort of decorative cushion. The ladies bore it uncomplainingly, proudly, *"pour la France."*

Morale was high throughout the summer, and by autumn the rumor began to fly that d'Estaing had relieved New York. This was officially denied, but everyone still felt confident that the war would be a short one. Surely the brave American army, supported by d'Estaing's fleet, would bring the British to their knees at least by the following year, 1779.

Instead all the plans went wrong. D'Estaing was to have attacked Lord Howe's fleet in Delaware Bay, but he moved so slowly that Howe was able to slip away to New York. The French followed only to be met by the British drawn up in a battle array which so terrified the local pilots that they would not take d'Estaing through the Narrows. There was nothing for it but to sail for New England, where, after an abortive struggle with the British during a storm so severe that there could be no real battle, the battered French withdrew to Boston for repairs and then sailed for the West Indies. A gallant man, Admiral d'Estaing was not running away. The West Indies sugar islands were of vital commercial importance to both British and French interests. The Caribbean was a major theater of war.

The following year d'Estaing raced from the Antilles to the rescue of Savannah, which, with all of Georgia, had been reconquered by the British during the preceding winter. There were only 3,200 English soldiers to defend the city, and the French transports were carrying 6,000 troops. It could have been an earlier Yorktown, but again d'Estaing had bad luck. Unable to find a safe anchorage for his ships, which were threatened by an autumn gale, he attacked with reckless impatience and insufficient preparation. Suffering heavy casualties and wounded himself, he withdrew and sailed for France. The Bailli de Suffren, who served under him, said of d'Estaing: "Had only his seamanship equalled his courage!"[4]

The French, seeing their proud fleet return after fifteen months in American waters with nothing to show for the expensive effort, became discouraged with the war. It was said that French sailors had been roughed up by gangs in the streets of Boston, and one of d'Estaing's officers wrote a popular book describing the annoyances he and his men had suffered at American hands. The fall of Charleston and the defection of General Benedict Arnold increased the gloom. When Congress devalued the currency to a fortieth of its former value, it seemed obvious to all that America was finished. The certainty of defeat was whispered at Versailles and sung in the streets.

Encouraged, the British stepped up their propaganda efforts, and the works of two skillful writers, Tucker and Pownall, were influential. Their theme was that, once the war was over, Great Britain would regain her monopoly of American commerce and the French would have wasted their men, their time, their money, and their enthusiasm. On a lower level, ugly pamphlets circulated attacking Vergennes, Sartine, and Franklin. They were rather well done, especially two entitled *La Cassette Verte de Monsieur de Sartine* and *The History of a French Flea*. Their style was as intimate as a modern gossip column. They named grand names and quoted what the holders of these were purported to have said about the weakness of America. Court gossip was their mainstay. Necker was reported to have told the King that he was as worried about the financial strain of the war as had been his predecessor, Turgot. (This was quite true—Necker had been sympathetic to the American cause but against direct intervention.) The French Flea was right there during the private conversations of the King and Queen and overheard the King saying how much the impudence of the incessant

American demands for money irritated him and the Queen replying that she was equally incensed.

Here the Flea slipped up. It is unlikely that Louis XVI would have had a serious discussion about the American war with his wife. More than a year before, the watchful Empress Maria Theresa had written to Mercy-Argenteau, the Austrian Ambassador: "My daughter would do well not to show her predilection for the English so openly. I know that this has already annoyed the French." The King and Vergennes kept Marie Antoinette out of the discussions that led up to the treaty of alliance, and like most women, she disliked politics that she could not influence. Once the war started, she and her entourage did not follow the course of it closely, as is revealed in a fascinating memoir, recently published: the diary of the Marquis de Bombelles. Bombelles was a diplomat living at Versailles between posts abroad. Both his wife and her mother held positions in the Royal Household, and Bombelles was a keen observer of the intrigues that absorbed the courtiers. No reminiscences of Versailles since those of the Duc de Saint-Simon in an earlier reign are as penetrating or amusing as his. But it is striking to note that between 1780 and 1784 he never mentions the American war, except to give news of some friend who is about to leave France to serve or who has been wounded or killed. Neither Yorktown nor the peace treaty is referred to, nor the negotiations that led up to the latter. There were two Versailles, that of the Queen and her intimates and that of Maurepas and Vergennes.

Vergennes fought back against the wave of defeatism that threatened to bring down his policy. Realizing that it would be foolish to defend the Americans, charge by charge, he responded instead with an inspired propaganda campaign. The French people had fallen in love with the American cause in 1775 for idealistic reasons. Now Vergennes employed the weapon of sentiment once more. He worked hard to make a hero of George Washington. Here was the Fabius of the New World; the legend that was built on Washington's name compared him to that great republican leader of ancient Rome, Quintus Fabius Maximus Verrucosus. Brave, uncorruptible, modest in his glory, virtuous without need of priests or dogma, Fabius had been called "Cunctator," he who delayed. Vergennes's flair for knowing what people wanted never failed him. The discouraged French found in Washington the new hope that they needed; after all, they reminded themselves, Fabius, that model of delaying tactics, had taken sixteen years to achieve the defeat of Hannibal. Was it not natural that their beleaguered American hero could not provide an instant end to the war? One great advantage to the cult of George Washington was that, being very far away, blemishes on his perfection went unseen.

Franklin was impressed and delighted with the success of Vergennes's propaganda. He knew, as the French did not, how much Washington had suffered from the intrigues and cabals of his enemies at home. And worse than these attacks was the attrition of inflation. Washington had asked: "When a rat in the shape of a horse could not be bought for less than 200 pounds, what funds can stand the present expenses of the army?"[5] Not only were the soldiers wretchedly supplied, but the pay they sent home was hopelessly inadequate to support their families. At the time that Paris was singing the praises of their hero Fabius-Washington, the Commander-in-Chief was in fact grimly expecting mutiny. The Connecticut line had already emerged from their miserable huts threatening to go home. Had they not been dissuaded, the whole army might well have followed.[6]

Franklin wrote a fine letter to cheer up Washington:

> *Passy, March 5, 1780*
>
> *. . . Should peace arrive after another Campaign or two, and afford us a little Leisure, I should be happy to see your Excellency in Europe, and to accompany, if my Age and Strength would permit, in visiting some of its ancient and most famous Kingdoms. You would, on this side of the Sea, enjoy the great Reputation you have acquir'd pure and free from those little shades that Jealousy and Envy of*

a Man's Countrymen and Cotemporaries [sic] are ever en-
deavouring to cast over living Merit. Here you would
know and enjoy what Posterity will say of Washington.
For 1000 Leagues have nearly the same effect as 1000
years. The feeble voice of those grovelling Passions cannot
extend so far either in Time or Distance. At present I
enjoy that Pleasure for you, as I frequently hear the old
Generals of this martial Country (who study the Maps of
America, and mark upon them all your Operations) speak
with sincere Approbation and great Applause of your con-
duct; and join in giving you the Character of one of the
greatest Captains of the Age.[7]

A French historian has written: "The sincerity and loyalty of
Franklin during his long mission are the finest examples of
'moral diplomacy' that have been seen before or since. The only
trick in which he indulged was his manner of affecting such exhaustion and decrepitude when he came to see Vergennes, that
his advice and warnings were like those of a grandfather on his
deathbed, saying his final goodbyes to a beloved grandson."[8]
This commentary conjures up a vivid picture of Benjamin
Franklin tottering across the courtyard of Versailles, painfully
dragging his way up the steps of the Aile des Ministres and into
the minister's office; of Rayneval, or one of the other officials,
rushing forward with a footstool for the gouty leg; of Vergennes,
imbued with the profound veneration for age innate in the
French, listening closely and respectfully, nodding his agreement.

Franklin would have been justified in using every trick in the
diplomatic book to keep Vergennes friendly. John Adams had
returned to Paris in February 1780—it must have seemed to
Franklin as though he had just left. Congress had elected him
minister to negotiate treaties of peace and commerce with Great
Britain—a high title which would have made a lesser man than
Benjamin Franklin extremely jealous. As there was no question
of peace being in sight and no commerce, Adams had nothing to
do. He took to visiting Versailles in order to lecture Vergennes

on foreign affairs and he must have been very tactless, for he irritated the minister so much that the French government came close to demanding his recall that spring. Fortunately, it did not come to that, but everyone was relieved when Adams left for Amsterdam in July, commissioned by Congress to negotiate a Dutch loan.

Anyone who has examined Vergennes's papers for that period may well wonder how he got through his work. His correspondence with the European powers filled volumes as he struggled with the intricacies of their different interests. His aim was to isolate Great Britain, and he achieved it brilliantly. Spain, France's laggard ally, at last signed a secret treaty in 1779. The price Vergennes paid was to agree to assisting Spain in the capture of Gibraltar from the British, which was the primary Spanish target. Vergennes tried hard to insert a clause which would have bound Spain to insist on the independence of the United States should the expected war with England break out, but the Spanish Foreign Minister, Floridablanca, refused to accept it. The Spanish colonies in America were too important to Madrid to allow them to view the independence of the United States with sympathy. In this instance Vergennes was, therefore, only partially successful, but in his anxiety to get Spain into the war he felt that concessions were worth making. Spain declared war on England in June 1779.

Vergennes's next objective was to organize the northern powers into a neutral bloc. Central Europe had been quieted by the Peace of Teschen, in which Vergennes had arbitrated a settlement between Austria and Prussia. The Netherlands, the principal bankers of Europe, were eager for the profits of neutral trading and had been sending their cargo ships to the Dutch-owned West Indian island of St. Eustatius, from where they engaged in a brisk, clandestine trade with America. However, the Dutch were tied to England by an ancient treaty. One of Vergennes's greatest successes was to persuade the Netherlands to dissolve this alliance by declaring neutrality in 1779. During that year further good news came from Russia, where Catherine the Great invited the other neutral nations to join her in an Armed Neutrality agreement.† Sweden and Denmark accepted, and the Baltic was closed to belligerent vessels. Thus, from Scandinavia to the Iberian Peninsula, was formed a continuous border consisting of neutral states and two powerful allies, France and Spain.

Franklin, watching Vergennes's diplomatic maneuvers with admiration, was ready when called upon for help in the war at sea upon which much depended. He knew that it was a subject beyond his competence—but when asked to plan with the French a joint attack on the British coast in 1779, he drew up the instructions for John Paul Jones, the American naval officer who was to command the fleet, with the land forces led by Lafayette. Versatile as he was, the difficulty of the task weighed heavily on him. He wrote to Lafayette, "I have not enough knowledge in such matters to presume upon advising it."[9] It was a bold plan, especially as, much to Lafayette's chagrin, his part in it had to be abandoned. Jones set out alone with his flagship, the *Bonhomme Richard,* and a makeshift Franco-American fleet.

John Paul Jones was one of the most flamboyant figures of the war. Born in Scotland, the son of a gardener on the property of a prosperous landowner, he had emigrated to America. After an adventurous early career at sea, he had arrived in Philadelphia in 1775 just as the navy was being formed. Commissioned lieutenant, he had risen fast in rank. Two years later he sailed to France a commodore aboard the sloop-of-war *Ranger.* In early 1778, he made a lightning raid on the English port of Whitehaven and continued on to Scotland. The cruise ended with the successful capture of H.M.S. *Drake.* His name was becoming known and feared in the British Isles.

John Adams knew Jones and wrote of a dinner given by the latter at the port of Lorient on the thirteenth of May 1779. While Adams admitted that the dinner for sixteen officers and

† *It had been Vergennes who secretly inspired Catherine the Great's Armed Neutrality. While the members did not declare war, they assumed a hostile attitude toward Great Britain, which they viewed as the "tyrant of the seas."*

gentlemen was an elegant one, he found that the conversation was "not very instructive," although he noted that, according to the Commodore, there were two ways of learning French: "Take a Mistress and go to the Commedie." Adams added in his puritan way: "The language is nowhere better spoken than at the Commedie." He continued: "After which Jones came on Board our Ship. This is the most ambitious and intriguing officer in the American Navy. Jones has Art, and Secrecy, and aspires very high. . . . Eccentricities and Irregularities are to be expected from him—they are in his Character, they are visible in his Eyes. His voice is soft and still and small, his eye has keeness and Wildness and softness in it."[10] In his portraits Commodore Jones has a most attractive face. His low voice, which Adams mentions, was said to be particularly appealing to women. His quarterdeck voice they never heard. Certainly he was ambitious, and his heart was set on gathering a squadron to accompany him in the amphibious assault with Lafayette.

The French government put a large commercial vessel, the *Duc de Duras,* under the American flag, and Leray de Chaumont provided the money for the purchase. A tired old ship which had made the long voyage to China many times, she required six months of refitting to be ready to sail out as the ship-of-war *Bonhomme Richard.* However, Jones, according to his biographer, "enjoyed fitting out more than anything except fighting and making love."[11] He had a splendid time with Chaumont's money, and the financier for his part was probably delighted to have Jones out of Paris, for all the world knew of the love affair between the dashing officer and Madame de Chaumont.

Eventually the fleet was ready. The *Bonhomme Richard* was the largest ship that Jones had ever commanded. She carried a crew of 380 representing eleven different nationalities; the officers were all Americans. Next came the new frigate *Alliance,* the French frigate *Pallas,* and the two smaller French vessels, all under the American flag although the captains were French. They went to sea on August 14, 1779, and sailed around the

View of a Paris boulevard

Silas Deane
America's first envoy to France

Conrad Alexandre Gérard
The first French Minister to the United States

John Ad

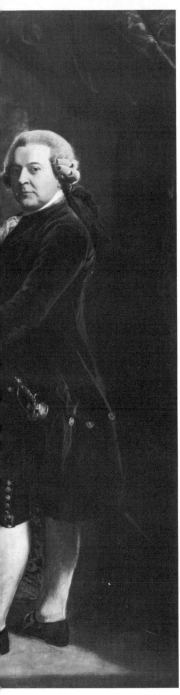

Abigail Adams

The courageous wife of John Adams

Arthur Lee

The most difficult American in Paris

John Jay
after the signing of the Definitive Peace Treaty
by Gilbert Stuart

Sarah Livingston Jay
The beautiful wife of John Jay

Maison de Santé.

St

depicting the unhappy prostitutes of Paris ha

...cene

...eir heads shaved following a new police order

William Carmichael

Robert Livingston
First American Secretary of Foreign Affairs

British Isles, taking prizes and terrifying the whole coast. The climax came on September 23 in the North Sea off Flamborough Head, where Jones in *Bonhomme Richard* engaged H.M.S. *Serapis* for four hours in a ship-to-ship battle. Long after any other captain would have surrendered, Jones fought on in his almost disabled ship. At last Captain Pearson of *Serapis* struck his colors, and Jones, with his ship sinking, transferred his flag to the English vessel and sailed her and the rest of the squadron into a neutral Dutch port.

John Paul Jones's autumn victory may have seemed all the more triumphant as it had been a bad year for his nation's cause. The French particularly liked the story of the exchange between the two captains at the height of the battle. The two ships had been so close that Captain Pearson could be clearly heard on the quarterdeck of the *Bonhomme Richard*. Sure that no commander in his right mind would continue the fight, he called, "Are you surrendering?" Back came the now famous answer, "No, I have not yet begun to fight."

Returning to Paris a hero, Jones received an ovation when he entered the Opera House; he was fought over by the salon hostesses, pursued by beautiful women, and elected a member of the Freemason society of the Nine Sisters, which also commissioned Houdon to sculpture his bust. The King gave him a golden sword and hung around his neck the order of a Knight of the Order of Military Merit. Even the Queen forgot her dislike of republicans and greeted him with unusual warmth. It was a splendid hour, and Franklin, who was a stranger to envy, rejoiced in the popularity of his compatriot.

Yet Franklin was growing tired, bone-tired. One contributory cause of his letter of resignation in 1781 was that he was always being ordered by Congress to undertake tasks that were truly beyond his experience, as in the case of the John Paul Jones task force. He knew nothing of naval matters, but in addition to his daily grind—the endless visitors who asked favors, wished information about America, wanted to emigrate, desired his opinion on a new scientific discovery—he was obliged to become a director of naval operations and, worse still, commercial and financial representative of the United States in Europe.

Of all the tasks Congress imposed on Franklin, the most onerous was extorting loans from the French to finance his government. Congress had no ready source of income as it had no power to tax and the states were unwilling to tax themselves. Its solution to the problem was to print paper money, issue after issue. Already in 1775, Franklin, as a member of that body, had been opposed to this dangerous practice and had urged that the courage be found to tax the citizen rather than risk the depreciation of the paper currency. But he had been overruled. So it was that in its fifth year the unpopular war could only be supported by loans from the French, who had already been generous and were now carrying the additional burden of their own war with the British. What was particularly trying for Franklin was that, instead of being allowed to choose the most propitious moment to approach the French, he was told to apply for monetary aid immediately upon receipt of instructions from Congress, which, without waiting to hear whether he had been successful, would draw upon the amount Franklin had been instructed to borrow.

The reckless drafts made Franklin feel like a permanent beggar. He wrote to John Jay in Madrid on October 2, 1780: "The storm of bills which I found coming upon us both has terrified and vexed me to such a degree that I have been deprived of sleep, and so much indisposed by continual anxiety as to be rendered almost incapable of writing."[12] An order he received in the middle of 1779 called for the procurement of military equipment to the tune of twelve million livres. An additional problem was that the terms used in these orders were often unintelligible to him and to the French merchants to whom he showed them, for the Americans, having been accustomed to buy what they needed from England, spoke a technical English which meant nothing to the commercially inexperienced Franklin. At last he resorted to sending to England for one of each article to use as a model for the French workmen.

The account of this particular venture has been beautifully told by Madame Claude-Anne Lopez.[13] Franklin pared down the order—he could never have managed to borrow twelve million in one gulp from the French—and obtained three million, which was still a great deal of money. Lafayette, back from America, had been clamoring for uniforms for Washington's army. The troops, he said, were "naked, shockingly naked." Therefore, Franklin gave priority to cloth and uniforms, making up the balance with ammunition and weapons. Leray de Chaumont undertook the financing, while Franklin's grandnephew in Nantes, Jonathan Williams, was responsible for the negotiations with the merchants.

From the beginning everything went wrong. It was eighteen months before the important cargo was on its way. There had been three false starts, caused by a combination of inefficiency, bad luck, and acrimony between the Williams-Chaumont team and the men who were to carry the supplies. John Paul Jones had looked like a likely candidate. He was due to sail with Rochambeau in the *Alliance* and, had he joined forces with the French fleet, the crucial cargo would have reached Washington by the early summer of 1780. But the turbulent Jones had a row with Chaumont—the plan fell through. To Franklin it must have seemed as if fate was against him. Hardly had he learned that Jones's overwhelming pride had caused yet another delay to the unlucky shipment, when news reached Paris of the devaluation of the Continental currency to one fortieth of its value. The frantic French merchants rushed to Passy to implore his help in the catastrophic situation in which they found themselves. Worse was to come.

In the course of a government reshuffle, Sartine, Chaumont's patron, was dismissed from office, and the financier's credit fell to zero. He had overextended himself and was faced with bankruptcy. Franklin, who had been in bed for weeks with acute gout, dragged himself out to Versailles for a useless consultation with Vergennes and, finding no help in that quarter, offered to put up his own private fortune to save Chaumont. In the middle of the drama, Congress dispatched a letter to Franklin scolding him for his delay in completing the last order and enclosing a further request for a new loan and more supplies. Back in America, the unforgiving Arthur Lee wrote that Dr. Franklin, "whose conduct I consider as injurious to the honor and the interests of the United States," should be removed. He alluded to considerable supplies having been furnished Franklin a year previously and stated that "not having expedited them has every appearance of designed neglect."[14] Designed neglect! Chaumont was saved by a miracle: the arrival of remittances from America in January 1781. What Mrs. Lopez rightly calls "the most troublesome cargo ever to leave for America" was at last embarked.

It had been intolerable for Franklin to feel that Leray de Chaumont was in trouble. Not only was he the generous landlord who had put his house at the disposal of the mission, rent free, but his wife and his daughters were Franklin's intimate friends. Chaumont held great positions which had seemed to make him invulnerable. As the archaic etiquette of the Court rendered it impossible for the Director-General of Finances, Jacques Necker, to sit with the Privy Council at Versailles because he was a Protestant, Leray de Chaumont took his place at all meetings with the King. He also was the Intendant of the Invalides, a remunerative sinecure which was conferred only on honored and privileged individuals in whom the King had complete confidence. He was the owner of a former royal château, Chaumont, on the Loire, as well as the beautiful Hôtel de Valentinois in Passy. His fleet of ships was impressive; his mercantile interests were flung across all Europe; he was, it would appear, a Maecenas whose position was as solid as a rock. A man whose hatred of England had been the motive of his original support of the American colonies, he had become, with Beaumarchais, the lifeline on which the Continental army depended.

Franklin was still worrying about Leray de Chaumont when he left France and continued to concern himself with the Chaumont family until the day he died. He had reason to do so, for the niggardly behavior of the Congress brought two of the most loyal friends of America to ruin. Chaumont, armored with the prestige that his position gave him, waited a long time before complaining. Beaumarchais, the adventurer who had started life as a poor watchmaker's son, became uneasy as early as 1777. By September of that year he had sent over cargoes worth five million livres without receiving a word of thanks or even a reply to the letters addressed to Congress which accompanied the shipments. He was waiting not only for thanks but for the ships full of indigo and tobacco which were supposed to be returned in payment, according to his original agreement with Silas Deane. Deane was more and more embarrassed as the months passed, but it occurred neither to him nor to Beaumarchais to look to Arthur Lee for an explanation. Lee, smoldering with jealousy of Deane, had lost little time in giving his side of the story to Congress. His first confidential letter to the Committee of Secret Correspondence was dated from Paris, January 3, 1777:

"Monsieur de Vergennes, the minister and his secretary, have repeatedly assured us that no return was expected for the cargoes sent by Beaumarchais. This gentleman is not a merchant; he is known to be a political agent, employed by the Court of France."[15]

This first drop of poison was followed by other similar envenomed epistles, and it is interesting to note that, although correspondence from the commissioners in Paris to Congress in Philadelphia was normally signed by all three names, these letters carried only the signature of Arthur Lee, although he constantly spoke in the plural, "Vergennes has assured *us*,"‡ etc.

Lee's information was perfectly intelligible to the committee. It explained why the invoices accompanying the goods of war had been so confusing to them. The practical Americans had wondered what sort of merchant this fellow could be who sent them such mixed-up lists from France. They knew nothing of the scenes of the wharves of Le Havre as Beaumarchais and his men packed and repacked the ships, often by night, to avoid the

‡ *Author's emphasis.*

attention of Lord Stormont's spies. The lack of order that attended the frantic last-minute rearrangements was inevitable, and perhaps the members of Congress would have been less critical could they have witnessed the playwright's determination. His only daughter, Eugénie, had been born in Paris while he was in Normandy attending to the loading of the cargo of the *Amphitrite*. It was many days before he was free to return to see the long-awaited baby.

Most confusing of all to the Americans was the style of Beaumarchais's letters. This romantic figure, this compulsive actor was perfectly incapable of writing the sort of straightforward business letter to which members of Congress, many of them merchants themselves, were accustomed. He now saw himself not merely as the statesman who had changed French policy with the famous memorials which Vergennes had inserted into his state papers, but also as a man of action, the admiral whose fleets would combat the wind, the waves, the English navy. Also, he was Beaumarchais the philosopher, the lover of liberty, the ally of the oppressed. His missives, signed Roderigue Hortalez et Cie (". . . and what kind of a name is that?" they must have asked themselves in Philadelphia), were impassioned tirades, with political advice and exhortation interspersed with requests for salt fish and indigo. He would sign off with a paragraph sounding, if not imperial, at least proconsular:

> *Gentlemen, consider my house as the head of all operations useful to your cause in Europe, and myself as the most zealous partisan of your nation,* THE SOUL OF YOUR SUCCESSES, ETC.
>
> *Roderigue Hortalez et Cie*

Did the man really exist? they asked themselves as they read the letters—perhaps he was a fictitious person. No, Arthur Lee had said that he did exist and that the merchandise he sent over was the free gift of the King of France. So be it. They were busy men with more important things to do than to reply to the protestations of enthusiasm from the man in Paris with the funny name. He could wait for his indigo and his salt fish.

After two years, his money and credit all but exhausted, he did receive a letter from John Jay, then President of the Congress:

> Philadelphia, 15th January 1779
>
> Sir,
>
> The Congress of the United States of America sensible of your Exertions in their favor present you with their thanks and assure you of their Regard.
>
> They lament the Inconveniences you have suffered, by the great Advances made in support of these States. Circumstances have prevented a compliance with their wishes, but they will take the most effectual measures in their power to discharge the debt due to you.
>
> The liberal Sentiments and extensive views which alone could dictate a Conduct like yours, are conspicuous in your Actions and adorn your Character. While with great Talents you served your Prince, you have gained the Esteem of this Infant Republic, and will receive the merited Applause of a new world.
>
> By order of Congress
>
> John Jay
> President[16]

This was an encouraging letter, statesmanlike in tone. Beaumarchais waited eagerly for the promised payment. What he received, nine months later, was not the money he so badly needed but a series of bills of exchange* to the value of 2,544,000 livres tournois, drawn to Franklin, signed by Jay, and payable in three years' time. Beaumarchais's biographer, Louis de Loménie, puts it succinctly: "bills which were signed by a nation hardly acknowledged as such could scarcely pass for ready money."[17]

It is difficult to excuse the Congress for its stinginess, hard-pressed as it was! Beaumarchais, of course, fought back with the full support of Franklin, and the story of Figaro was not yet finished. To both men there was only one redeeming feature to

---

* The bills of exchange are today in the possession of Madame Jacques de Beaumarchais. The family retains them as amusing souvenirs.

the summer of 1779 as they waited for news with sinking hopes, and that was the electrifying return of Lafayette. The tall young man who had slipped out of France in 1777 in his own ship, the *Victoire,* to offer his services to the Americans without remuneration, had come back a popular hero. Men crowded around him from the moment he landed, seeking his opinion of the war. Was there a hope that Washington would regain his momentum, or was all lost as people feared?

He went everywhere, seeing the ministers, being received at Versailles by the King and Queen, dining out every night in Paris. As he talked, his listeners forgot the weary realities of finance and supply and thrilled to hear him speak in glowing words of liberty and independence. It was as if a crusader had come back from the Holy Land to inspire those who had remained at home with the wonder of the cause. Especially the young men of his own generation and class listened and asked themselves how they could have tarried so long when before them beckoned a new frontier.

Maurepas and Vergennes had the courage to back up Lafayette as he begged, implored, cajoled the government to accept his pet project: the dispatch of a French expeditionary force. Without Lafayette's enthusiasm the Comte de Rochambeau would never have sailed, and it is greatly to the credit of the twenty-two-year-old general that, when he was passed over for the command of the four crack regiments that comprised the expedition, he never complained, much as he was disappointed. Rochambeau had been thirty-seven years in the army and was on the point of retirement when he was chosen for his competence and, above all, for his vast experience.

When the force embarked on May 2, 1780, the list of the names of the senior officers read like a page from the Almanach de Gotha, that Social Register of European aristocracy. "The Duc de Lauzun, the Chevalier de Chastellux, the Vicomte de Noailles, the Comte de Charlus, the Comte de Custine." These men, and others like them, were the sons of the greatest families of France. They were ready to risk their lives for American independence and were proud to be called *"les Américains."*

Count Axel de Fersen, the Queen's devoted Swedish admirer, was one of Rochambeau's aides-de-camp—another volunteer was a young German, Baron Ludwig von Closen, whose journal is an important source on the expeditionary corps. There were many more eager volunteers than the crowded ships could carry —Captain Alexandre Berthier, who was later to be Napoleon's chief of staff and a Marshal of France, wanted so much to go that he clung to a rope ladder on one of the ships, begging to be taken on, even as one of the crew. (He failed, but managed to join Rochambeau later.)

They landed in Newport, Rhode Island, and what a show it was! To the stupefied Rhode Islanders accustomed to the ragged dress of the Continental army, the appearance of the four thousand French as they disembarked seemed a picture out of a fairy tale. The troops wore spotless white uniforms, with the regiments distinguished by the color of their lapels, coat collars, and buttons. "The Bourbonnais wore crimson lapels, pink collars, and white buttons; the Soissonais rose-colored lapels, sky-blue collars, and yellow buttons; and the Saintonge green lapels and yellow buttons."[18] This dazzling force settled down in the quiet little town of Newport for eleven months of frustrating inaction while they waited for the arrival of the promised French reinforcements that would enable them to strike. Twice General Washington came up to Connecticut to meet his French opposite number and his staff in order to plan the operations that would eventually take place. The second conference, the most important of the war, was held in Silas Deane's hometown of Wethersfield, in the house of his first wife's family. Washington was so hard-pressed for funds that he gratefully accepted the offer of Governor Trumbull of Connecticut to pay the expenses of the meeting.

An inactive army is usually a badly behaved army, but the discipline of the French in Newport was remarkable. The inhabitants of the town had greeted the flashy soldiers warily; for all they knew their farmyards would be pillaged and their wives raped at gunpoint. Instead, the troops paid for their supplies with hard money; the fruit in the orchards among which they pitched their tents remained on the trees; and the women went unmolested. Rochambeau's orders were "that the King's army would maintain as strict a discipline in America as though they were encamped under the walls of Paris." He was obeyed. The officers were billeted here and there in the charming white colonial houses of the residents—the Duc de Lauzun, for example, found himself living on Thames Street with the widowed Mrs. Hunter and her three daughters. Lauzun was one of the greatest rakes in Europe—merry, dashing, charming—he had been in and out of every fashionable bed in Paris, and his escapades used to provide Madame du Deffand with rich material for her letters to Horace Walpole. In America, he was circumspection itself and became a devoted friend to Mrs. Hunter, without a hint of flirtation. Probably the good widow was bitterly disappointed, for Lauzun was a very attractive man and a famous hero to whom the King had given a regiment bearing his name as a reward for the capture of Senegal from the British.†

The Chevalier de Chastellux, a passionate sightseer whose book describing his travels in America is still good reading, was that unusual combination of a first-class professional soldier and literary man. He had been a friend of the Encyclopédistes and a writer in his own right; the American Philosophical Society was proud to elect him a member when he visited Philadelphia. In Newport he lived on Spring Street, where he entertained as if he had been in Paris, according to Ezra Stiles, the president of Yale College. President Stiles recorded in his diary dining "at General Chastellux in a Splendid manner on thirty-five dishes. He is a Capital Literary Character, a member of the French Academy. He is the glory of the Army."[19] Stiles also dined with General de Rochambeau, with whom he conversed amiably in Latin, which the General spoke "tolerably."

† *Typically, Madame du Deffand wrote to Walpole that the garrison at Senegal consisted of four men, three of whom were sick.*

Rochambeau, like the good commander that he was, did everything in his power to keep up the spirits of his inactive army. He encouraged the officers to acquire horses and take long rides about the island; he built them a sort of club where they could entertain and play cards. Now and then they gave a ball there which must have been a great event for Mrs. Hunter and her daughters and their friends. Little is said of recreation organized for the benefit of the enlisted men, but such a thought would hardly have penetrated the consciousness of an eighteenth-century general.

For the commander himself, the strain was considerable. He had dispatched his own son, the Vicomte de Rochambeau, to France with an urgent message following the first conference with Washington at Hartford. The sense of it was that the American army was melting away from lack of funds to pay the soldiers, and Washington was at the end of his rope. The gloomy news did not come as a surprise to Vergennes when young Rochambeau presented himself at Versailles in late December 1780. Dispatches from the French Minister in Philadelphia, the Comte de la Luzerne, and the letters he had received from General de Rochambeau in the preceding months had prepared him for the crisis.

How many times Vergennes, who was mocked by the Parisians for his prudence, laughed at for his caution, caricatured as a coward, had taken the riskiest of gambles! It was five years since he had presented to the startled King and Cabinet his two great policy papers, the Considerations and the Reflections, backing them up with the evidence of his agents, Bonvouloir and Beaumarchais. It was thanks to his implacable will that America had received gifts amounting to ten million livres tournois and loans totaling forty-seven million.[20] And what had he got for it? As Bernard Faÿ, the historian, put it, "All that was most cynical, sceptical and jealous at Court was in league against Vergennes."[21]

Indomitable, he summoned his resources for one last effort. The call for help from Rochambeau could not have come at a more difficult time. The Empress Maria Theresa of Austria had just died. Until it was seen what effect her death might have on the equilibrium of Europe, it would be impossible to send reinforcements to America. War might well break out again, with the removal of the force for peace that the Empress had represented in her later years. England had just declared war on the Netherlands, and the French had sent a naval force to the East Indies to support the Dutch. Above all, Jacques Necker, as Director-General of Finances, was pleading for economy; the cautious Swiss banker was appalled by the effect on the treasury of the millions poured across the ocean.

The eager young Rochambeau was told that his father and Washington could not have what he had come to ask for—ten thousand men and an immediate dispatch of naval power. Nor would the Americans receive the immense sum of twenty-five million livres which they requested. But six million was forthcoming, extracted by Vergennes from the protesting Necker, and this important sum was to be a free gift to Washington for the supply and pay of his army. This generous aid was perhaps the most crucial transaction of the war. To the Vicomte it did not seem enough, and he returned to Newport "tired and dissatisfied" with the results of his mission.[22]

His father also was chagrined. On assuming command he had been promised that a second division of the expeditionary corps would follow the first, and for months he had been straining his eyes over the horizon looking for the expected troopships. He wrote a polite but cold letter to the Minister of War, the Maréchal de Ségur, mentioning that his son seemed to have come back to him "very much alone."[23]

The Comte de Rochambeau and his son had both underestimated Vergennes. While Maurepas was still what we would call Prime Minister, he was now eighty years old and increasingly grateful to be able to leave the difficult decisions up to the Minister of Foreign Affairs. And Vergennes now had two energetic and powerful allies—the Marquis de Castries and the Maréchal de Ségur, the new Ministers of the Navy and of War. Castries had a son serving as an officer with Rochambeau's forces, and Ségur was an old comrade-in-arms of the General's. Both men were well aware of Necker's dire warnings, but both agreed with Vergennes. It was time to make one gigantic effort to end the stalemate in America.

Rochambeau received a letter from the Marquis de Castries, announcing that Admiral de Grasse had sailed from Brest with a fleet powerful enough to assure command of the seas to France and her American allies. It was a tremendous commitment on the part of Louis XVI: twenty ships of the line, with ten more to join them in the West Indies, all under the command of a formidable fighting sailor. Washington rushed to concert his plans with Rochambeau—he personally was anxious for the combined attack to take place on New York, but if Admiral de Grasse preferred Virginia, the choice must be his. Washington had early grasped the crucial importance of superior naval power and had expressed his longing for it again and again. Rochambeau shared his views exactly—*"Rien sans la marine prépondérante* [nothing can be done without an overwhelming navy]" was his conviction.

Once "this new and radiant light shone from France"[24] the dragging war followed a pattern of brilliant cooperation between the two armies and the French fleet. Events moved with miraculous speed. De Grasse, remembering his colleague d'Estaing's trouble in the Narrows three years before, chose the Chesapeake and bypassed New York. On August 31, Washington's and Rochambeau's armies marched south from Philadelphia, and the allied forces moved on Yorktown, Virginia. A decisive naval battle off the Capes of the Chesapeake was a French victory, and the British forces in New York remained where they were. General Sir Henry Clinton was completely taken in by an adroit deception scheme of Washington's. Not one of his soldiers went to the aid of Lord Cornwallis' army at Yorktown, so sure was Clinton that the attack would come on New York City via Staten Island. The siege of Yorktown was a classic battle, with mines, redoubts, trenches. The casualties were fairly light but Cornwallis knew he was beaten on October 17 and on that day sent out a white flag, surrendering two days later. "One by one, the British regiments, after laying down their arms, marched back to camp between two lines, one of American soldiers, the other of French, while the military bands played a series of melancholy tunes, including one which all recognized as 'The World Turned Upside Down.' "[25]

Washington's dispatch announcing the surrender reached Philadelphia at 3 A.M. on October 22, and an old German watchman awoke the sleeping population by bellowing through the town: "Basht dree o'clock und Gornwallis ist gedaken!"[26] People ran out onto the streets in their nightclothes, candle in hand, and embraced each other. As soon as day broke, Congress convened for a service of thanksgiving.

Vergennes received the news at Versailles on November 19 and sent a note to Franklin which arrived at Passy at 11 P.M. At dawn the next day, Franklin sent his friends copies of Vergennes's note which he had made himself on the copying press he had invented. Happy as he was, the wise old man refused to be too hopeful. He had little reason to believe that the English would change as a result of bitter experience. "Depend upon it," he wrote to Lafayette, "the King hates us cordially and will be content with nothing short of our extirpation."

He girded his loins for his last great task. A month before, he had been informed by Congress that he, John Adams, John Jay, and Henry Laurens had been named commissioners to negotiate the peace with Great Britain at the end of the war. It was well that his letter of resignation had not been accepted.

XI

Failure of a Mission

THE FRENCH MINISTER TO the United States, Conrad Alexandre Gérard, was returning to France. In a courteous gesture, the Congress had offered him the U.S.S. *Confederacy*, one of the finest frigates in the Continental navy, to transport him and his party. It was convenient to send the newly appointed American Minister to Spain, John Jay, with his family and staff by the same ship.

Wartime crossings of the Atlantic were dreaded ordeals in the eighteenth century, but this looked like rather an easy one. The *Confederacy* was commanded by Captain Seth Harding, an experienced Massachusetts-born officer. She carried thirty-six guns and a crew of nearly three hundred. The sailing date was October 20, 1779, and Captain Harding planned a fast North Atlantic run, once he was free of the Delaware Capes and two British frigates which were rumored to be lurking about in anticipation of the appearance of his ship with her important passengers.

Jay, who had just resigned from his post as President of Congress, had seen a good deal of Monsieur Gérard during the year he had represented his country in America, and he liked and respected the minister. Gérard had been Vergennes's adviser on American affairs and had arrived in Philadelphia to find a welcome that was almost euphoric in its enthusiasm. A warm, sentimental man, he had loved his job; it was the worst of luck that the Deane-Lee imbroglio should have developed shortly after he had settled down, tearing apart the Congress. Eager to defend the honor of Louis XVI, accused by Lee of having helped America secretly while still at peace with England, he threw himself into the middle of the row with more passion than discretion. Wining and dining congressmen nightly in order to persuade them to join the Deane, or pro-French, side, he was ready, too ready to give his advice. As a result, the Lee faction formed a tight group in Congress which made life so disagreeable for him that he at last preferred to "retire for reasons of health" and return to France. It was a sad waste of a first-class man; there were many, including Jay, who were sorry to see him go.

What Jay could not have known was how desperately eager Gérard was to get home in order to clear his name and reputation. Vergennes had been anything but pleased with the way he had become so intimately involved in the factional congressional struggle and was replacing him with the Chevalier de la Luzerne, a careful man who hardly needed Vergennes's warning "*contre les excès de zèle et l'indiscrétion sentimentale.*" The pressure he was under was to make Gérard a difficult and, indeed, dangerous traveling companion, but in the first easy days after departure from Chester there was no hint of the coming trouble.

The Jay party consisted of the thirty-four-year-old minister and his twenty-three-year-old wife, Sarah Van Brugh; Sarah's younger brother Henry Brockholst Livingston, who was to serve as Jay's private secretary; William Carmichael, secretary of legation; Peter Jay Munro, a twelve-year-old nephew; and Abigail, a black servant. Five days out Brockholst Livingston wrote to his mother that they were still becalmed in Delaware Bay, that the ship was delightfully comfortable and well supplied, that they were all talking French at meals with Monsieur Gérard serving as teacher. His sister was already making great progress with her French and the sea air was a tonic for her appetite.

The Livingstons were a cheerful, close-knit clan. William

Livingston, Mrs. Jay's father, was a son of one of the most powerful families in New York. He had moved across the Hudson
River to New Jersey, where he built his famous house, Liberty
Hall, near Elizabethtown. An intellectual and political leader of
the Whigs, he served as patriot governor of the state throughout
the war. Ever hospitable to the young, the governor and his wife
kept open house for the friends of their seven children: William, Jr., Catharine, Susannah, Judith, Henry Brockholst, Sally,
as the family called Sarah Van Brugh, and John Lawrence.

They laughed, they danced, and they played battledore and
shuttlecock on the green lawn; above all they talked and their
talk became more and more political as the young men became
involved in the patriot cause. Kitty and Sally seem to have been
the ringleaders. While neither girl was well educated they attracted some of the cleverest minds of their generation. It was
Sally who invited the young Alexander Hamilton down to Liberty Hall over Sunday, where he met John Jay, neither of them
guessing that years later they would collaborate with James
Madison on the political tracts that would be known to history
as the *Federalist* papers. Gouverneur Morris was always in and
out; so were the Robert Morrises, and Sally's cousin Robert Livingston, Jay's law partner and intimate friend. The swarming,
lively crowd was just what John Jay needed, and his proposal of
marriage to Sally in 1774 was the wisest thing this son of a som-
ber family ever did.

The Jays were French Huguenots who had come to New
York in the seventeenth century seeking a land offering religious
toleration. Auguste Jay, the first emigrant, married into one of
the great Dutch families, as did most of his descendants. Peter
Jay, father of John, married Mary Van Cortlandt and settled
down to what the young couple expected would be a pleasant
and prosperous life in their house on Broad Street, from which
Peter could manage his mercantile interests. But their story became a tragic one, even by the hard standards of the eighteenth
century. Of their ten children, seven lived to adulthood, which
was unusual for the time, but, of the seven, four were physically

or mentally handicapped. Eve, the oldest, was emotionally disturbed from girlhood onward. Augustus, the next child, was mentally retarded and never learned to read or write. Peter and Anna Maricka, the third son and second daughter, were blinded in the smallpox epidemic of 1739. This left James, John, and Frederick, the baby of the family. James, referred to later on by his brothers as "the black sheep," was thirteen years older than John.

Peter and Mary Jay did what they could to make the existence of their handicapped children easier. The country, they felt, would be safer for "the little blind ones" than life in Manhattan. Abandoning his business interests, Peter Jay moved his family to Rye, New York, in 1745. There he built a big white house overlooking Long Island Sound and also invested in a farm. It was a lovely place for the boy John to grow up in. The house was surrounded by woods full of birds, and the seashore beckoned just below. But when he was still a child his worn mother's health began to break down; he could hardly remember her except as a semi-invalid. She died in 1777. His father, laden with cares, was a melancholy, overburdened figure, seeming older than his years. It must have been a joyless house, one in which people tiptoed and closed doors quietly.

What a relief for the boy to discover the hurly-burly of student life at King's College in New York City, the excitement of opening his own law office with his friend Robert Livingston, the shouting merry family at Liberty Hall, and above all, his beautiful Sally. Jay was a complex, highly strung man. His shyness and reticence were taken throughout his life for arrogance and coldness by those who knew him little. To his family and close friends, he was an excellent companion, fun-loving, even ribald, and capable of the deepest affections. The marriage was a close and happy one, with Sally's gaiety the ideal complement to Jay's public reserve.

Neither of the Jays wanted in the least to go to Madrid. It meant for Mrs. Jay leaving behind her adored three-year-old son Peter Augustus, as the voyage was considered too hard for so small a child. Jay, a devoted father, also minded leaving little Peter, besides which he was gravely concerned by the thought of what would happen to his aging father and his afflicted siblings in his absence. Brother James, the black sheep, was certainly not to be counted on; Frederick, while kind and amiable, was not particularly intelligent or competent. Although family concerns were the principal deterrents, Jay was also aware of the diplomatic difficulties that he could expect to encounter as a result of his many conversations with the experienced Monsieur Gérard in Philadelphia; but it did not occur to him to refuse to undertake the mission. Foreign affairs had been his specialty since he first entered Congress and was put on the Committee of Secret Correspondence. What he longed for was not to go abroad but to stay at home and eventually be given the job that Robert Livingston was to undertake—today it would be called Secretary of State. But envy of his friend never entered his mind when he heard in Spain that Livingston had been named our first Secretary of Foreign Affairs. It is perhaps because of Jay's generosity toward his friends that he had so many among his colleagues. He appears to have been the one "Founding Father" who liked all the others and was liked by them; the clash of personalities that so often affected the relationships of our early statesmen seemed to pass him by. He got on well with both Adams and Franklin, and the former said of him: "In my opinion, the greatest mass of worth . . . collected in one individual resided here."[1]

There was no question of leaving Mrs. Jay behind when Jay went to Madrid. No other American official assigned abroad during the war had been accompanied by his wife, but this pair were inseparable. Sarah Jay had followed the New York Assembly as it retreated from place to place up the Hudson, just one jump ahead of the British, and it had irked her when John went alone to Philadelphia to assume the presidency of the Continental Congress. Her letters to him all began, "My dear Mr. Jay," in formal eighteenth-century style, but the contents were tender and loving. They are the letters of a courageous woman who was endowed with charm and a sense of humor. Lacking the intellectual capacity of Abigail Adams, she was a cheerful extrovert who made those around her happy, and Jay's letters to her, addressed to "My dear Sally," reflected his dependence on her presence. Her appearance would have made any husband proud. Dark-haired, blue-eyed, she was tall and carried herself superbly. Later, in Paris, she was taken for Marie Antoinette by the crowd when Benjamin Franklin and she entered their box at the opera. From the portraits the two women did not resemble each other closely, but both had what the French called *allure,* which can be roughly translated in modern terms as style, elegance, and that elusive touch of star quality which makes heads turn when the person who has it enters a public place.

When the *Confederacy* sailed, the Jays were bid farewell with a profusion of affectionate wishes and earnest prayers. In a sentimental moment, Sally had written to General Washington asking him to send her a lock of his hair to bring them luck. He replied, enclosing the desired token, and said he hoped that "prosperous gales, unruffled seas, and everything pleasing and desirable, may smooth the path she is about to walk in."[2]

Both Peter Jay and the William Livingstons promised to cherish their little grandson Peter Augustus, and from neither family came a word of self-pity as they said goodbye. William Livingston's farewell letter to his daughter was a model of restraint, and all the more moving as he thought it likely that, in view of his age and "the mortality of man," he would not see her again. Sally's brother William sought to cheer her with a teasing letter telling her that he expected reports on "every piece of knight errantry" she would encounter in the land of Don Quixote. Robert Livingston and other close friends write more serious letters to John Jay, expressing their admiration and respect.

Once clear of Delaware Bay, Captain Harding could breathe a sigh of relief, for there was no sign of the British frigates believed to be looking for him. The weather was worsening, but the *Confederacy* had been built to withstand Atlantic storms. She was a handsome ship, long and lean, 160 feet in length and about 35 feet wide. However, the majority of the passengers took to their bunks groaning with seasickness, from which John Jay suffered continuously for five weeks "and was surprizingly reduced," his wife wrote home. Mrs. John Adams, making her first crossing in the *Active* in 1784, has left us a vivid description of the misery of those ships. She spoke of the horrid dirtiness everywhere, the fumes given off by the cargo which increased her nausea, "the water from the deck leaking into the cabin to wash vomit and other slop across the floor. She could do little but lie in her cabin, where the door opening upon the men's quarters was the only source of air. With her own servants and the other women passengers too ill to nurse her, she depended totally upon male strangers for even the most intimate services."[3]

Mrs. Jay was lucky enough to escape seasickness; she was awake and alert on the terrible morning of November 7 when catastrophe struck. The *Confederacy* had run into a frightful gale just as she was moving from the North Atlantic into the Gulf Stream. Between 4 and 5 A.M. she was completely dismasted: foremast, mainmast, mizzen, bowsprit, everything over the side. A full report of the damage was given in the report of the officers of the *Confederacy*: "Boatsprit, Foremast, Main Mast and Mizen Mast, together with all Rigging . . . Rack, Foresail, Fore top sail, Jibb Fore Stay Sail, Main top Mast Stay sail, Middle Stay Sail, Main top Gallant Stay Sail, Sprit Sail, Sprit Sail Top Sail, Fore top Gallant Steering Sail, Mizen Stay Sail, Mizen top Gallant stay Sail and Royal Mizen top Sail, Mizen top Gallant Sail, Mizen top Gallant Royal. The next day at 7 a.m. found the Rudder Head to be gone."

Hearing the shouting and crashing above, Sally and her brother Brockholst scrambled up on deck, where they grasped the horror of the situation at a glance. All hands were attempting to cut away the wreckage while the ship rolled in the heavy seas, as the surgeon worked on the members of the crew who had been wounded by falling timber. A gunner whose legs had to be amputated was a fatal casualty; it is astonishing that there were not more deaths. Five hours after the dismantling the rudder went, its shank split by the gale-high winds. Thereafter the *Confederacy* wallowed uncontrollably in the waters southeast of Newfoundland, over a thousand miles from the Capes of the Delaware and nearly nine hundred from the Azores. Two weeks later, thanks to the frantic efforts of the officers and crew, temporary jury masts and a provisional rudder were in place, but it must have been a terrible two weeks for the passengers. The ship creaked as she rolled, and the ropes holding the rudder would snap every day, causing the terrifying sound of wild banging against the stern. As if this was not frightening enough, the improvised sails were blown to tatters, and twine to repair them was in short supply. Water leaked into the stern to ruin the bread supply.

By November 23 the winds had moderated, and it was decided to proceed. But to where? Captain Harding held a council of his six officers, asking each one of them the same question—"Do you think it prudent to proceed to Europe with the *Confederacy* in her present condition?" One by one the answers were returned: a unanimous negative. The carpenter, Mr. Storer, put it in one terse sentence: "No, the rudder can't be secured so as to proceed with safety." Their opinion, with which the captain agreed, was that their best chance was to head south for the first safe port in the West Indies, counting on the trade winds to carry the disabled ship.

Captain Harding reported accordingly to Gérard and Jay, as the final decision on the destination of the *Confederacy* was theirs by order of the Marine Committee of Congress. Jay concurred with the captain, but a first-class row ensued when Monsieur Gérard was asked his opinion. Worn out by the ordeal of the last weeks, obsessed with his personal reasons for returning to France, the diplomat lost his temper badly. Again and again Jay and the captain patiently explained that the lives of three hundred persons and the safety of a valuable ship could not be risked on a gamble that was almost certainly suicidal. Again and again Gérard refused to listen: the Congress, he said, had given him the *Confederacy* in order to transport him to his own country, and he was willing to risk the odds against them. If not France, he argued, why not the Azores, from which he could get passage in another ship?

They were exhausting sessions held in the stuffy main cabin which served as the passengers' dining room, the ship rolling helplessly, the rudder banging on the stern. Jay, still reeling from seasickness, must have looked like a ghost. He never appeared particularly robust at the best of times, with his tall, thin figure, pale complexion, penetrating dark brown eyes, aquiline nose and sharply pointed chin. Normally he wore black, with hair highly powdered, but for the stormy scenes with Gérard he must have felt too queasy to get formally dressed, for he was attired in a dressing gown, his hair its natural black, and his face paler than usual as he fought to keep his temper.

The Azores, Captain Harding told the irate Frenchman, offered only an open roadstead which would not be a safe anchorage for a vessel in the condition of the *Confederacy*. Furthermore, no facilities for repair and refitting existed there. Back and forth went the argument, with William Carmichael taking Gérard's side. It is surprising that he should have done so, thereby infuriating his new chief, but it will be remembered that Carmichael was the curious young man who may have gone over to the British side while serving as Silas Deane's secretary. After Vergennes's suspicions of his loyalty forced Franklin and Deane to send him home, he had applied to Congress for the position of secretary of legation at Madrid, and the post had been accorded to him. Speaking excellent French and Spanish and already possessed of some diplomatic experience, he seemed just the man for the job. John Jay's biographer, Professor Richard B. Morris, has written that by taking Gérard's side on the *Confederacy*, "he began his systematic intrigues to undermine the authority which the American minister plenipotentiary jealously guarded."[4] In the end Gérard was obliged to concede and the ship lurched southward, still rolling heavily.

There never was a more dispirited, bedraggled company than

the passengers of the *Confederacy*. Confined in a very small space for several weeks more, it was impossible to continue on terms of icy avoidance of one another as the Gérards and the Jays literally fell over each other every time they opened their doors. Sally Jay then did the impossible—she gave a successful party, which must be described in her own words. The extract comes from a letter to her mother begun on December 12; in the first part she described their trials, carefully editing the letter so that Mrs. Livingston would not be unduly distressed.

> . . . *We are now in smooth seas, having the advantage of trade winds which blow directly for the Island; nor are we, if the calculations made are just, more than 220 miles distant from the destined port. Thus while our American friends are amusing themselves by a cheerful fire-side, are we sitting under an awning, comforting ourselves with the expectation of being soon refreshed by some fine southern fruits. I expect to write to papa and the girls from Martinico, and if what I hear of crabs, fresh fish, and Oysters be true, I'll make papa's mouth water, and make him wish to forego the pleasure of pruning trees, speechifying assemblies, and what not for the pleasures of messing with us. And now let me recollect—is there nothing that has occurred in the space of seven weeks* worth mamma's attention? Why let me see—there's the celebration of Mrs. Gérard's birth-day. When we first came on board, Monsieur Gérard among other subjects mentioned that he hoped for the pleasure of our company at his house the 7th of December, as it was customary for his Lady to entertain her friends on the anniversary of her birth day. The accidents I've related account for our not arriving in France. Mr. Jay therefore surprised our Friend by inviting all the officers of the ship and gentlemen who were passengers to breakfast and spend the day with us, mentioning in the cards the occasion. Early in the morning we were amused by a small band of musick, and the discharge of a number of cannon, which led Mr. Gérard to enquire the*

---

* *It had been seven weeks since the accident.*

reason that gave rise to the present joy; and when the gentlemen waited upon him to congratulate him upon the occasion, he received them very politely, and waited upon them in the Dining-room (alias Cabbin) where a very genteel breakfast was prepared. The vessel rolls so intollerably, and Mr. C. and the Colonel† who are playing drafts at the same table leave me no chance to write legibly, so that I must lay aside my pen 'till some quieter opportunity offers. Thank fortune the gentlemen have thought fit to walk out and leave me at leisure to proceed with my narrative, and as to waiting for an easy motion of the ship, I believe it will be needless, for I begin to be of the Carpenter's opinion, that she would hardly lay still again were she put upon the stocks.

So much by way of digression, and now I think we'll return to the gentlemen in the Cabbin, and as they have had quite time enough to finish their breakfast, I'll conduct them upstairs, where the whole deck is covered with an awning for their reception. There they continued to amuse themselves with chess, cards, and drafts; musick still heightening their pleasure, 'till 4 o'Clock, when they were invited to (what in our situation might be called) a elegant dinner: after which a number of pertinent toasts were drank, to each of which was a discharge of cannon. I then withdrew, and the gentlemen had coffee, tea and cakes sent them, and then concluded the evening with dancing.

December 14th

Our calculation nearly expired and no signs of land, so I'll e'en please myself with continuing my scrawl relying upon your indulgence.

. . . A land bird! A land bird! Oh! the pleasure of being near land! A pleasure I, more than once since I left Chester, had reason to fear never being sensible of.[5]

The ten days in Martinique, "the most verdant, romantic country I ever beheld," were a delight to Sally Jay. The *Confederacy* was sent back to America for refitting, and the Gérard and

† *Brockholst Livingston was referred to as "the Colonel."*

Jay parties sailed off on the French frigate *Aurora*, bound for Cadiz. The heading of Mrs. Jay's letter of January 9, 1780, to her father-in-law expresses her mood in a line:

> *Aurora frigate, sailing sweetly before the wind.*
> . . . *Our voyage from America to Martinico was rather an unpleasant one, rendered so by several accidents and the degree of uncertainty naturally attending then; but the pleasure we received there would have amply compensated for the inconveniences we sustained in our passage . . .*

She went on to describe the beauties of the West Indies as if the ordeal of the *Confederacy* voyage had been an unimportant episode, not worth recounting. In none of her family letters did she refer to the multitude of discomforts, or to the unpleasantness of Monsieur Gérard, or to a pertinent fact that would certainly have greatly alarmed her loving family at home had they known it. She had conceived a child shortly before leaving the United States or soon after sailing, and ahead lay months of difficult traveling. How they were going to get from Cadiz to Madrid they had no idea; it was known to be a long hard journey over impossible roads, the rough carriages pulled by mules, and the only shelter flea-ridden inns. Not a word about the disappointment of missing a stay in Paris, from whence the journey across France would have been comparatively comfortable. They were plucky letters; Sally Jay could not refrain from expressing her longing for her little boy, but she always stopped short of self-pity with a sharp rebuke to herself: "But what am I saying? Pardon me, mamma, I forbear. And may God Almighty bless you. God bless my child."

They stayed in Cadiz for seven tedious weeks, living in lodgings, knowing no one in the dismal seaport. Mrs. Jay spent much of her time in bed, unable to throw off a heavy bronchial cold. Her brother, Brockholst, who had joined the party in order to enjoy the delights of diplomatic society, found himself very bored and uncomfortable. He wrote to his mother on February

20: "Though we are told by everyone of the millions of fleas, and other vermin we shall meet with, not one of them has yet told us of any remedies against their attacks—which from the specimen we have of those here are much to be dreaded . . . the fleas are here so numerous, that I have frequently by walking once, or twice across my Chamber seen above six or seven at a time on my stockings, and in bed it is not uncommon to feel them at a dozen different places at once."[6]

Jay took an instant dislike to Cadiz. As a lawyer, it revolted him to learn that a man could be hanged for murder after having been imprisoned for that crime for twenty-three years. It distressed him to discover that all mail was tampered with, even personal letters to friends had to be written in cipher. Although Cadiz had long been the center for Spanish trade with America, not one Spaniard appeared even remotely interested in the rebel cause. What a contrast to Franklin's landing at Auray in 1776, while all Paris awaited his triumphant arrival! With the exception of those hours spent in the company of some Irish officers quartered in the town, friendly souls whose enthusiasm for American liberty warmed the hearts of the lonely little party, the weeks in the squalid lodgings were a poor, disheartening start for a mission that Congress considered as crucial as Franklin's.

Jay's decision to linger in Cadiz was prudent, however. While he was to receive the chilliest of welcomes in Madrid, at least he spared himself the humiliation suffered by his predecessor Arthur Lee, who had pushed on from Paris in 1777 only to be informed at Vitoria that he would not be permitted to come any closer to the court of Carlos III. Jay sent William Carmichael ahead to Madrid to determine the situation.

The instructions given to Jay by the Congress were clear enough: to persuade Spain to join the Franco-American alliance. In return, the United States would guarantee the Floridas to Spain if they were reconquered from the British. Freedom of navigation of the Mississippi was an unconditional demand on the American side. Jay was to negotiate a loan of five million dollars at not more than 6 percent, Spain having already joined France in the loan to Beaumarchais in 1775 that had provided the original seed money for the firm of Roderigue Hortalez. Clandestine aid for the colonies as an instrument to hurt England had seemed perfectly acceptable to Carlos III and he had given the million livres willingly, but the prospect of openly helping rebels against their legitimate sovereign appalled him.

As a result of American independence in 1776, the "Family Pact" that had united the Bourbons of France with those of Spain had become a frayed strand of thinnest silk instead of the stout rope on which Vergennes had depended. In hindsight it is hard to see why, in either Paris or Philadelphia, an alliance with Spain seemed so fruitful a possibility. France was interested in preserving the balance of power in Europe and in destroying British commercial ties with her former colonies. Territorial conquests and a new French empire were the last things Vergennes sought. Spain, on the other hand, desired above all to preserve her huge colonial empire in both Americas and, if possible, to expand it. A weak America, with Spain in firm control of the Mississippi Valley and the Gulf of Mexico, was a primary goal of her foreign policy. The pro-French party of the Conde de Aranda, Ambassador of Spain at Paris, and the Marquis de Grimaldi, Chief Minister of the King in 1775, had been overthrown a year later and Grimaldi replaced by the Conde de Floridablanca.

Floridablanca cared nothing for the Family Pact, or for republican principles and republican governments. A vain, intensely chauvinist anti-French and anti-British lawyer who had risen from the middle classes to his high position, he was determined to free Spain from the domination of Vergennes. However, he needed French power to regain Gibraltar—and to that end signed a treaty in 1779 committing Spain to war with Great Britain. One secret condition of the treaty bound both Courts to make no peace or accept any truce until Gibraltar was restored to Spain.

On the French side, Vergennes's almost desperate efforts to

keep the Spaniards in the ring were based on the hope of assistance from their navy in the worldwide struggle. He was to be disillusioned, for Spanish policy toward France was to "ask everything and grant nothing," as the Comte de Montmorin, French Ambassador to Madrid, accurately phrased it. If Vergennes, the most experienced statesman in Europe, was naïve in his hopes of support from France's southern neighbor, it is hardly surprising that the Congress in Philadelphia was equally so. To the Committee for Foreign Affairs, drafting John Jay's instructions, it had seemed inconceivable that the great Spanish Empire, lord and master of three-quarters of North and South America, as well as the great riches of West Indies, could feel threatened by the poor new nation whose frontier marched with Spain's on the Mississippi. Yet the realistic Spanish saw the successful rebellion as a grave threat and the United States as a future rival. It was totally unrealistic to send an American envoy to this unfriendly nation to ask for alliance and help, but so innocent were the members of Congress, so urgent the need for money, that before Jay had sailed from Martinique bills were drawn upon him.

News from Carmichael reached Cadiz on February 20, followed by a letter from Floridablanca himself. Jay could proceed to Madrid, where he would be amiably received as a private person, in order to discuss with the Court the possibility of an alliance between the United States and Spain. But there were many questions to be settled before such a union could be effected, so, for the present, there could be no recognition of American independence. Hence Jay would not be officially welcomed as the U. S. Minister.

It might well have been better if Jay had spared himself and his country the humiliations that awaited him and taken the next ship back to Philadelphia. He might have done so could he have known of the headshaking of the neutral diplomats in Madrid who saw no hope for his mission, or could he have read the tense correspondence between Vergennes and his ambassador, the Comte de Montmorin. Gérard, who had gone on to

Madrid at the same time as Carmichael, had not been received by the Spanish Court in his official role as late French Minister to the United States on the grounds that the United States did not exist. Vergennes's rage at this insult was as unbounded as it was impotent, and Montmorin could only attempt to conceal the incident by putting it about that Gérard had not had time to buy the proper clothes to go to Court before proceeding to Paris. It was said that no more absurd excuse had ever been invented, as the Spanish tailors, known for their speed, could have produced any suit the French Minister desired in forty-eight hours.

Jay mistrusted Floridablanca's communication, "divested of the gloss which politeness spreads over it,"[7] as he put it, but as a public servant he could only follow his orders and the party set out for the capital during the second week in March. Traveling in Spain during the eighteenth century was an expedition rather than a journey. The Jays had had plenty of time in Cadiz to prepare and had been warned that, as well as strong mules and carriages, they must carry with them beds, blankets, mattresses, sheets, eating and cooking utensils, and guns. Mrs. Jay had been rather amused by the preparations—the Catalonian beds, for instance, were trunks rather than beds, and could be carried under the carriages. They included bed, bedstead, and mosquito net. She had taken trouble over the commissary, which included all their food for the voyage, to be cooked by their own servants. Yet she had forgotten one essential item, and when they stopped for the first night at Xeres she wrote: "Was ever a broom deem'd a part of traveling equipage before!" The broom was vital, and the party waited in the courtyard of the inn while someone rushed out to buy one so that the two Jay servants could sweep the filthy rooms. While this was being done, Mrs. Jay had time to notice that the mules were to be stabled in the room next to her bedroom, with only a thin partition separating them. This was to be a habit at every stopping place, and as each mule wore around his neck a garland carrying six or eight bells and the animals never seemed to sleep, she suffered through the night "the mortification of being serenaded with the tinkling." Sleep in any case was not easy, as the fleas and lice were worse than they had been led to believe by even the gloomiest reports before leaving Cadiz.

Both Jays thought the adventure so extraordinary that they each wrote long letters home describing the details of the journey. Jay, on the whole, thought that the discomforts were more bearable than he had expected, but Mrs. Jay wrote: "so greatly did the awkwardness and filth of everything exceed description . . . my surprise was not less than if silence had been observed on that subject." The long days in the crude carriages over abominable roads must have taken a heavy toll on a woman who was in her seventh month of pregnancy, but her spirits rose as they wound their way into the beauty of early spring in Andalusia. Cordova was a joy, and she longed to dally there, but Jay was impatient to reach Madrid. His wife permitted herself a sigh over his "maxim to put business before pleasure," but it was not her habit to argue with him.

They reached Madrid on April 4 and moved at once into the house that had formerly been the Legation of Saxony on the Calle San Mateo. For Mrs. Jay an important advantage was that there was a fountain in the courtyard. She wrote home that this was "a circumstance that but few of the inhabitants can boast as they are supplied with all the water they use from publick fountains."

Madrid, arid, hot and dusty in summer, freezing cold in winter, depended on its multitude of fountains and wells. It was a city in which to water a tree or plant was a luxury, and drinking water was carefully conserved. A common sight, unknown in the rest of Europe, was the troop of *aguadores* who wandered the streets twenty-four hours a day wearing short pants and painted hats and carrying huge jugs of "fresh" water from which they would sell a cup to the thirsty. The dryness of the summer heat turned women's skins into parchment and their hair into bristly bushes. To counteract the effects of this drought every good housekeeper employed porous clay jugs which were in a constant state of evaporation—they gave a smell of dank cellars to even the most elegant boudoir, but the Jay household probably had six or seven of the large clay jugs in the larger rooms and at least one or two in the bedrooms. The streets were narrow, offering merciful shade, but Mrs. Jay was too busy to explore the quarter around the Calle San Mateo immediately, curious as she was to see it. She had first to unpack and settle little Peter Jay Munro, who had proved a sturdy and courageous companion on their six-month journey from home.

Jay turned to his correspondence. Carmichael handed him letters from Franklin, Adams, Vergennes, Robert Livingston, and Floridablanca. The last was a tedious request for detailed information on "the civil and military state of the American Provinces," with three pages of subjects upon which information was desired. Evidently Floridablanca was marking time and had no wish to negotiate with the new minister-designate. Jay, determined to show his desire to please the Spanish government, worked on his answer for three weeks and sent off the lengthy document with a sigh of relief.

He had been received civilly enough by the Chief Minister the day after his arrival, but letters arriving on April 27 from America brought the alarming news that, while Jay had been writhing with seasickness in his bunk aboard the *Confederacy* in November, the Congress had drawn bills upon him for 100,000 pounds sterling, payable on sight in six months. It was the beginning of the same nightmare that had reduced Benjamin Franklin to sleeplessness and largely led to his letter of resignation. "You will find," the Committee for Foreign Affairs wrote breezily, "that we are become more dependent upon your vigorous exertions for the amelioration of our currency, than perhaps you expected when you left Philadelphia."[8] This understatement was to be frequently repeated to the unhappy minister-unrecognized, and the desperate urgency underlying it was obvious. In March, hoping to control the runaway inflation of the Continental currency, Congress had called in and burned two hundred million dollars, replacing them with a new issue of ten million. Then, to avoid further inflation, it was decided to start spending the money it hoped to obtain abroad, such as the bills drawn on John Jay. Such frivolous financial practice of course arose from the dire need to support an unsuccessful and unpopular war, but was compounded by Congress's total ignorance of the state of mind of the Spanish government. Carlos III was the best of the Bourbon Spanish rulers, a kindly man whose domestic reforms had surprised his European contemporaries. But why should the Committee for Foreign Affairs have expected him to sympathize with the aspirations of the colonial rebels who not only offered a dangerous example to the inhabitants of his vast possessions overseas, but had nothing to offer in return for the sums of hard money they so naïvely demanded? It was natural and normal for the Spanish to resent and rebuff the American appeals; it was extraordinary that the Congress expected otherwise.

For Jay, faced with the bills that would be due for payment within a month, there was nothing to do but to leave his Sally in Madrid and set out on the first of his begging missions to Floridablanca. Taking Carmichael, his only interpreter, he established himself in rooms at Aranjuez, where the Court was then in residence. The King hardly spent a month a year in his palace in Madrid, far preferring four country palaces which provided him with the hunting he loved and a constant change of scene and climate. There was El Pardo, just nine miles from Madrid, where he spent much of the winter. Aranjuez, twenty-six miles south of the capital, was a ravishing place, surrounded by ornamental gardens full of shady walks and cascades of running water; statues of nymphs and goddesses accompanied the visitor down the wooded *allées*. To the north lay the magnificent, forbidding Escorial, and in the mountains near Segovia was another country residence, San Ildefonso. All diplomats attached to the Court of Spain objected strongly to the expense the post entailed as they followed the royal peregrinations from place to place, taking houses as near the seat of power as they were able.

Jay and Carmichael sat down to wait in the cheapest inn they could find. Floridablanca received them on May 11, and the interview was encouraging. The King, acting as a private individual, would consider advancing 40,000 pounds by the end of the year, meanwhile pledging his credit toward the payment of the maturing bills. The next day, Jay wrote a happy letter to a friend in Philadelphia, describing the beauty of Aranjuez in the seductive Spanish May: he called it a fairy place and spoke of wandering in lonely recesses of the gardens made for those who, like himself, sought solitude.

> *The beau monde preferring a grand public walk, planted by Charles the fifth, where they see and are seen, where the Courtier bows to his Patron, the Belle displays her charms, the petit maître his pretty Person, the Grandee his equipage, and all have the happiness of seeing the Princess of Asturias‡ take her evening Ride in a splendid carriage, drawn by six fine Horses, richly caparisoned, and surrounded by Guards well dressed and well mounted, and holding naked sabres in their Hands.*
>
> *This pageantry may be proper in Monarchies, and may entertain those who seldom entertain themselves. For my own Part I readily exchange it for the lonely devious walk, the waterfalls, the fountains, the Birds, and above all the ancient Elms bound to each other by innumerable vines of Ivy, and whose tops intermixing exclude the sun. But as much as I am in love with these, I would gladly leave them for less decorated scenes on your side of the water . . .[9]*

This mood of romantic reverie could not last. Within a month, Floridablanca was asking for unacceptable terms from the Americans, and Jay's situation became critical. His letters to the Chief Minister went unanswered; interviews were granted more and more rarely. His cup of humiliation all but overflowed when on June 19 his funds were so depleted that he could not meet a bill for $333. He was forced to write to Floridablanca, who accepted the small bill but warned that "it will be impossi-

‡ *Louise Maria of Parma, daughter of Carlos III.*

ble to show the same complaisance for other bills without consulting the pleasure of the King."[10] In July came the news of the loss of Charleston to the British. Jay noted sadly that "the effect of it was as visible the next day as that of a hard night's frost on young leaves."[11]

Among men who knew him little, John Jay held the reputation of being vain and proud. Yet his self-control during this first difficult summer was remarkable. His repeated letters to Floridablanca were models of temperate equanimity. The French Ambassador, Montmorin, a helpful and useful friend and ally, was his only confidant, and the two men debated how best to deal with the ugly situation. Montmorin, who knew the Spanish Court well, urged his colleague to write again and again, even if the appeals met with silence, and on one occasion suggested to Jay that he open his next letter to Floridablanca by saying that he was "praying" for an interview. This was too much for Jay to swallow, even in his newfound humility. He thrust copies of his last four letters to the Chief Minister into Montmorin's hands, asking him to read them. The French Ambassador found them excellently drafted, but implored his friend to write just one more. Jay did so, leaving out the suggested phrase of supplication.[12] But it was to be some time before he saw Floridablanca again, for Sally's baby was due in July and he stayed with her in Madrid until September. It was now up to William Carmichael, who remained with the Court at Aranjuez.

Sally Jay was very much alone while she waited for her child to be born. It was May 14 before the first letter from America since she had left it arrived. Her devoted family had been writing constantly, especially her two merry sisters Kitty and Susan, but it has been seen how few letters reached their destinations during the war. She wrote to Kitty: "The variety of emotions that possessed my breast upon reading the first letter from America agitated me so much as to cause a slight fever; Joy to find that my dearest and most intimate friends were still happy and sympathy for the misfortunes that had fallen to the lot of others for some time divided my attention." She replied cheerfully, commenting on the news of home contained in Kitty's letter. Throughout the two and a half years that she was to remain in Spain it was the sisters' letters that were her great support. They wrote every detail concerning little Peter Augustus' health and welfare, of his intelligence and good looks—of his cheerful life between his two grandfathers' houses, accompanied by his faithful nurse Hannah. He was the solace of Grandfather Livingston in particular, who printed careful letters to him when he was away at Grandfather Jay's, and he was such a clever boy that he was already able to read them. Of course he missed his parents terribly—Kitty and Susan never forgot to put that in, but Sally really must not worry about him.

As for the news, Liberty Hall had been attacked for the second time, but by the greatest luck there was a thunderstorm and, when Kitty appeared at the head of the stairs, a stroke of lightning illuminated her and she must have looked like a ghost to the drunken Hessian soldiers below, who ran away screaming that they had seen an apparition. The Jays' house also had been entered and robbed, but nothing of much value had been taken. Both sisters were too well aware of the danger of their letters being opened to write anything that was not public knowledge, but they wrote well and Kitty especially was amusing on the subject of all the doings at Philadelphia, where she frequently visited the Jays' great friends Robert and Mary White Morris.

Besides the letters from home, Mrs. Jay's chief comforts were thirteen-year-old Peter Munro's society and the devotion of her black maid Abby. Brockholst Livingston was in and out. At twenty-two it would have been too much to ask that he should be the companion of his very pregnant sister, besides which he had his job as John Jay's private secretary. While she wrote of the pleasant walks she took in the public gardens of Madrid, she never once mentioned that summer or at any time later the names of any friends she might have made. A gregarious soul, accustomed to the company of her loving family and countless friends, Sally Jay must have been heartrendingly lonely. The explanation for this beautiful young woman's failure to make even one friend in over two years can only be that Madrid society of the eighteenth century was a closed circle, uninterested in novelty. The wives of other foreign diplomats would have been natural companions; but as the Jays had no official position, they were not invited to Court where Sally would have met them. Besides, the other diplomats followed the King on his royal progress from residence to residence and were seldom in Madrid. Sally could not leave Madrid, even to join Jay at Aranjuez or San Ildefonso, for his financial situation was so precarious that he could never afford decent lodgings, let alone a rented house. While on begging missions to Floridablanca he spent the long weeks in a small room in an inexpensive hotel.

Hence the "pleasant walks" that his wife described to her family were taken with only Peter Munro and a servant for company. There was much to see and observe that was wholly new to her. The houses, constructed for the most part of lath or brick and plaster, were painted vivid colors. The doorways were often of colored granite, and the windows surrounded by carved garlands hung about with flowers. It was the habit to hang fanciful cages full of crickets and plaited baskets of quail on the outside of the houses—a custom which filled the air with whistling and squeaking. The brilliant colors, the strong light, the silhouettes of the projecting balconies and *miradores* (glassed-in balconies embroidered with lacy metalwork) seemed to a foreigner, brought up in sober eighteenth-century New York, theatrically unreal.

Among the women of Madrid there was no "Spanish type," for the dark-haired, dark-eyed beauties so often described existed chiefly in southern Spain, and the physical attributes of the women Sally Jay saw on the streets must have been very like those of the French. She was as yet too ignorant to judge the fashions, but the upper-class Spaniards, both men and women, aped what they believed to be the Paris styles of dress with very limited success. To the French who visited Madrid, it all seemed dowdy and provincial beyond words, the only saving graces being the women's mantillas, worn on high combs, and the dexterous use of the fan. The poor mixed with the mantilla-decked ladies and gentlemen, dressed in horrible rags, covered summer and winter in loose cloaks like bathrobes, on the theory that what keeps out the cold also keeps out the heat. The most fetching costume in Madrid was that of the *grisette* (working girl), who wore a short skirt heavily embroidered with bright flowers, a long mantilla, silk stockings, satin shoes, and, of course, carried a fan.

Mrs. Jay mentioned the evening walk as the main social event, other than the bullfights, which she never attended. The promenade took place from seven-thirty to ten in the evening on the tree-lined street called the Prado. The women wore very décolleté dresses, as if for a ball, their arms bare, the inevitable mantilla on their heads. They walked unattended by any partners, it being considered extremely loose to take the arm of any man except father or husband. These walkers strolled in the dust on the sides of the street, calling greetings to those in carriages or on horseback who went down the middle. The carriages were undistinguished conveyances by English or French standards and were, for the most part, drawn by fat-bellied, flop-eared mules. Only the horses were dashing and beautiful, with long braided manes, tails that swept the ground, and richly decorated saddles. The crowding, heat, dust, and noise must have been indescribable, until at last the streets cleared and everyone, including women (unlike Paris), went to the cafés to pass the evening. Everyone, that is, except lonely foreigners like Sally Jay, who went home to sup alone with her young nephew or, if Brockholst happened to be free, with her brother. As they wound their way home it was necessary to listen for the warning cry "*Agua baja* [water below]," ducking into the nearest doorway to avoid the contents of a chamber pot about to be emptied from above.

It was months before anyone offered the Jays a meal in Madrid and then their hosts were not Spanish, but the Piedmontese nobleman Prince Masserano and his wife, who was born a daughter of the great French house of Rohan. This was such an event that Jay wrote to Franklin of how grateful he was to Masserano, adding that "except at his table" he had "eaten no Spanish bread" that he had not paid for himself since his arrival in Madrid six months before.[18] Dr. Franklin's kind heart must have ached for the Jays on getting this letter. His position was difficult in many ways, but the French had embraced him eagerly the day of his arrival and his popularity had never lessened. As has been seen, he had only to choose between a dinner with Turgot, an evening with his fellow scientists, a fashionable salon in which he would inevitably be the lion of the occasion, and a carpet-slipper sort of evening with the Chaumonts or Brillons or other Passy neighbors.

The Jays' second child, Susan, was born on July 9, 1780, to live for only twenty-two days. She had seemed perfectly healthy —"Ah, my Susan was a lovely babe," wrote the heartbroken mother. Jay had written the happy news to all his friends and was about to leave to rejoin the Court at San Ildefonso when the infant was taken ill and died four days later from "fits and convulsions." It was August 28 before Sally could summon the strength to write to her mother. When she did so, she apologized for the tear stains on the letter, explaining that it was the best she could do: "Would you believe that this is the third time I have tried to finish this?" The tragic letter was a gallant effort. She reassured Mrs. Livingston about her own health, describing how easy the confinement had been and how wonderful a nurse was Abby. Mr. Jay had been perfection throughout, as usual. He was at present in San Ildefonso, thirteen or fourteen leagues away, but imagine his kindness to her—he had just sent a servant riding all night to bring her some letters from America.

Jay, during late August and all of September 1780, was like a blind man struggling through a fog. He could not understand why Floridablanca should be wasting his time playing with him like a cat with a mouse. On July 5 loan discussions had been brusquely suspended, with the excuse given that a very important personage indeed would eventually appear to talk to Jay.

This mysterious individual suddenly turned up at the beginning of September, after a summer of suspense. He was Don Diego de Gardoqui, a trusted agent of the Spanish government. Meeting Jay in the office of Floridablanca's secretary, Bernardo del Campo, he offered a loan of a hundred thousand pounds contingent on America's abandoning her claims to free navigation of the Mississippi. The two men, treating Jay with the scorn to which he was becoming accustomed, reminded him that he was in no position to bargain in view of the bad military news from America and the low morale of General Washington's army. The Mississippi was not negotiable; Jay felt just as strongly as Benjamin Franklin, who wrote to him a few weeks later to back him up:

> Passy, October 2, 1780
>
> . . . Poor as we are, yet as I know we shall be rich, I would rather agree with them to buy at a great price the whole of their right on the Mississippi than sell a drop of its waters. A neighbor might as well ask me to sell my street door.[14]

Floridablanca then dropped the question of the Mississippi and came up with a new offer through Gardoqui. The King could not lend money himself, but would guarantee a loan by someone else for $150,000 spread over three years. This was a long way from the five million dollars that Jay had been sent to Spain to borrow, but he had to accept what he was offered. Somehow, by pleading for help to Franklin, who always gave what he could, he managed to keep afloat—just barely covering the expenses of the mission and meeting some, but not all, of the bills that Congress recklessly drew on him.

But why was Floridablanca willing to offer even this comparatively paltry sum? Why did he bother to keep talking, with the Mississippi an apparently immovable obstacle to the success of any negotiations? The explanation lies in the murky world of spies and double agents that made the diplomatic game of the late eighteenth century a wildly erratic one for the players.

By 1780 Spain was quite ready to discuss peace terms with the British. Her financial situation was far less stable than the Americans knew, besides which she had been badly disappointed by the failure of a reckless Franco-Spanish plan of the preceding year to invade England. She was totally uninterested in the independence of the United States; her main objective remained the acquisition of Gibraltar. Two highly unlikely intermediaries now thrust themselves forward. One was Thomas Hussey, an Irish priest who had been educated in Spain and had served as chaplain to the Spanish Embassy in London, where he was also the head of the Spanish intelligence service. The British government knew this, but permitted him to accompany an English agent, Richard Cumberland, to Spain to open peace negotiations. Cumberland was a playwright, and while he was not one of William Eden's men, he was the protégé of the Secretary of State for the Colonies, Lord George Germain. Carmichael, who had run into Father Hussey in Aranjuez in June and instantly suspected him, told his chief that he "had a conscience as smooth and pliable as a lady's kid glove."

The pair remained in Spain for over a year, and Cumberland brought out from England his wife and daughters, who were made much of by the Court. In sharp contrast to the miserable neglect of Jay, the enemy agent was flattered by the grandees of Spain, entertained by the ministers of the government, and given fine presents by the King himself. Jay observed bitterly that it was unique for "the licensed spy of an enemy government to be so honored in a capital."

Fortunately for the United States, the fashionable British agents turned out to be a pair of bunglers. They had raised false hopes in England. When the Spanish terms became known, George III turned them down icily, and Cumberland was recalled in 1781. Meanwhile Jay's presence had been convenient to Floridablanca, who could blackmail Cumberland with the threat that Spain might at any moment form an alliance with the United States. It was for this reason that Jay was given the $150,000, ultimately raised to $174,011, to keep him going for two years and to pay a measure of the drafts that Congress drew on him. The debt to Spain was paid back after the Revolution by Alexander Hamilton as Secretary of the Treasury of the United States.

It was not long before Jay realized that he was being used by Floridablanca as a counterweight to the British peace negotiators. Back and forth the talks went, an exercise in frustration. The hardest part was that the letters he received from his closest friends at home showed so little understanding of his situation. To Robert Livingston and Gouverneur Morris he had fired off letter after letter ever since his arrival begging them to use their influence to arrest the flood of bills drawn upon him, but they seemed not to listen. A letter from Gouverneur Morris is typical of those that reached him in reply to his appeals:

> *Philadelphia, 7–9 May, 1781*
>
> . . . I lament very much the Loss of your little Infant chiefly on Mrs. Jay's account. You have more Vigor of Mind than to sink under Misfortunes. Present to her my tenderest Condolences. Comfort her. There is one thing indispensable, SIX MILLION DOLLARS AT LEAST MUST BE LANDED HERE BY THE SPANISH COURT.* This I say is indispensable and I mean that Word should be taken in its fullest force.

If Gouverneur Morris was driven to writing like this things must have been very dark. The two men were in the habit of mixing gossip with politics in their letters—all the fathers of our country were great gossips, with the exception of General Washington, whom no one but Lafayette dared to tease. The last exchange between Morris and Jay had concerned a bawdy accusation made by Jay concerning an affair between Morris and a Mrs. Plater, which had been passed on from Paris to Madrid by Silas Deane. That the terse demand for six million dollars could have been made as late as May 1781 must have made Jay feel that no one had been reading his reports and that he was more alone than ever.

* *Words printed in small capitals were in cipher.*

The family letters were sometimes as gloomy reading as were the ones from official friends. Mrs. Jay's brother John, a young naval officer, was lost when the sloop-of-war *Saratoga* went down. Jay's father, Peter Jay, was failing. He died while his son was still in Spain. Eve Jay Munro continued to fall in and out of deep depressions and was at last deserted by her Tory husband, Harry Munro. To the John Jays, Munro was a good riddance and they were happy to have young Peter Munro with them in Spain where they could watch over him, but it was disquieting to hear that his mother Eve had left the family home and disappeared. As for the oldest brother, Sir James Jay, the black sheep, his career became more embarrassing and notorious every year. Faithful to his habit of changing sides when it seemed opportune to do so, he at last managed to be captured by the British and sent to England, where he later attempted to set himself up as a rival peacemaker to his brother John.

Just as Franklin's house in Passy had been a scene of great tensions during the pre-Saratoga period when Arthur Lee and Silas Deane could only bring themselves to communicate in writing, there was little harmony in the house on Calle San Mateo. Jay had begun to dislike Carmichael when he took Gérard's side during the argument over the *Confederacy*'s route. He disliked him increasingly in Madrid. During the time that the secretary was left to carry on affairs in Aranjuez while the minister remained at his wife's side, he had showed a tendency which worried Jay to take on responsibilities that were not his and to talk imprudently to important people. Jay brought him up sharply with a cold letter of reprimand, to which Carmichael replied with an "I am more hurt than angry" apology for having annoyed his chief, and he went right on doing what he had been ordered not to do. A bouncy man with considerable charm and a manner that ingratiated him to all classes of people, his letters written from the Court showed that he was enjoying himself immensely. Jay was not without the usual human frailties, and it must have irritated him to read that while he, the minister-designate, was stewing in baking-hot Madrid, William

Carmichael was disporting himself with Spanish grandees and beautiful Court ladies among the fountains of fairy-like Aranjuez. Here is a typical Carmichael letter:

Aranjuez, 19 June, 1780

Dear Sir,

. . . I dined with the Embassador today, where we had a great deal of company. Not only the Foreign Minister but the Duke d'Arcos, the Duke de Ossada and others. The Comte de Montmorin took great care to express publicly his regret at not having the pleasure of seeing you.

. . . I had the pleasure of making a very pleasing acquaintance today with the Abbé Casti, an Italian, who has travelled with The Imperial Ambassador and is a great favorite of his and his fathers, the Omnipitent [sic] Minister of Vienna. He brought me a letter of Introduction from Paris.

. . . I visited the Princess Masserano this afternoon who made many kind inquiries for Mrs. Jay's health. I hope her Spirits will not leave her, and that she may not fear the heats of Madrid.

I have the honor to be with respect Your Most Obedient and Most Humble Servant

William Carmichael[15]

This sort of letter sounds innocent enough and the secretary could not be accused of not being hard-working. He spent far more time waiting about in the antechambers of Floridablanca's office than he did flirting with princesses and dining with ambassadors, but at some moment which is unrecorded Jay definitely decided that he was a spy. As has been written earlier, even today the diplomatic historians are still arguing about William Carmichael. Some think that he may have been an even more dangerous spy than Bancroft, others that he never stepped over the border of treason. He is an intriguing character, apparently so gregarious that he had enjoyed the company of drunken sea captains and their mistresses in Paris just as much as he did that of the highest in the land in Madrid. What is certain is that two great men, Vergennes and Jay, neither of them paranoid, became convinced of his disloyalty. In Jay's case, the discovery was a great inconvenience, for he felt himself obliged to copy and encipher his more important dispatches to Congress himself, with the exception of those he confided to his private secretary, Brockholst Livingston. In September 1781, writing to Gouverneur Morris about some of his epistles to Morris which had "gone astray," he openly blamed Carmichael. He raged in code at the secretary:

THIS SAME MAN IS IN MY JUDGMENT, THE MOST FAITHLESS AND DANGEROUS ONE, THAT I HAVE EVER MET WITH, IN ALL MY LIFE. THIS IS STRONG LANGUAGE, BUT TWENTY-TWO MONTHS CONSTANT EXPERIENCE ASSURES ME IT IS JUST. IF I COULD HAVE TRUSTED MY CYPHERS WHEN AT MARTINICO I WOULD FROM THENCE HAVE WRITTEN TO YOU OF THIS SUBJECT, GIVEN A HINT OF HIS SHAMEFUL DUPLICITY AND UNKIND CONDUCT. TO DO HIM HARM IS NOT MY WISH, REVENGE NEVER HAS NOR EVER SHALL ACTUATE ME, BUT HAPPY SHALL I BE TO SEE THE DAY WHEN I SHALL CEASE TO HAVE ANYTHING TO DO WITH HIM NO MORE BE PLAGUED BY HIS TRICKS. THERE IS SOMETHING VERY DISAGREEABLE IN THUS MENTIONING MATTERS OF THIS SORT . . .[16]

For Mrs. Jay, Carmichael became the devil incarnate. Besides her brother Brockholst, there was living in the house a young American called Lewis Littlepage to whom Jay had offered hospitality as a favor to a fellow member of Congress. Like Brockholst, Littlepage had arrived expecting a glamorous diplomatic life; instead he found a quiet house whose master was snubbed and unrecognized by Spanish society and the Royal Court. A rather attractive and romantic young man, Littlepage sought military adventure by volunteering his services to the Spanish army. Time and again he had to be bailed out by Jay, as the Spanish army did not reimburse a volunteer, and his expenses were considerable. This would have been a trivial nuisance, had not eighteen-year-old Lewis Littlepage and twenty-two-year-old

Brockholst Livingston come much under the influence of him whom they called "the third Merry Knave," William Carmichael, who was their senior by more than ten years.

It was the Paris story again—nights of pleasure in the lowest quarters of Madrid, debauchery led by the sophisticated Marylander whose knowledge of the world impressed the two younger Americans as much as it had Captain Hynson and his fellow seamen. The effect on Livingston was deplorable. Littlepage was a passerby who could not affect Sally Jay's peace of mind seriously, but she grew distraught as she watched the demoralization of her brother's character and behavior. He became sulky, irritable, and so lazy that he complained of being treated like a slave by his chief and brother-in-law. Trusted by Jay, who was remarkably patient with him, he was permitted to copy official letters when Carmichael was no longer entrusted with the task, and it horrified his sister when one day she understood, from overhearing a remark between them, that her brother was showing the correspondence to his friend. She wrote sadly to sister Kitty of the men near her husband: "One of them [Carmichael] is the most insidious and deceitful man I have ever known and is unfortunately the other's tutor."[17]

At length it was agreed that Brockholst should sail for home, and Sally, alarmed at what lies her beloved father might hear from his angry youngest son about his sojourn in Spain, sat down and wrote the most devastating letter of her life. In it she detailed Brockholst's shocking behavior—it would infuriate his patriot father as it had infuriated her at the time to hear him denouncing the manners and habits of the American Congress to a French guest at their table; there had been angry words when she had suggested that attacking one's own country when abroad as a diplomat was poor taste as well as unwise. This was only one example of Brockholst's bad manners, for which she blamed Carmichael's sinister influence.

> But think not, sir, I ascribe the whole of my brother's conduct solely to the dictates of his own head or heart. No, there is another cause and one that has not given us

less pain. Good God! papa, so dearly as we love America! that all our unquiet should proceed from those who received their birth in that favored Country. My emotions are very great when I reflect upon the insidious and cruel manner in which Mr. Carmichael has treated Mr. Jay. The friendly part he had assumed while we were at Philadelphia was thrown aside soon after the Confederacy was dismasted, and though the masque has at times been reassumed, the cloven foot was not concealed as formerly. With this gentleman the Colonel [Brockholst] has formed the greatest intimacy, swallowing unwarily his artful baits. I soon perceived the seeds of jealousy grow in the breast of Mr. Carmichael. He knew the reputation which you sustained in America and feared a rival in your son . . .[18]

Old Governor Livingston never received his daughter's long, agonized letter. John Jay had sent it to Kitty with a note suggesting that she should not show it to her father unless Brockholst behaved so badly that it was absolutely necessary for him to know the sad story. Evidently Brockholst became his old self once released from the company of Carmichael. He rejoined the Continental army, in which he had previously served with General Schuyler, and had a distinguished later career. Nevertheless, neither of the Jays ever forgave Carmichael, and the remaining year of the mission was a time of increasing strain. In 1795, Jay summed up his assessment in a note attached to a bundle of correspondence:

"Care should be taken of these Papers. They include Letters to and from Wm. Carmichael—a man who mistook cunning for wisdom; and who in pursuing his Purposes, preferred the Guidance of artifice and Simulation to that of Truth and Rectitude. He finally yielded to Intemperance, and died a Bankrupt."[19]

Floridablanca, speaking of Jay, had written to the Conde de Aranda, his ambassador in Paris: "His two chief points were: Spain, recognize our independence; Spain, give us more money."[20] He saw the American as a tiresome and importunate rebel, occasionally useful as a means of twisting the British lion's tail. The Congress, desperate for financial aid, instructed Jay to weaken his demands for U.S. freedom of navigation on the Mississippi, and he was obliged to do so in the last year of his mission. Seeing the dangers of the concession, he wisely worded it with ambiguity and reserve in the draft of a treaty of alliance which was turned down after months of negotiation. He spent most of these in his lodgings at Aranjuez, driven mad by Spanish procrastination and suffering badly from indigestion as a result of the food at the local inn. Always something of a hypochondriac, he considered himself poisoned by the bad oil in the gazpacho, an Andalusian soup which is today considered a delicacy in America, but probably was very different, made with rancid oil in the kitchen of a Spanish country inn in the eighteenth century. His views on the officials with whom he dealt were expressed in one of his letters to Gouverneur Morris: "They have Pride without Dignity, Cunning without Policy, Nobility without Honor."[21] To his old law partner, Robert Livingston, now Secretary of Foreign Affairs, he described the affairs of the mission as being "in forma pauperis."

Livingston wrote back sympathetically, for the victory at Yorktown had so radically altered the military situation that, while the war limped on spasmodically, it was obvious that peace negotiations were around the corner. The Secretary of Foreign Affairs had already suggested to his harassed friend that he might be asked to go to Paris to assist in them.

Philadelphia, 28 November, 1781

. . . Congress are occupied taking measures for an active campaign and they feel themselves satisfied with every thing both at home and abroad EXCEPT THE RECEPTION YOU MEET WITH. *Plain and ingenuous* THEMSELVES THEY ARE *astonished* AT THE FINESSE OF THE COURT, THE CANDID MANNER IN WHICH FRANCE HAS TREATED WITH THEM LEADING THEM TO EXPECT LIKE CANDOR ELSEWHERE. THEY FEEL THEIR PRIDE HURT AT *the measures* OF SPAIN AND IN SPITE OF ALL THEIR *attachment* to *the* MONARCH AND PEOPLE OF THAT COUNTRY THEY *begin to talk of ceasing to*

APPLY WHERE THEY ARE CONSIDERED NOT AS AN INDE-
PENDENT PEOPLE BUT AS HUMBLE SUPPLICANTS.

*Tell me seriously what your opinion is about being
directed to* GO TO PARIS. IF NO LOANS CAN BE OBTAINED, IF
NO TREATY CAN BE OPENED, WHY STAY WHERE YOU ARE
AND EXPERIENCE NOTHING BUT MORTIFICATION?

*The Marquis de Lafayette is the bearer of this . . .
his aide waits. Adieu my Dear Sir, Believe me to be with
the highest respect and esteem, Your Most Obedient Humble Servant,*

Robert R. Livingston[22]

John Jay must have sighed with deep relief. At last his old
friends had understood what purgatory he had been undergoing
during his failure of a mission. It was just like Livingston to be
worrying about him, and the formality of the address did not
disturb him—he had written to the Secretary that on assump-
tion of his high office the two men must abandon the "Dear
John" and "Dear Robert" openings of their long correspondence,
and the informal closing "affectionately." The next letter, written two weeks later by Livingston to Jay, caused a momentary
friction and is worth quoting in part as an illustration of the lack
of reliable communication between Philadelphia and Madrid.

"We wait with utmost impatience your next dispatches, we
have heard THAT YOU HAVE OFFERED THE NAVIGATION OF
THE MISSISSIPPI, BUT WE ARE IGNORANT UPON WHAT CONDI-
TIONS, and what is still worse we hear that the ANSWER TO
THIS IMPORTANT OFFER IS DELAYED THOUGH the ground on
which we stand ENABLES US TO SPEAK IN A FIRMER TONE
THAN WE HAVE DONE. You are acquainted with the facts.
The rest may be safely left to your Judgement, on which we
have the greatest reliance . . ."[23] Livingston added peevishly
that "it is not without some degree of pain that we receive our
earliest Intelligence frequently from the Minister of France."

Good God! Robert must be out of his mind. John Jay would
have given away his only son Peter Augustus before he would
have given away the Mississippi. He had written to Silas Deane

in an earlier-quoted letter that he loved his country better than
he did his friends and even his family, and he meant it. D—n
the French Minister for spreading such slanderous nonsense.
Evidently his own painstaking dispatches describing the recent
negotiations had not reached Philadelphia. There was nothing
for it but to copy out duplicates and pray that they would cross
the Atlantic without interception. Happily they did, and Jay
was free to concentrate on his work during the last months in
Spain without further misunderstandings.

The spring of 1782 was a time of mixed pleasure and pain.
On February 20 a strong, healthy little girl was born to the Jays
and christened Maria. Her godfather was Robert Livingston.
However, her father had little time to rejoice over the event, for
a real crisis confronted him. He had no funds to meet the heavy
bills that were to fall on him in March, nor could he repay the
debt he owed the Spanish banker Cabarrus for earlier loans. He
spent the weeks after the baby was born at El Pardo, frantically
consulting the French Ambassador, Montmorin, and conferring
with the stony-faced Spaniards. Cabarrus finally agreed to cover
the March bills if Montmorin would guarantee repayment, but
the ambassador reluctantly refused on the grounds that he did
not have the authority to back the Americans without orders
from Versailles. Jay wrote letter after letter to Benjamin Franklin, but all doors seemed shut against him. The creditors arrived on March 14, and the United States defaulted. The humiliation was agonizing.

On March 26, twelve days later, a letter from Franklin at
Passy lifted the dark cloud. A six-million-livre French loan
would enable John Jay to meet all of his obligations! "Our
credit," he wrote triumphantly, "was re-established."

In Paris, Franklin was growing impatient that he should be
carrying the entire burden of the peace negotiations. Of the
peace commissioners appointed by Congress, Thomas Jefferson
could not leave America (he was never to come to Paris until he
later succeeded Franklin as minister); Henry Laurens was a
prisoner on parole in London; John Adams was in Holland, en-

gaged in crucial negotiations with the Dutch; and John Jay was still in Madrid. Franklin wrote urgently on April 22, "Render yourself here as soon as possible. You would be of infinite service. Spain has taken four years to consider whether she should treat with us or not. Give her forty, and let us in the meantime mind our own business."[24]

Jay received this letter on May 10. Eleven days later, he and his family were packed up and out of Madrid forever. With the exception of the Comte de Montmorin, there had been no friends to say goodbye. Into the carriage went Peter Munro, baby Maria, the faithful Abby, and another servant. Farewell to those snubbing Spanish officials, farewell to the perfidious William Carmichael, farewell, tragically, to the grave of Susan. Traveling as fast as they were able, the Jays arrived in Paris on June 23, where Temple Franklin had taken rooms for them at the Hôtel de la Chine near the Palais Royal. Mrs. Jay, unlike other American letter writers, did not mention being shocked by the poverty in the streets on entering the capital, probably because she had seen worse in Madrid. Nor did the filthy, noisy streets seem to upset her; viscous French mud was a welcome change after two and a half years of Spanish dust. On the contrary, she was delighted with everything.

Having deposited his family at the hotel, Jay drove immediately to Passy to see Franklin, without stopping to unpack. In his luggage was a brand-new suit of clothes to wear the next day when he accompanied Franklin to Versailles. Congress, feeling slightly guilty about Jay's hard mission, had magnanimously sent him as a token of esteem the sum of 30 pounds sterling to be spent on a costume suitable to be worn at the Court of Versailles. The suit still exists, displayed at the family homestead. It is not as fine as if it had been made in France, and by now the brocade is a little shabby, the colors of the waistcoat a trifle faded, but all the same a faint aura of elegance lingers about it.†

† *Story told to the author by her father, Peter Augustus Jay (1876–1933), corroborated by Mr. Lino S. Lipinsky, Curator, John Jay Homestead, Bedford, New York, who heard it from his predecessor.*

✤ XII ✤

Violation of Instructions

THE COMTE DE MAUREPAS, who had been known as "the Mentor" throughout his long career, lay dying in his lovely apartments under the mansard roof of the Palace of Versailles. Franklin had often struggled up the stairs that led to them, his gouty legs aching, as had the King and the Comte de Vergennes, to consult with the Chief Minister as his health declined. It had been there that the bold decision had been made to form the Franco-American alliance of 1778. Now, as the old statesman was about to relinquish office forever, the news of the victory at Yorktown was brought to him and his response was: "I die content."[1]

In London, the report of Maurepas's death arrived almost simultaneously with the tidings of Cornwallis' defeat. The Secretary of State for the Colonies, Lord George Germain, received the news of the disaster in America on November 25, 1781, and drove immediately to Downing Street to break it to Lord North. North took it, according to Germain, "as he would have taken a ball in his breast." "Pacing up and down his apartment, he repeated again and again, 'O God! It is all over!' "[2] Incredibly, King George III remained calm and unmoved. While the country demanded a speedy peace and a change of government as a result of Yorktown, the King lumbered forward blindly and his ministers lurched behind him, attempting one expedient after another to avoid the inevitable. Germain was thrown to the wolves as a scapegoat, and the aged Welbore Ellis chosen as his successor. Of him Horace Walpole said that he possessed "all the activity of an Aulic counsellor, the circumstantial minuteness of a church warden, and the vigour of another Methusalah."[3]

In its death throes it seemed to the North ministry that perhaps separate peace arrangements could be made, thus avoiding the concession of total American independence. To this end, William Eden's band of spies entered the scene once more. First, Paul Wentworth was sent to Holland to investigate the possibility of reviving the old Anglo-Dutch treaty of 1674, thereby destroying the alliance so carefully composed by Vergennes, but the reward was not sufficient to interest the Dutch. He returned empty-handed, as did a second British spy, Maryland-born Thomas Digges, sent to the Netherlands, this time to see John Adams. Digges evidently thought it would be cunning to mystify Adams and wrote to him from the First Bible Hotel in Amsterdam asking for an appointment and requesting that the reply be directed "to the gentleman who arrived this night, and lodges in the room number ten."[4] Adams received him but gave him short shrift. So the British thought that he still nourished resentment against the French because of his well-known altercation with Vergennes in 1780, did they? He told Digges coldly that under no circumstances would America make a peace that would not satisfy her ally.

Desperate as they were, the ministers in London did not bother wasting an agent on a mission to Franklin, but they did dispatch a steady old workhorse of a spy, Nathaniel Parker Forth, to see Vergennes with some rich concessions in his pocket in return for a deal. These included Dunkirk, parts of the Indian possessions, and possibly the return of Canada to France. News of Forth's attempt leaked out, and Vergennes was careful to immediately inform Madrid and Philadelphia of the overture. "If the King of England wishes to throw an apple of discord among the allies, we have prevented him so doing," he wrote to Montmorin.[5]

While the secret agents intrigued futilely on the Continent, two crucial votes were taken during the month of February in the House of Commons. A resolution by General Conway moving an address to the King demanding that the American war should be halted failed by a single vote, but five days later a similar resolution, also introduced by Conway, passed by nineteen votes. The jig was up. "At last," sighed George III, "the fatal day is come."[6] He had for some time been talking of abdication and return to Hanover, but after a last, tragic interview during which he accepted Lord North's resignation, he forced himself to the task of forming a government from the Whig opposition, every member of which he loathed.

The safest of the lot, it seemed to the King, was the Marquess of Rockingham, who was named First Lord of the Treasury, or Prime Minister, of the new peace ministry. Rockingham, cruelly referred to by Horace Walpole as "the wet blanket," was a pleasant, liberal Whig grandee of the old school. Lacking the force to be a strong party leader, he was further handicapped by bad health in the early months of his administration. The summer of 1782 was the worst and wettest England had known for years, and Rockingham, who suffered from bad lungs, diminished visibly as the weeks went by. However, even had he been a tower of moral and physical strength, it is hard to see how he could have succeeded in driving the extraordinary tandem with whose reins he was entrusted. The King, in forming the Cabinet, gave to Lord Shelburne the post of Secretary of State for Home, Colonial, and Irish Affairs. The other Secretaryship of State, designated for Foreign Affairs, was given to Shelburne's chief political rival, Charles James Fox. Thus, at the very outset of the peace negotiations, dissension between the two men responsible for their success was inevitable. Both were individually remarkable in an age of remarkable men.

Charles James Fox, son of the politician Henry Fox, first Baron Holland, had entered the House of Commons at the age

of nineteen. The British historian Sir Lewis Namier has remarked, "Men ripened more quickly in the 18th century than
they do now."[7] At twenty-one Fox served in Lord North's Cabinet as a Lord of the Admiralty and moved on to become a Lord
of the Treasury until his dismissal in 1774 for what was
regarded as insubordination. He then joined the Whig opposition.

It was in opposition that this blazing star made his name in
history, and it is in opposition that one always imagines him
strolling onto the floor of the House, his tall frame and swarthy
countenance—some said "saturnine"—his bright eyes dominat-
ing the members as he began to speak. Adored by his friends for
his gaiety and good nature, warmhearted and generous, original
in his genius, abandoned in his love of drink and gaming, he
was anathema to King George III, who saw him as a dangerous
influence on the Prince of Wales. Irrepressible in his brilliance,
he never prepared a speech in advance. On one occasion he
spoke in defense of the Church, having just finished what he
called "the pious exercise" of passing twenty-two straight hours
playing hazard (a gambling game of the time), at which he had
lost 11,000 pounds. So clear were his thoughts, so compre-
hensive his understanding of the complex argument, and so
plain his presentation that the House hung on his words. He
was never obscure, he never bored the members, and when his
heart was in his cause as during his opposition to the American
war, he was considered by many people to be an even greater or-
ator than Edmund Burke. His speeches attacking North's coercive measures against the colonies, especially the tea duty, were
considered the best he ever made. As Foreign Secretary in the
Rockingham administration, he was indefatigable and even
abandoned his addiction to gambling. This most attractive figure
was too popular for the King to have avoided awarding him his
high office, much as he hated doing so, but in the end it was the
King who won, and it was Fox's bitterest rival who was to conduct the peace negotiations.

William Petty, first Marquess of Lansdowne, better known as

the Earl of Shelburne, was a most unpopular man, yet today it is hard to see why he was so universally disliked by his contemporaries. His attacks on the North government's American policy were as strongly expressed as Fox's had been, and he too was a fine speaker. He also had fought against the Stamp Act—he too deplored the series of coercive measures to which Fox objected. In a speech in 1775, he condemned "the madness, injustice, and infatuation of coercing the Americans into a blind and servile submission." He opposed the American Prohibitory Bill as being "to the last degree hasty, rash, and ruinous," and declared that "a uniform lurking spirit of despotism" had pervaded every administration with regard to their American policy.[8]

Thus his philosophical credentials as a crusader for the opposition cause were impeccable and should have rendered him as odious to the King as was Fox had not the two leaders varied on one significant point: Shelburne was a dedicated believer in the indissolubility of the Empire. Much as he deplored the injustices suffered by the colonies and wished to reform the system of governing them, he could not bring himself to concede the principle of total independence. As late as the surrender of Cornwallis at Yorktown, he held to this view, saying in the debate of February 1782 that "he would never consent under any possible given circumstances to acknowledge the independency of America."[9]

What Shelburne wanted was not unlike what Jefferson and Adams had hoped for in 1774–75, a sort of dominion status for America within the Empire. It was not for this that he was unpopular—it was a perfectly respectable, if outdated, concept. He seems to have been distrusted for other reasons by nearly everyone in British public life. Horace Walpole declared that "his falsehood was so constant and notorious that it was rather his profession than his instrument . . ."[10] Burke said, "If Lord Shelburne was not a Catalina or a Borgia in morals, it must not be ascribed to anything but his understanding." Thomas Gainsborough, attempting for the second time to draw him, flung away his pencil, exclaiming, "D—n it! I never could see through varnish, and there's an end." Illustrations of his unpopularity could be extended indefinitely—"perfidious liar," "hatred of his very name" are some of the phrases occurring in the memoirs referring to him and often the writers were members of his own party.

Yet Shelburne was a generous patron of the arts and entertained magnificently at his London house in Berkeley Square and in his two country houses, Wycombe Abbey in Buckinghamshire and Bowood in Wiltshire. At Bowood the scientist Joseph Priestley was the custodian of the superb library, and the list of cultivated men who stayed with Shelburne is a dazzling one. Benjamin Franklin had greatly enjoyed his visits to Wycombe during the prewar years. Other guests to both houses were the renowned actor David Garrick, the philosopher Jeremy Bentham, the witty French moralist the Abbé Morellet, and another Frenchman who was later to play a crucial part in his country's history, the Comte de Mirabeau. Dr. Samuel Johnson was often at Bowood; and if the sheer brilliance of the conversation of such company overpowered the occasional unintellectual guest, he could always wander in the gardens, newly created by Capability Brown, which surrounded the beautiful house. However, there was hardly a gentleman in England who, given the choice, would not have turned down an invitation to Bowood for one to drink a glass of wine in a tavern with Charles James Fox.

Franklin, waiting in Paris for the arrival of his fellow peace commissioners, was visited by emissaries from the two archrivals. Richard Oswald, who was to be Shelburne's chief intermediary throughout the negotiations, got there first and had an interview with Franklin on April 15. He was a Scottish merchant of mediocre talents who had been chosen principally because he had lived in America and was known to have an acquaintance with Dr. Franklin. Thomas Grenville, Fox's man, was not particularly distinguished either, but with London just across the Channel there was no need for envoys capable of taking independent initiative. One of them wrote, "We can consider ourselves as little more than pens in the hands of the government at home . . ."[11] The Americans were, of course, still handicapped by the length of time that it took for Congress to receive diplomatic correspondence from Europe and to reply to it. In one vital instance the commissioners were forced to rely on their own judgment rather than wait months for new instructions.

The negotiations could not legally commence until Parliament had passed an official act enabling the King to treat with the former colonies. While waiting for this, Franklin's talks with Oswald and Grenville were necessarily inconclusive, but he was able to guess, correctly as it turned out, what were the main objectives of both Shelburne and Fox. England was facing three allied enemies—France, Spain, and the Netherlands—besides the United States. Clearly it was in her interests to keep them separate rather than deal with them as a united front—the tottering North ministry had realized this fact when they made their useless efforts through secret agents. By now even Shelburne had seen that it was futile to offer the Americans less than independence, but he hoped to do it in such a way that they could be weaned away from their French allies. Thinking to influence the American Congress and nation even before the negotiations began in Paris, Sir Guy Carleton, who had been sent to the United States to arrange for British military withdrawal, was ordered to let it be known that the ministry in London planned to acknowledge American independence immediately. Congress, uncertain what was behind this, coldly refused to deal with Carleton and left everything to their trusted commissioners abroad.

Curiously, it was Benjamin Franklin who was the first to break the united front. In an informal conversation with Oswald, he suggested that Canada be ceded to the United States in reparation for British war crimes and to prevent future border friction. Shelburne and Fox heard the proposal with astonishment and discussion of the matter was postponed. Franklin, usually so scrupulous in his dealings with the French, did not inform Vergennes of his maneuver. In his three months without Jay and Adams, Franklin had established a reasonably friendly relationship with Shelburne, and he evidently preferred to keep certain secrets from Vergennes—a memorandum of great importance prepared by him was transmitted to Oswald orally, its terms known only from the words in which Oswald transmitted them to Shelburne.[12] In it he proposed what he considered to be the essential points of peace. Four of them he called necessary: (1) full and complete independence and the withdrawal from the United States of all British forces; (2) a settlement of the boundaries of *their* colonies and the loyal colonies; (3) the confinement of the boundaries of Canada to at least what they had been before the Quebec Act of 1774 extended them below the Great Lakes to the Ohio; (4) freedom for Americans to fish on the Newfoundland banks, for fish as well as whale. Four more points he called advisable, the last one being the cession of the whole of Canada.[13]

The passing of the Enabling Act by Parliament on June 17 meant that the time of informal discussion was ended and real negotiation could commence. The Rockingham Cabinet was torn by differences and Rockingham himself lay dying of influenza. They did not dare to inform the King of his condition until nearly the end. The stubborn monarch had had his hopes rekindled by Admiral Rodney's naval victory over the French Admiral de Grasse two months before and could not realize that it was now too late to extract diplomatic concessions as the result of a single victory. Louis XVI had said resolutely, "I have lost five ships, I will build fifteen to take their place and one will not find me on this account more tractable at the peace."[14]

Despite all evidence to the contrary, George III still believed that an ignominious settlement could be avoided, and when at last the decision had to be made he came down hard on the side of Shelburne. Fox, unable to block Shelburne's succession, resigned, refusing, in Burke's words, to "act as a clerk" in his rival's government.[15]

In Paris, Jay had arrived from Spain just before Shelburne

formed his government. Franklin was recovering from a minor attack of the influenza that had killed Rockingham. Jay wrote of Franklin to Robert Livingston that he was "in perfect good health" and that "his mind appears more vigorous than that of any man of his age I have known."[16] The two men conferred daily about what was to be expected from the change in the British administration; Franklin, despite his pleasant acquaintanceship with Shelburne, suffered from "nagging doubts" about his intentions.[17]

Then Jay fell a victim to the influenza epidemic and lay in bed for the first half of July, leaving Franklin to continue his discussions with Richard Oswald alone. Henry Laurens, the fourth commissioner, appears to have been one of those unlucky men who, through no fault of their own, seldom arrive at their assigned destination on time. A successful South Carolina merchant who had been elected to Congress in 1777 and had succeeded John Hancock as president of that body, he was chosen in 1779 to negotiate a loan and treaty of alliance with the Dutch. The ship on which he was traveling was seized by the British and a sack of official papers which Laurens had thrown overboard too late was fished out of the water. It contained the draft of a projected treaty with Holland which served as a pretext for the British declaration of war on the Dutch. Laurens himself was confined for over a year to the Tower of London on suspicion of high treason. His treatment there was at times fairly harsh. Through the efforts of Franklin and Edmund Burke he was released on heavy bail in December 1781 and was eventually exchanged for Cornwallis. Named to Paris to serve with Franklin, Adams, and Jay, he arrived only just in time for the signing of the preliminary articles of peace and was absent when the final peace treaty was signed. His health having deteriorated as a result of his imprisonment, he was never strong again. He died seven years later in his native Charleston, South Carolina. Laurens' bad luck had necessitated his replacement in the Netherlands in 1780 by John Adams—a mission that lasted nearly two years.

Adams was never better than during his Dutch mission. It was not easy, for he was received with suspicion and as he wrote himself: "I can represent my situation in this affair of a loan, by no other figure than that of a man in the midst of the ocean negotiating for his life among a school of sharks."[18] Yet he handled himself with tact and ability, playing his cards with ingenuity and patience. His personal life among what he called "the sharks" sounds happier than his Paris life had been. He was proud of his sons John Quincy and Charles, who had accompanied him from America in a voyage nearly as unpleasant as that of the Jays the same year. John Quincy left Amsterdam in 1781 to join Richard Dana, the American Minister to Russia, in the capacity of private secretary, from where he wrote letters that were the delight of his parents. He was only fourteen years old, but as quoted earlier, "Men ripened earlier in the 18th century than they do now." Charles, aged eleven, returned to America to pursue his studies in the same year that John Quincy went to St. Petersburg, causing his anxious mother torments of anxiety as she waited for his delayed arrival. But Mrs. Adams also was happier than she had been during the years that her husband was in Paris. Peace was in sight and there was hope now that either he would come home for good or she would be allowed to join him abroad.

During the summer of 1782, Adams kept in close touch with his fellow commissioners as the talks began. His letters were supportive and encouraging to Franklin and Jay. He longed to join them, but his unfinished business was too important—he had been recognized as minister plenipotentiary by the Netherlands in April and had taken up residence in the first American legation building purchased in Europe, known in The Hague as the Hôtel des États-Unis, a big, pleasant brick house. In June he contracted with a syndicate of Dutch bankers for a loan to the United States of five million guilders. October found him compounding this triumph with the signature of a treaty of amity and commerce. He said himself that his work in Holland "was the greatest blow that has been struck in the American cause, and the most decisive."[19] John Adams was never unduly modest, but he deserved his laurels. Hardly was the ink dry on his treaty when this engaging, capricious, occasionally reptilian, marvelously patriotic figure was in his traveling carriage, dashing to the help of his friends in Paris. In his jaunty mood, he could not resist writing that everyone in the Hague was showering praise on him—*"Monsieur, vous étes le Washington de la négotiation* [you, Sir, are the Washington of negotiation] was repeated to me by more than one person. . . . A few of these compliments would kill Franklin if they should come to his ears."[20]

It had been an uneasy summer, the sort of summer in which people shivering under the gray skies of Paris and London said to each other: "What can you expect with weather like this?" Fox had made an important speech on July 9 in which he told the House that his resignation as Foreign Secretary "had been prompted principally by his having been outvoted by the Cabinet on the issue of an unconditional grant of independence to America, a concession which he deemed necessary to the salvation of his own country."[21] Forced to reply, Shelburne made a grudging admission of "the fatal necessity" of granting independence, ending, "the sun of England would set with the loss of America . . ." but that he was resolved "to improve the twilight and to prepare for the rising of England's sun again."[22]

What did these last fine words mean? The already suspicious mood of the American peace commissioners darkened as the British Cabinet vacillated. The loss of Fox was felt by them to be a disaster to their cause, and Franklin's informal negotiations with Richard Oswald were moreover overshadowed by the dispatch of June 15, 1781, in which Congress had manacled its commissioners by ordering them "to govern themselves by the advice and opinion of the King of France."[23] This meant that Adams, Franklin, and Jay were in effect formally instructed to operate as servants of the French Foreign Office, although the Congress, recalling the national interest at last, did remind the commissioners on January 22, 1782, not to forget the importance of boundaries and fisheries, "in the obtainment of which objectives the United States . . . counted upon the backing of the French."[24] The importance of the congressional order shackling Franklin and Jay to the French cannot be overestimated. Without the aid of France, the War of Independence would have been lost and America's debt to her generous ally was a tremendous one. However, the interests of the two countries were in many ways dissimilar, and the three diplomats, feeling themselves tied down like so many Gullivers by the strings with which Congress had seen fit to ensnare them, struggled for freedom of maneuver. Franklin, as described, had already given Oswald his suggestion for the accession of Canada and his memorandum containing his "hints" for the points to be contained in the future treaty without informing Vergennes. John Jay, on recovering from his influenza, was to prove an even tougher customer than his more famous colleague.

John Jay, to the British, was an unpleasant surprise. He was known to have come late to the revolutionary cause and to have fought against the concept of independence as late as 1775, when John Dickinson and he had drafted the Olive Branch Petition, that last desperate appeal from Congress to the King. He should have been a most conciliatory sort of colonial, with every reason to hate the French in memory of his Huguenot ancestors who had been forced to leave their country for the sake of their Protestant religion. But his attitude toward the French appeared to be ambiguous to Richard Oswald, who wrote of Jay, "we have little to expect from him in the way of indulgence."[25] The first interview of the Scottish merchant with the New York lawyer had proved a nasty shock to Oswald, who had hastened to Paris with the commission in his hand which would permit him to commence the peace talks. It empowered him to treat with "commissioners named by *the said colonies or plantations*."*[26] A quick perusal had satisfied Franklin, who told Oswald that he hoped they could agree and get on with the job. Jay was obdurate. He did not trust Shelburne, and the phrasing of the doc-

* *Author's emphasis.*

ument seemed to him deeply offensive. John Adams from Holland lent him full support. Both men were lawyers, but to them this was no mere legal quibble. Adams wrote, "I think we ought not to treat at all until we see a minister authorized to treat with 'the United States of America' . . ."[27] Like Jay, it infuriated him to be considered the representative of "the said colonies," and his strong letters agreeing that explicit recognition must be demanded reinforced Jay's stand. Richard Oswald was aghast by what he called "the unpleasant reception from Mr. Jay."[28] Dr. Franklin had been benign, understanding, and only eager to pursue the negotiations as soon as possible. Now everything was held up by the stubbornness of this tall, cold man who dared to say to Oswald, "I would not give a farthing for any parchment security whatever"[29] unless the British terms were altered.

The issue was resolved on August 29 in a knuckling-down memorandum written by Thomas Townshend, Oswald's chief. It began: "That we are ready as Mr. Jay desires to Grant the Independence of the Thirteen Provinces in the Preliminary or First Article of a Treaty either of Peace or Truce." The last paragraph spoke of "Treating with the 13 Provinces of N. America in all things as with a Free and Independent State Over whom the Crown of England Pretends to hold no authority."[30]

The hated word "colonies" had been eliminated at last, and the wording now satisfied the American commissioners. But much time had been lost. While Jay was engaged in the talks with Oswald that the latter found so singularly unpleasant, he was also involved in some important conversations with the Spanish Ambassador to France, the Conde de Aranda. The two men liked each other on sight, although, obliged to follow his instructions from Madrid, the ambassador could only receive the peace commissioner as a private gentleman. Aranda was a powerful figure in Parisian society. A rich grandee who was said to have the finest wine cellars in Europe, he lived in splendor in that fine house overlooking the Place de la Concorde which was subsequently occupied by Talleyrand, then by the Rothschild family, and most recently by the United States government. Jay wrote to Montmorin after meeting Aranda for the first time, "He appears frank and candid as well as sagacious."[81] It is a pity that the subject the two men had to discuss was such a thorny one, for had it not been Jay might at last have made a Spanish friend.

Aranda was empowered to discuss the boundaries of the possessions of Spain in America, and a French edition of Mitchell's huge map of North America was put on a table in front of the diplomats. "What does the United States expect?" asked the ambassador. "Jay drew his finger along the Mississippi from its source to 31 degrees NL, which was the old northern boundary of West Florida. Now Jay's finger moved east along that degree to the Chattahoochee, and then followed the undisputed northern boundary of East Florida to the sea."[32]

Aranda asked for a few days to consider these limits and then gave Franklin and Jay a map marked by himself with a red line showing that Spain planned to allow the Americans only a fairly narrow piece of coastal territory *five hundred miles to the east of the Mississippi*. This startling proposal came as more of a shock to Franklin than it did to Jay, for the memory of months of fighting with Floridablanca about the Mississippi was agonizingly fresh in his memory. He wrote to Robert Livingston that Aranda's line "would leave near as much country between it and the Mississippi as there is between it and the Atlantic Ocean."[33] Looking at the map of the boundaries of the United States today, it is hard to imagine the country that the Spaniards were proposing as the one we know—except for a bit of Pennsylvania and Virginia lying to the west of the Appalachian Mountains, we should have been limited to a long, thin strip on the Atlantic. Franklin put it well when he wrote to Livingston on August 17 that Spain desired "to coop us up within the Allegheny Mountains."[34]

The two commissioners, sadly perturbed, traveled together to Versailles on August 10 to consult Vergennes. With the Minister of Foreign Affairs was his undersecretary, Joseph-Matthias

Gérard de Rayneval, who had been of the greatest help during the conversations with Aranda, for Jay's French and Spanish were far from adequate to conduct negotiations without the services of a translator, and he had been grateful to have Rayneval at his side throughout the talks. What the Americans could not have known was that the French intermediary was far from neutral, nor was his chief. Both thought that the United States was asking for too much and their sympathies were with Spain. "Two weeks before Vergennes had told Aranda that if Jay would not modify his demand for the Mississippi as America's western boundary, there was the alternative of setting up a neutral Indian state, about which Aranda himself was dubious."[35] While careful in his remarks to the Americans, Vergennes made it very clear that on this question they would get no help from France. The conversation that followed between Franklin and Jay has been reconstructed by Professor Richard B. Morris in his book *The Peacemakers*—it was a heated exchange.

"Have we any reason to doubt the good faith of the King of France?" asked Franklin.

"We can depend on the French," Jay countered, "only to see that we are separated from England, but it is not in their interest that we should become a great and formidable people, and therefore they will not help us to become so."

"If we cannot count upon France, upon whom else may we depend?" Franklin inquired.

"We have no rational dependence except on God and ourselves," Jay replied.

"Would you deliberately break Congress's instructions?" Franklin pressed. (He was referring to the earlier-mentioned instructions of 1781 ordering the commissioners to govern themselves by the advice and opinion of the King of France.)

Jay did not hesitate. "Unless we violate these instructions the dignity of Congress will be in the dust," he asserted. "I do not mean to imply that we should deviate in the least from our treaty with France," Jay added. "Our honor and our interests are concerned in inviolably adhering to it, but if we lean on her love of liberty, her affection for Americans, or her interested magnanimity, we shall lean on a broken reed that will sooner or later pierce our hands. If you don't believe that, consider the fates of Geneva and Corsica!"

"Then you are prepared to break our instructions," Franklin pressed, "if you intend to take an independent course now."

Jay had made up his mind. "*If* the instructions conflict with America's honor and dignity I would break them—like this!" Family tradition has it that Jay stood up and hurled his long clay pipe into the fireplace. Strewn among the ashes and embers, the shattered pieces might well have betokened the grand alliance itself.[36]

When John Adams heard the news, he too was ready to hurl some shatterable object into the fireplace. Writing later, on what he called "these tainted instructions," he said, "Congress surrendered their own sovereignty into the hands of a French minister. Blush! Blush! ye guilty records! blush and perish! It is a glory to have broken such infamous orders. Infamous, I say, for so they will be to all posterity. How can such a stain be washed out? Can we cast a veil over it and forget it?"[37]

Some thirty years later Gouverneur Morris remarked, "Jay, what a set of d—d scoundrels we had in that second Congress." "Yes," replied Jay, "that we had. . . ."[38]

It was unfair of the two old diplomatists to have put it so harshly, for there had been men like James Lovell on the Committee for Foreign Affairs in 1781 who had spoken vehemently against the instructions to the peace commissioners which shackled them to the decisions of the French. He had been voted down, but his fellow congressmen were not scoundrels, they were purely ignorant of power politics and genuinely grateful to France. It was Vergennes who said that relations between powers should never be governed by reason of gratitude.

It never seemed to occur to either Adams or Jay to reflect on Vergennes's complex problem. In order to get the laggard Spaniards into the war against Great Britain, he had been obliged to promise the support of France for their obsessive aim of regaining Gibraltar. Thus, in 1782, combined French and Spanish forces had been flinging themselves fruitlessly and at great financial cost at the stubborn rock for months. Vergennes, unable to deliver on Gibraltar, felt obliged to back up Spain on a question that seemed to him of secondary importance—the American boundaries between the Alleghenies and the Mississippi. It was not his wish to betray America, although of the three peace commissioners only Franklin, who had known him longest, trusted him. He might have trusted him less if he had had access to the documents available today. As early as 1778, Vergennes had written to Montmorin: "We ask independence only for the thirteen states of America. . . . We do not desire that a new republic shall arise which shall become the exclusive mistress of this immense continent. . . ."³⁹

John Adams put it this way: "Vergennes means to keep us down if he can," to hold "his hand under our chin to prevent us from drowning but not to lift our heads out of water."⁴⁰

Vergennes didn't give what in the eighteenth century they always called a d—n for the words of the Declaration of Independence which still cause the heart of any American to skip a beat. To Adams and Jay they meant a great deal, as indeed they did to Benjamin Franklin, above all men the one the most responsible for the success of the effort described in this book.

The French statesman would have read Jefferson's words with some admiration for the cadence—but the notion that Americans should dedicate themselves to "certain unalienable rights . . . Life, Liberty, and the Pursuit of Happiness" would have seemed to him a romantic one, wholly unrelated to the pursuit of the national interest which was his own religion, his consistent creed. While he had risked again and again the fortunes of France and his own career on behalf of the American cause, his aims remained the same as he had pronounced them in his "Considerations" and "Reflections" of 1776: i.e., do down England, revenge the humiliations of 1763, and make a good thing if possible out of seizing the monopoly of trade with the colonies from greedy British hands. A powerful, continent-wide America in the distant future was to be avoided, unrealistic as such a possibility seemed. It is important to recall that in 1783 the population of the United States was about 3.5 million, that of the United Kingdom 18 million, and of France approximately 26 million. Thus Franklin, Adams, and Jay were bargaining with superpowers, comparable in today's terms to an underpopulated third world country taking on Russia, population approximately 245 million, or the United States, roughly 226 million.

The surprise for Vergennes was the tenacity with which the representatives of the new tiny power were capable of fighting for their own national interests. On September 9, Jay learned that Rayneval, following an early-morning conference with Vergennes and Aranda, had hastily and mysteriously left for England. To him it seemed certain that a Franco-Spanish conspiracy was afoot to interfere with American affairs. In point of fact, Rayneval's primary object was to discuss the French and Spanish treaties with Shelburne, but Jay was not too far off the target, as the Frenchman did hint to the British Foreign Secretary that France did not support the American demands entirely and that it would be well to conceal from the peace commissioners what the French, Spanish, and English were planning."[41]

Jay decided that he must act immediately and alone to save America from these dangerous plotters. To this end he sent Benjamin Vaughan to London on September 11 with instructions to inform Shelburne that Oswald could get on with the peace negotiations at once without further quibbling about words. Furthermore, he was to tell the Foreign Secretary that "prompt action on the part of the British government would cut the cord which tied America to France. The American commissioners had still to fulfill their treaty obligations, but were determined not to let the French alone say what those obligations were."[42] Vaughan was an Englishman. An old friend and editor of Franklin's, he was in Paris as an agent of Shelburne's. He left with dispatch, neither he nor Jay having informed Franklin of the mission. The British were wary but delighted by the sudden eagerness of the commissioner who had been impeding the progress of the talks all summer with his tiresome insistence on the phraseology of Oswald's instruction. It had of course been their desire from the start to separate America from France.

From then on events moved fairly rapidly. Vaughan went back to Paris on September 27, accompanying the courier who carried a new commission for Oswald. A set of Preliminary Articles of Peace were in shape by October 5, drafted by Jay with Franklin's approval. Franklin was ill—Benjamin Vaughan wrote to Shelburne that he found him "very much indisposed this week with gravelly complaints, but today is somewhat better. In the warm bath he has for some days voided small stones."[43]

The burden of the work fell upon Jay. The Preliminary Articles that were signed on November 30, 1782, in Richard Oswald's rooms were highly satisfactory to the United States. Summing up the concessions made by the British, Shelburne confided to Oswald: "We have put the greatest confidence, I believe, was ever placed on men, in the American commissioners. It is now to be seen, how far they or America are to be depended upon," adding: "I hope the public will be the gainer, else our heads must answer for it deservedly."[44]

The text of the Preliminary Articles of the Peace of Paris varies very little from the text of the final articles that were signed the next year. It can be found in an appendix to this book. It is a simple document, settling the boundary lines and the fishing rights of the United States, the rights of the Loyalists (a point on which Shelburne had laid much stress), and other details of lesser importance—to read it today it appears a primer that could be memorized by an intelligent sixth-grader, provided that he or she had a map. There are only nine articles, written in the plainest English. The first article is one that is truly moving to an American:

"His Britannic Majesty acknowledges the said United States, New Hampshire, Massachusetts Bay, Rhode Island and Providence Plantations, Connecticut, New York, New Jersey, Penn-

sylvania, Delaware, Maryland, Virginia, North Carolina, South Carolina, and Georgia, to be free Sovereign and independent states; That he treats with them as such; And for himself, his Heirs and Successors, relinquishes all Claims to the Government, Propriety, and territorial Rights of the same, and every part thereof; and that all Disputes which might arise in future, on the Subject of the Boundaries of the said United States, may be prevented, It is hereby agreed and declared that the following are, and shall be their Boundaries."

The said "Boundaries" were the ones that Adams, Franklin, and Jay had been fighting for from the beginning. It had been a great source of strength for the sick Franklin and the lonely Jay to have John Adams, exuberant from his Dutch successes, arrive in October to lend his great heart and skilled mind to the completion of the document above summarized, every word of which required hours of exhaustive negotiation with the British. Bounding out of his carriage after the journey from The Hague, he was unable to find Jay at home when he called on him. This annoyed him, and he confided to his diary that he saw he would have "a delicate, a nice, a critical part" to act between "two as subtle spirits as any in the world." Jay was probably honest, Adams thought, but "Franklin's cunning will be to divide us; to this end he will provoke, he will insinuate, he will intrigue, he will manoeuvre."[45]

This was nothing more than the reflex action of Adams in any new place or situation—it was simply a manifestation of the same suspicions he had formed of the rich New Yorkers when passing through on his way to the First Continental Congress, of the French aristocrats to whom Franklin had introduced him on his first arrival in Paris in 1778. There was little that his friends could do about Adams' quirky mind, and the men with whom he was intimately involved were too accustomed to him to be disturbed by his crotchety ways. The very next day he was closeted with Jay for three hours, assimilating the complex details of the stage of the negotiation in which they were involved together and agreeing with his fellow commissioner on every point. Breaking down his aversion to Franklin was a knottier problem. At first, he refused to make even a courtesy call at Passy; however, after a few grumbling days in his hotel, he was persuaded to do so. On the evening of October 29, he went to see Franklin and during the course of the discussion told him that he praised the "principles, wisdom, and firmness" which Jay had shown (he was referring to Jay's intransigence toward France) and announced that he would support Jay to the utmost of his power. Franklin knew this already—the vehement letters from The Hague had been pouring in all summer—but the actual presence of the fierce little figure before him must have reinforced the written word, for at the conference of all the British and American commissioners the next morning, Franklin turned to Adams and Jay and said: "I am of your opinion, and will go on with these gentlemen in the business without consulting this Court."[46]

Neither Jay nor Adams had ever doubted Franklin's loyalty to their unified stand. It had been he who had first broken the orders from Congress by his oral suggestions to Oswald on what might compose the articles of peace, without informing Vergennes. But now it was Franklin's task to inform the French Minister of Foreign Affairs that the Preliminary Articles had been settled on November 29 between the British and American commissioners and signed the next morning, without a word to France. In the history of diplomacy there can never have been a heavier burden of reporting, for they had been through so much together. It had been Vergennes in 1775–76 who had seized the implications of the dispatches from his agents and had forced the first loan for America from an undecided King and a reluctant Cabinet. It had been Vergennes who had fought off Lord Stormont and kept the undeclared aid to America going at a time when France was unprepared for war. Saratoga had been the reward for his faith which permitted him to risk a Franco-American alliance of 1778, a bold move presaging certain war with England. Then had come the bad years, with failure after failure for Washington's armies and report after report of the

George Washington
by Charles Willson Peale

Marquis de Lafayette

Marquise de Lafayette
born Adrienne de Noailles, a loyal, long-suffering wife

Conde de Floridablanca

Foreign Minister of Spain by Goya – the artist is depicted on the left

Comte de Rochambeau
Commander of the French forces that turned the tide of the war

Surrender of Lor

by Jo

...rnwallis at Yorktown

...umbull

Signing of the Treaty of Peace, Paris
by Benjamin West
It was West's intention to add the British commissioners, but they never appeared to pose
Left to right, John Jay, John Adams, Benjamin Franklin,
Henry Laurens, William Temple Franklin (grandson of Benjamin Franklin)

unpopularity of the war itself in America and of the general who was conducting it. The Rochambeau expedition which won the war at Yorktown would have faltered and stopped had not Vergennes summoned his resources for the loan which made the victory possible. A very human man, the minister had minded the calumnies and insults which had been shouted in the streets of Paris with relentless animosity since he had taken office seven years before. Nevertheless, when Franklin drove out to Versailles to talk to him (he had already sent the minister a copy of the treaty signed behind the backs of the French), he found an urbane figure confronting him on the other side of that superb desk that is still known as *le bureau de Vergennes*. Reprimanded mildly for the haste in signing "which had not been particularly civil to the King,"[47] Franklin excused himself as best he could. Vergennes said that he had done very well for his country and gave the impression that if he had been in Franklin's place he would have done the same thing.[48] The conversation sounds implausible, but two things must be remembered. Both were experts at the game of statecraft, and Vergennes was too big a man not to admire a fellow player who had achieved a triumph. More importantly, he was sick to death of his involvement with Spain and wished that he had never committed France to the hopeless task of regaining Gibraltar as a bribe for keeping the Spanish in the war against England. Now he would be free of that burden, for the defection of the United States with consequent strengthening of England would force Spain to make peace and forget, for a moment, the struggle for Gibraltar.

Nevertheless, it would be foolish to suppose that Vergennes did not resent the American action. His rebuke to Franklin, written two weeks later, reads as follows:

> *I am at a loss, sir, to explain your conduct and that of your colleagues on this occasion. You have concluded your preliminary articles without any communication between us. . . . You are about to hold out a certain hope of peace to America without even informing yourself on the state of the negotiation on our part.*

> *You are wise and discreet, sir; you perfectly under-*
> *stand what is due to propriety; you have all your life per-*
> *formed your duties. I pray you to consider how you*
> *propose to fulfill those which are due to the King?*[49]

Franklin replied to this with one of his most famous diplomatic letters. In it he said that in failing to consult with Vergennes the Americans had indeed been guilty of neglecting a
point of *bienséance* (propriety) but not from any "want of respect to the King, whom we all love and honor."[50] He hoped that
this unhappy incident would cause no break in the ranks of the
allies, for if this should happen all their common expenditure of
blood and treasure would probably be for naught. Then came a
brilliant touch: "The English, I just now learn, flatter themselves they have already divided us. I hope this little misun-
derstanding will therefore be kept a secret, and that they will
find themselves totally mistaken."[51] (Dr. Bancroft had this letter
on Shelburne's desk within three days.)

Then, incredibly, in the same document, Franklin asked the
bankrupt French government for another loan of six million
livres and got it immediately. As one historian has commented,
"France could not afford, as Franklin slyly pointed out, to let the
already costly fire die out for lack of fuel."[52]

When the terms of the Preliminary Articles reached America
at the end of the year, Congress eventually voted for ratification,
but there was many a dissenting voice to question the ethics of
making a separate peace with England in direct violation of the
congressional instructions to the commissioners. In point of fact,
Franklin, Adams, and Jay would have been censurable had they
acted in any other way. Nowadays our representatives abroad
can ask for new instructions by telephone or telegraph as the occasion demands; in 1782 it would have taken months to acquire
them and the men in the field were obliged to act as they saw
fit. The boundaries delineated by France and Spain would have
kept us a small, feeble country. However, the pro-French elements in the Continental Congress and the Secretary of Foreign
Affairs, Robert Livingston, did not have access to Vergennes's

papers as we do today. The French minister had been perfectly consistent in his policy of desiring an independent but weak America.[53]

The commissioners in Paris, without access to secret information, had smelled the way the wind was blowing and taken their decision accordingly. They waited nervously, but hopefully, for a word of approbation for their hard work in Paris. The negotiations with the English commissioners that had produced the clear wording of the nine articles that read so simply had been exhausting. Fishing rights off Newfoundland, for example, were to remain a bone of contention between Britain and the United States for over a hundred years. It had been the New Englander John Adams who had been in charge of the question of the fisheries, and at the dinner following the signing of the articles —a quiet meal shared by the British and American commissioners—he had declined the fish offered him, saying that he was really too worn out by the very word to feel like partaking of fish tonight.

Such was the slowness of communication that it was May 1783 before Robert Livingston's reaction to the Preliminary Articles reached the men who had drafted them. When it came, it was a harsh rebuke, far more unkind than anything Vergennes had had to say. It was John Jay, Livingston's best friend, who was the chief target for his anger. In a laborious, five-page letter to him, the Secretary stated that Jay had misunderstood the French negotiating stance and had held unworthy suspicions of Vergennes which Franklin unquestionably did not share. Jay replied with a curt letter in which he stated that a dispatch already on its way "affords an answer to the greater part of your inquiries." Later on the three colleagues took joint action in the form of a strongly written reply to Livingston's strictures, in which they hotly defended their treaty and their behavior. John Adams could hardly contain himself. He wrote to Robert Morris: "If any man blames us, I wish him no other punishment than to have, if that were possible, just such another peace to negotiate, exactly in our situation."[54] To Livingston he addressed three letters in as many days, boiling with indignation.

The American historians have generally had nothing but praise for the work of the plenipotentiaries that produced the Peace of Paris. "The greatest victory in the annals of American diplomacy was won at the outset by Franklin, Jay, and Adams," is how Samuel F. Bemis put it in his classic *Diplomacy of the American Revolution*, written in 1935.

French historians, until recently, have been extremely hostile to the American negotiators, feeling that they ill repaid the government of Louis XVI for the aid without which the war could not have been won. As late as 1975 the Duc de Castries of the Académie Française wrote his version of the events.[55]

According to him, Franklin, a true friend of France, would have cooperated with Vergennes until the end and no separate peace would have been made had it not been for the bad luck of the old man's poor health which kept him off the scene during the late summer of 1782. Thus he was unable to defend the interests of France (which he saw as identical to those of America) against the machinations of two second-rate men, John Jay and John Adams, both of whom were eager to play great roles in public affairs. Adams, says the Duc, was the cleverer of the two but the ambitious Jay was the greater traitor. In a passage written in beautiful French, he is compared to General Benedict Arnold, who had attempted to sell his country for 20,000 pounds in gold. The key phrase is "Jay was on the field of diplomacy what Arnold was on the field of war."[56] As the Duc de Castries cannot prove the bribery of Jay by the English, he does not give any source for his theory, and the reader is left with the picture of the wretched Franklin, pinned to his bed, impotent to deal with his two wicked colleagues.

This is an extreme example of how earlier French historians, outraged by what they considered betrayal by the United States, presented American peace moves. More typical of the modern school of French writers on the subject is the dispassionate technical analysis of the negotiations published in 1976 by Monsieur

Robert Lacour Gayet.[57] The author agrees with the American historian Professor Richard B. Morris that the tenacity of our diplomats was remarkable and points out that, new as they were at the game of power politics, they never gave in on any but the unimportant concessions. From the beginning to the end, they were intractable on the two vital issues—absolute independence and the right to extend their thirteen seagirt provinces across the continent.

The last sampling to be offered here from the rich crop of French histories of the peace treaty is a brief one, from Mr. Pierre Salinger: ".The delegation chosen to negotiate the peace accords was certainly the best the United States has ever put into the field. It comprised three giants of American history. . . . These men, all profoundly attached to their country, were as different one from another as the countries which faced them across the negotiating table."[58]

❧ XIII ❧

End of a Story

FRANKLIN HAD WRITTEN TO Congress as soon as the preliminary peace articles were signed that he wished "for the little time I have left to be my own master."[1] This wish was not accorded him, and it was to be another two years before he was permitted to return home. He still suffered from gout, and the bladder stones which had suddenly attacked him in the middle of the peace negotiations in August 1782 never left him. The pain could be excruciating, but he felt himself too old to risk an operation and refused all drugs. Writing to John Jay, who was in England, on January 6, 1784, he was as cheerful about this new enemy as he had been humorous about the gout: "You may judge that my disease is not very grievous, since I am more afraid of the medicines than of the malady."[2]

At least he finally had some leisure. The war was over, and the last loan from France had been negotiated. Now it was up to John Adams to extract any needed monies from the Dutch. It was an infinite relief to abandon the commercial responsibilities which he had never liked to Thomas Barclay, who had been sent over from America to handle consular affairs. The daily strain was eased, and he employed his new freedom in answering some of the many questions about his country which had been addressed to him during the years of his mission. *Information to Those Who Would Remove to America* was printed in

French and English at Passy on March 9, 1784. In it he sought to warn those who wanted to emigrate against overoptimism. Summing up his report in a letter to a friend, he said: "Our country offers to strangers nothing but a good climate, fertile soil, wholesome air, free governments, wise laws, liberty, a good people to live among, and a hearty welcome. Those Europeans who have these or greater advantages at home would do well to stay where they are."[3]

The French had often asked about the red Indians—to answer them he wrote *Remarks Concerning the Savages of North America,* which was translated by the Duc de la Rochefoucauld, the same friendly scholar who had earlier translated the state constitutions and the Declaration of Independence. The winter of 1783–84 was the coldest that anyone in France could remember, and Franklin, ever the scientist, sought an explanation in a paper called *Meteorological Imaginations and Conjectures* on the cold. He ascribed it to the long fogs of the summer of 1783, which so chilled the ground that the early snows in December could not melt. Perhaps there is now a true meteorological explanation for the severities of the late-eighteenth-century climate in France, which was quite different from what we know today. The reader who has shivered in a sweater in Paris in July must have been astonished by the description in an earlier chapter of the courtiers all but fainting from the heat at Versailles during the summer of 1778, or of the young court of Marie Antoinette sleighing down the frozen Seine in 1775. But the Seine did freeze every three or four years, the climate was much crueler then, with extremes of temperature unknown in modern times.

For Franklin it was a period of reflection and summing up. His personal life was a cheerful one; the Passy friends, like the Chaumonts and Monsieur Le Veillard, remained close to him; Polly Hewson, the widowed daughter of his London landlady, Mrs. Stevenson, brought her three children to spend his last winter in France with him; and until they returned to America in 1784, the John Jays were constantly in and out of the house.

They spent the summer of 1783 at Passy, and Jay kept a sort of diary, which today we would call oral history, of Franklin's anecdotes. The old man was touchingly devoted to Maria Jay, aged a year and a half. Ann Jay was born in the house in August. The invitations from great people in Paris continued to pour in, the honors accumulated, but to drive in his carriage over the bumpy roads exhausted Franklin, and he gave up his weekly visits to Versailles, sending Temple in his place. He was not closing himself off from the outside world, for solitary contemplation would have been anathema to him. But while he continued to be on excellent terms with Madame Brillon and her family just around the corner, there was an air of detachment about the relationship. For some time Franklin's letters to her had been more sparing; perhaps, as his vitality diminished, her archness and her selfishness drained him.

He knew where to go in order to replenish his supply of spiritual oxygen, and it was to Madame Helvétius in Auteuil that he went, as he had done again and again over the years. Auteuil is next to Passy, but Madame Helvétius and Madame Brillon were not friends. They might as well have lived poles apart instead of the five kilometers or so that separated them physically. Madame Brillon was a very well-to-do bourgeoise of the most conventional kind. She would as soon have let her daughter marry for love as she would have appeared in her salon without her high coiffure arranged in the latest fashion, as dictated by Léonard. Every pin of her costume would have been in place—in those days women's dresses were not sewn together; a man's tailor made the skirts, a bodice maker the tops, a dressmaker the sleeves, the whole pinned on at the last moment by a maid. The most important feature of the ensemble was the pouf, that mushroom-like velvet or satin cushion worn on the top of the head, into which jewels, ostrich feathers, flowers, or any other sort of decoration could be thrust. Poufs were nearly twice as expensive as hats, and Madame Brillon probably went to the Queen's milliner, Mademoiselle Rose Bertin, or her rival Madame Eloffe, twice a year for a pouf. If the confection was admired, she would be sure to murmur, "Oh, well, Bertin is really becoming impossible with her prices, but you know what my husband is like—he positively forced me into the rue St.-Honoré to buy this silly extravagance." Madame Brillon had never known what poverty was, nor would it have interested her to hear a discussion of the economics of the ancien régime. As an artist, she would have said with her trilling laugh, she was perfectly ignorant of such things and always left public affairs to the men. It would have been impossible for her to have crossed that checkerboard of splendor and squalor that was Paris in her carriage without catching sight of the skeletons in rags who haunted the narrow, fetid streets just off the grand boulevards, hands outstretched, but such realities were remote from what Madame Brillon called *"notre monde."*

Madame Helvétius had known comparative poverty, and would not have minded talking about it in the least, had she not felt that there were more interesting things in her life to talk about: her garden, for instance, which she kept a profusion of colorful flowers in abundant disarray. It was as different from Madame Brillon's neat, geometric arrangement of flower beds as Madame Helvétius' cheerful, extrovert earthiness was from the nervous, introspective nature of the other woman.

Born to one of the great families of Lorraine, related to the Hapsburgs and hence to Marie Antoinette, Anne-Catherine de Ligniville d'Autricourt had suffered a hard youth. The tenth of twenty children, she was without dowry and so considered un-marriageable at the age of fifteen, which was the normal age for marriage of an upper-class girl. The only solution was a convent, in which she remained until the mature age of thirty, at which time the small pension which kept her there expired. She had no alternative but to live at home with a once-again pregnant mother and fifteen other children. A kindly aunt, Madame de Graffigny, had taken a fancy to her when she was small, and this good woman saved her niece from the dismal prospect before her by bringing her to Paris. In Madame de Graffigny's salon she was introduced to two brilliant men who were sufficiently charmed by her beauty and direct, engaging personality to overlook the lack of dowry. One, who loved her all his life and never married, was the young Anne-Robert Turgot, who was to become one of the most powerful men in France as well as an internationally respected economist. However, as Turgot was younger than she and nearly as penniless, a better match in the eyes of the world was the rich financier Claude-Adrien Helvétius. The marriage took place in 1751, when the bride was thirty-two and the bridegroom thirty-six.

It was a happy enough marriage by the standards of the time. Helvétius soon gave up finance for the pleasures of philosophy. Although he was never intellectually in the first flight and his books were later severely criticized by his contemporaries, he was a good talker and a delightful host. Madame Helvétius' Tuesdays in their Paris house in the rue Sainte-Anne became so famous that Madame Necker, who was herself to become a powerful hostess, was warned on her arrival in Paris that she must choose another day than Tuesday on which to receive, as it would be too dangerous to compete with the rue Sainte-Anne, where such men as Diderot, d'Alembert, Condorcet, the Baron d'Holbach, Turgot, David Hume, and many others were habitual guests.

This pleasant life went on serenely for twenty years, interrupted by visits to one or the other of the family's two châteaux, accompanied by the two daughters who had been born to the Helvétiuses. A son had died earlier in infancy. In a portrait painted by Louis-Michel Vanloo, Madame Helvétius appears strikingly beautiful in early middle age and very elegant. The nearly centenarian writer Fontenelle is supposed to have said, "Oh, to be seventy again," on catching sight of her.* When her husband died in 1771, she showed an independence of spirit that was unusual for a widow in those days. Instead of settling down with her daughters, she briskly married them off to men of their choice and gave each of them a family château. The Paris house

* *Claude-Anne Lopez,* Mon Cher Papa: Franklin and the Ladies of Paris, *p.* 247.

was sold, and she bought from the painter Quentin de la Tour a ravishing little three-acre estate in Auteuil on the edge of the Forest of Rouvray. Her traveling friends brought back from abroad specimens of every sort of flowering flora to fill her small park. She found room for all manner of shrubs: Lord Shelburne's gooseberry bushes from Bowood, lilacs from the rich soil of Normandy, roses from Picardy, rhododendrons from Cornwall, of which she was especially proud, were all jumbled together—a confusion of sweet-smelling delight. Animals, for which she had a mania, were everywhere: deer in the park, as well as ducks, chickens, and hundreds of birds in large aviaries. Any number of dogs and cats roamed about, coming to their mistress to be fed.

By the time Franklin met Madame Helvétius, introduced by her ever-faithful admirer Turgot, the household consisted of three permanent boarders in addition to their hostess. These were the Abbé de la Roche, the Abbé Morellet, and a younger protégé, Dr. Pierre-Georges Cabanis. Very disparate men, they provided the intellectual stimulation and amusing companionship that Madame Helvétius required. Cabanis, whom she took into her house as a half-starved medical student at the age of twenty-two, was the son she had lost long ago. He later became a brilliant medical theorist and a famous man of learning, but even after his marriage he never forsook his benefactress and was with her when she died. These three clever men brought their friends to see Madame Helvétius, and the gathering of intellectuals at her new home was soon referred to jokingly as *l'Académie d'Auteuil*. Franklin found nothing but pleasure in the ambiance, saw nothing to criticize in the arrangement whereby an elderly widow lived in the company of three younger men. For him the best of it was not the scholarly conversation, which he could have found elsewhere in salons where the standard would have been just as high, but the casual coziness of it all. He loved the simple jokes—one of the abbés had a passion for immense amounts of heavy cream, and they never stopped teasing him about it—Madame was hopelessly forgetful and thought nothing of inviting Dr. Franklin for breakfast and then going off to Paris, leaving him with the abbés and hardly a mouthful of food in the house. She could be laughed at for her absentmindedness without resentment on either side, and once, writing to tell her how much her intimacy meant to him, Franklin ended his letter with a heartfelt line: ". . . in your company we are not only pleased with you, but better pleased with one another and with ourselves."[4]

He proposed marriage to her insistently; she was flattered but unwilling to abandon her free, bohemian existence. It is curious that he was physically attracted to her as he evidently was, for by the time he knew her her beauty had long departed, and she took no trouble about her appearance. Coming in to call unexpectedly, a visitor might find her in the garden, feeding the chickens in a heavy gardener's apron and leather boots, her hair tucked under a shabby handkerchief from which unkempt wisps would escape. If an occasion arose on which she had to entertain, it never occurred to her to send for Léonard; indeed she had probably never heard his name, for fashion bored her and she would have been too lazy to study the prints that so engrossed Madame Brillon. Unless one of her daughters or nieces had thought to tell her, she would hardly have realized that a revolution in skirt lengths had occurred in 1777 and that ladies now universally wore short skirts—that is to say, to the ankle. As for poufs—she would have found them too much of a bother. John Adams, profoundly shocked by the ménage when Franklin took him to call shortly after his arrival, wrote a devastating passage in his diary which has been quoted in an earlier chapter, but Abigail Adams was even more horrified when Franklin took her to dinner at Auteuil after her arrival from America in 1784. Mrs. Adams must tell the story in her own words:

> *She entered the room with a careless, jaunty air; upon seeing the ladies who were strangers to her, she bawled out, "Ah! mon Dieu, where is Franklin? Why did you not tell me there were ladies here?" You must suppose her*

*speaking all this in French. "How I look!" said she, taking
hold of a chemise of tiffany, which she had put on over a
blue lute-string, and which looked as much upon the
decay as her beauty, for she was once a handsome woman.*

*Her hair was frizzled; over it she had a small straw
hat, with a dirty gauze half-handkerchief behind. She had
a black gauze scarf thrown over her shoulders.*

*She ran out of the room; when she returned, the Doc-
tor entered at one door, she at the other; upon which she
ran forward to him, caught him by the hand, "Helas,
Franklin!" then gave him a double kiss, one upon each
cheek, and another upon his forehead. When we went
into the room to dine, she was placed between the Doctor
and Mr. Adams. She carried on the chief of the conversation at dinner, frequently locking her hand into the Doctor's, and sometimes spreading her arms upon the backs of
both the gentlemen's chairs, then throwing her arm
carelessly upon the Doctor's neck.*

*I should have been greatly astonished at this conduct,
if the good Doctor had not told me that in this lady I
should see a genuine Frenchwoman, wholly free from
affectation or stiffness of behavior, and one of the best
women in the world. I own I was highly disgusted, and
never wish for an acquaintance with ladies of this cast.*

*After dinner, she threw herself on a settee, where she
showed more than her feet. She had a little lap-dog, who
was, next to the Doctor, her favorite. This she kissed, and
when he wet on the floor she wiped it up with her
chemise. This is one of the Doctor's most intimate friends,
with whom he dines once every week, and she with him.[5]*

Small wonder that Mrs. Adams was revolted. The sloppiness,
the bad manners of this great lady who so clearly preferred the
company of her lapdog to that of her female guests, the egotism
she displayed in holding the floor at dinner, her embarrassing
flattery of Franklin combine to make the modern reader grateful
that he or she never knew Madame Helvétius. Nevertheless, to
Franklin she came as welcome relief after the artificial ex-

changes he had had with the other ladies in his Paris life. Madame d'Houdetot, with her rhapsodical verses in praise of everything from Liberty to the locust tree, had been a mixed pleasure—his feet must have hurt for weeks after the famous party in his honor at Sannois.

Madame Brillon, attractive as he had found her, had nothing to offer him compared to the plain fun of a day at Auteuil, with its in-house jokes and the total disregard of fashion which so dominated the world in which his position obliged him to live in Paris. After a day beginning with several hours of wrangling with the Conde de Aranda on the question of the navigation of the Mississippi, followed by a tense meeting with Adams and Jay concerning the answer to be given to the British commissioner in response to his outrageous new argument re fishing rights off Newfoundland, it was the sheerest delight to find himself in company which cared nothing for such matters. There was never anything pretentious about the invitation—just a line from Madame Helvétius: "Do you want, dear friend, to have dinner with me on Wednesday . . . ?" and he would find himself with the abbés arguing heatedly over the authenticity of a new theory of magnetics on which they were eager for Franklin's counsel, while the lady of the house, assisted by Cabanis, occupied herself with a newly born litter of puppies in a corner of the linden-laden park.

It would be interesting to have a record of what Mrs. John Jay thought of Madame Helvétius, but, although she must have been to the house many times, she never described it or its owner. This writer's guess is that she would have been as unhappy there as Mrs. John Adams had been, but Mrs. Adams was, as Jefferson's biographer, Dr. Dumas Malone, has pointed out, an American in the tradition later made famous by Henry James.[6]

It was like her to correlate the decay of Madame Helvétius' dress with the ruin of her beauty, and together they typified the rotten, decadent structure of European society that she sensed surrounding her from the first night she was taken to the theater and was deeply shocked by what seemed to her the indecency of the actresses' costumes. Later Mrs. Adams grew to love Paris and regretted leaving it, but it was only at the end of her stay that she felt its charm. Intellectually she was more akin to Franklin than Mrs. Jay could hope to be, but morally Benjamin Franklin and Sarah Jay were birds of a feather—no Henry James-like inhibitions about *their* approach to the enjoyment of European life. The young woman, who had written to her mother from the *Confederacy* that brief, lyrical, lark-high song of joy after her great hardships at sea, known in the family as "the land bird letter," was an exuberant optimist. She took to Paris from the moment her dusty coach drove into the hotel courtyard. Paris took to her. She understood "douceur de vie."

"I fear, my dear, you begin to think that the idea of amusement is the only one I attend to," she wrote apologetically to her sister Kitty. Kitty and Susan Livingston and the other members of the family, far from being disturbed, were delighted, for they had worried themselves sick about her during the two and a half years of the Jays' virtual isolation in Spain. It was immensely comforting to hear that she was having fun. First of all there were the American ladies. Mrs. Ralph Izard, born Alice De Lancey, had stayed on after the departure of her husband for America, and the De Lanceys were connections of the Jays. There was Mrs. Matthew Ridley, the wife of one of Jay's closest friends. These were joined by others: "You would be surprised to see what a circle we form when collected. Mrs. Price and Mrs. Montgomery have the suit [*sic*] of rooms over my head in this same hotel and Mrs. Izard lives directly across and has two daughters that are grown up. There are three days in the week that we take tea and play cards at each others houses, besides meeting on other occasions."[7]

The end of the war encouraged the growth of an American colony in Paris, and Sally Jay loved catching up with the news she had missed for so long. American society was a small entity in those days, and over the tea table she could hear from the ladies just how many new babies there were in the families of her friends, just how many tragedies or pieces of good fortune the latter years of the war had brought to her acquaintances, what people really thought in Philadelphia and New York about General Washington and the prospects for a stable government at last—in fact, all the things that mattered. Kitty and Susan had done their best to keep her in touch, but so many letters had been intercepted, and in any case they had been too discreet to touch on political affairs.

Furthermore, the shrewd American ladies in Paris were a source of information on the vital question of Paris fashions. The names of "little dressmakers" were whispered across the tea table—"I pray you, dear Mrs. Jay, not to give this address to another soul—but take my word for it—a lady of my acquaintance who goes to Court frequently assures me that the price is half of Mademoiselle Bertin's and that she combined a sheaf of wheat and poppies so arrestingly in Madame de Polignac's pouf last Sunday that the Queen herself stopped to admire it." Such intimacies as these were pearls beyond price to a newly arrived young woman—Sally Jay must have gone home with her mind reeling as she considered the possibilities before her. She had come from Madrid without a dress fit to wear, and already piling up on the desk of the hotel apartment were a mass of invitations which were impossible to refuse. Fortunately, she was naturally elegant, and it was a period during which fashion was extraordinarily diffuse.

Except for the "grand habit," to be worn at Court on great occasions, the terrifying pannier, twenty-one feet around, was long gone by 1783, and fashionable young women wore dresses to the ankle that were not dissimilar from the fashions of the 1880's, bustles behind, with a bodice that could be pinned on by the wearer and her maid in whatever becoming and original manner they saw fit. Unlike the regulation panniers, or the midnineteenth-century crinoline, or for that matter the disciplined order of the first sixty years of the twentieth century, when the great Paris dressmakers could dictate a change in style that would be copied from Sydney to Saskatchewan, fashion was very free in the last years before the French Revolution. The satins and brocades and velvets employed were of a quality unknown, alas, today, and a beautiful woman with a good eye could set a fashion in one evening with a twist of the wrist. Before long Mrs. Jay was one of the most admired figures in Paris society, and we can be sure that Franklin had been of the greatest help in building up her confidence. He had been an amused student of women's fashions since his first days in France, noting them carefully—now he had a daughter figure, bursting, like himself, with gaiety and animal spirits, on whom he could practice the fruit of his observations. One can just imagine the pair of them enjoying themselves as Mrs. Jay sat at her dressing table preparing to go out, the maid hovering behind her with the ostrich feathers for the pouf, Franklin in a chair with baby Maria on his knee, peering keenly through his bifocals. "A little to the right, I think—no, that is too much—try two inches to the left and then center the top plume—ah, perfect."

The Jays were automatically part of diplomatic society, and then, as now, the most popular ambassadors were not necessarily the representatives of the dominant powers. Aranda was a famous host, but the Sardinian Ambassador and the Neapolitan Ambassador were just as fashionable as he was, and everyone was grateful to be invited by Baron de Walterstorff of Denmark. John Jay, who could be delightful in society and much enjoyed good talk, accompanied his wife cheerfully enough on these evenings, but he put his foot down at the suggestion of the theater or any musical entertainment, for he was bored by the plays and had no ear for music. He was delighted to let Sally go with Franklin and to remain at home, a book in his hand and a glass of madeira at his side. Although his nature was not cold, it was a delicate one, and he was instinctively drawn to those who possessed greater vitality than himself. Proud of his wife, he was undoubtedly pleased to have Franklin show her off.

We hear of only a single episode of disharmony among the close trio: On one of the rare evenings when there was no company at Passy, the skeptical old eighteenth-century philosopher wandered from the political and personal anecdotes which Jay so loved to record into a cynical, and no doubt caustic, attack on the validity of the miracles of Jesus Christ as described in the New Testament, speaking as a man of science. This was unbearable to Jay, a devout Christian of Huguenot faith, but it would have been unthinkably rude to enter into heated argument with his host. He waited until it was possible to change the conversation, and then requested Dr. Franklin to do Mrs. Jay and himself the great favor of playing the harmonica. As we know, Franklin had invented his own instrument, and it was surely with the greatest pleasure that he sent off a footman to fetch it and, quite oblivious to the torture that any music was to John Jay's ears, played until it was time for the party to go to bed.[8] It is a great pity that Sally Jay did not describe the episode. Although she once told Kitty Livingston, "I never yet wrote a letter that pleased me,"[9] she was, in point of fact, a very good letter writer, albeit not a reporter of daily gossip in the fascinating style of such contemporary letter writers as Walpole and Madame du Deffand.

Franklin's French friends were kind and hospitable to the Jays. Of the many houses they went to, the one they found by far the most congenial was the Lafayettes'. The Marquise de Lafayette welcomed Mrs. Jay to Paris with a pleasant letter asking permission to come to call the next day, and the acquaintance expanded into close friendship. Adrienne de Lafayette is one of the most attractive and appealing figures in French history. Born a daughter of the great house of Noailles, she had been married off at the age of fourteen to the sixteen-year-old provincial aristocrat Lafayette, whose pointed nose and receding forehead combined with a lanky awkwardness of appearance made people say that he looked like an undernourished bird. His only merit in the eyes of Paris society was his 140,000 livres a year.† As has been described, this gangling youth was

† *The historian from whom I have taken this figure, David Loth, estimates that Lafayette's income was worth two or three million in dollars of the year he was writing, 1952.*

metamorphosed by the American Revolution into a valorous hero whose example and inspiration were of inestimable value to the cause he served, and the Lafayette the Jays knew in 1783 was a most attractive figure, not yet weakened by the side of his character that Jefferson later called "a canine appetite for popularity and fame." His wife, Adrienne, a wise and loyal observer, fully cognizant of her husband's infidelities and weaknesses, stuck by him until the end. When he wrote to her after his arrest at Rochefort during the French Revolution, "You know that my heart would have remained republican had not my brain been affected by 'cette nuance de royalisme,'" she understood his confusion perfectly, for her mind was clearer than his. She wrote: "You are neither royalist nor republican, you are Fayettiste."[10]

Typically, even as she wrote the letter, she was preparing to cross Europe with her two daughters to join her husband in his grim dungeon at Olmütz in Austria, an experience that was to fatally undermine her health. She was a pious saint who was never priggish. Her servants adored her, and it was natural to her to commence letters to her maid, Madame Beauchet, "Ma chère amie," which was extraordinary for that place and time. As for the lifelong liaison of her husband and the beautiful Adelaïde de Simiane, which was public knowledge in Paris, she resigned herself to it.

There have been few more selfless women than Adrienne de Lafayette. Although she was more reserved than beautiful, merry Sally Jay, both women were open, direct, and shared a deep dedication to the American cause. It is hard to imagine a more American house than the Lafayettes'—the children, two of whom were called George Washington and Virginia, spoke English fluently. Invitations to the Jays were written in English, and were delivered by an American Indian, one of two whom Lafayette had brought over to live in his household. The guests at dinner always included "les Américains," as the French volunteers who had returned from the war were proud to call themselves. As old campaigners do, they relived their experiences over the food and wine—the Chevalier de Chastellux would turn to the Comte de Sarsfield to ask him to tell his story about Cornwallis' expression on the second day of Yorktown—or was it the third day? The Vicomte de Noailles would remind them of something he had never forgotten when he was first presented to Washington, which in turn reminded the Duc de Lauzun of something funny which had happened to him while marching through Maryland, and so on. While it was the greatest fun, there was an undertone of deep melancholy to those reunions. Jammed into crowded troopships, these men had returned to a France in which nothing had changed since they had left it. What were they to do now? Having seen what they had seen, felt what they had felt in the new young republic, the sterility of their own system of government appalled them, the tinsel of Versailles revolted them, and the reforms for which they longed seemed as far away as ever. Until the King could be persuaded to summon the long-unconvened legislative body of the realm, the States General, in order to discuss what must be done, they were impotent. Six years later, in 1789, this assembly gathered, and the Vicomte de Noailles was one of the first on the floor, calling, in a ringing voice, for the abolition of titles of nobility as a first step toward the constitutional monarchy that he and the other liberals demanded.

Besides enjoying the hospitality that was afforded them in Paris, the peace commissioners were engaged in winding up their work during the summer of 1783. Shelburne had been forced to resign in February as a result of the unpopularity of the Preliminary Articles and had been replaced by the unholy combination of Fox and North. Adams, Franklin, and Jay had begun their conferences with the new British commissioner, David Hartley, in April. Inevitably there were minor differences to be ironed out before the signing of the Definitive Treaty, but there were no major crises and it was possible for John Adams to return to The Hague in July. He went mainly on business to do with our loans from the Dutch, but also to join John Quincy, just back from St. Petersburg. The sixteen-year-old diplomat had performed with distinction during his two years' service as private secretary to the American Minister to Russia, and his father was rightly proud of him.

The letters exchanged between the American statesmen with whom this book is concerned are very different in tone after 1782 from their earlier tense correspondence. They had, after all, known little but strain, overwork, and worry for nearly ten years. The New Yorkers and Philadelphians resumed their easy, intimate correspondence. The Morrises, Robert and Gouverneur, wrote amusing, gossipy letters to Jay, no longer interlarded with those terrifying enciphered demands for more loans, desperate in their urgency. Not that things were easy; Robert Morris wrote from Philadelphia on July 26, 1783:

". . . My situation as a Public Man is distressing. I am cursed with that worst of all political Sins, Poverty. My engagements and Anticipations for the Public amount to a Million of Dollars; it racks my utmost intervention to keep pace with the demands, but hitherto I have been able to preserve that Credit which kept our affairs alive until you had the opportunity of Concluding a Glorious Peace, and now a little exertion on the part of the States would enable me to make payment and quit the Service with reputation."[11]

However, the Morris letters were usually full of family news, as were those of Robert Livingston, who forgave the peace commissioners for their defiance of instructions and returned to the "Dear John," "yours affectionately," epistolary style. He was much occupied in dealing with the estate of Jay's father and in seeing that the inefficient Frederick was taking proper care of his siblings. Everyone wrote about the remarkable beauty and charm of little Peter Augustus—Sally Jay, her heart aching for a sight of him, wrote back to her sisters that, happy as she was to hear such reports, she wished that someone would tell her what history he was reading. He was, after all, seven years old.

Another subject of correspondence that pleased his friends, Franklin, Adams, and Jay, was the splendid success in America of that shining social light, the master spy Dr. Edward Bancroft.

The Livingstons could hardly bear to have him leave Liberty Hall, but New York was clamoring for him, especially the circle around General Washington, to whom he had been warmly introduced by a letter from Lafayette. Kitty Livingston wrote to Jay that as hard as it had been to let him go, at least he had promised to pay a return visit in the spring.[12]

Nothing can better illustrate the new relaxation of tension among the Americans in Paris than a one-paragraph note, undated, written during 1783 by John Jay to John Adams:

> *Sunday, 10 o'clock*
>
> *On calling this Moment for my Man Manuel to comb me, I am told he is gone to shew my Newphew the Fair. I fear they will have so many fine Things and Raree Shows to see and admire, that my Head will remain in Statu quo till afternoon, and consequently our intended Visit to Count Sarsfield be postponed. Thus does Tyrant Custome sometimes hold us by a Hair; thus do ridiculous Fashions make us dependent on Valets, and the Lord knows who. Adieu my Dear Sir, yours sincerely,*   J. Jay

Manuel was a Spanish servant who had accompanied the Jays from Madrid. The most punctilious of men, John Jay would normally have been furious with him, instead of which he appeared to find it rather a joke that he should be trapped in the house with uncombed hair while his valet and Peter Jay Munro took off to the "Fair." It would, of course, have been unthinkable for him to attempt to deal with his hair himself. As has been mentioned earlier, since the disappearance of wigs in the middle 1770's, upper-class men were the slaves of the barbers or servants who attended them daily to wash, curl, pomade, and powder their hair.

Adams returned from The Hague in late August, the date for the signing of the Definitive Treaty having been set. The protocol arrangements for the great day were not entirely easy to arrange. According to custom, presents were supposed to be exchanged by the plenipotentiaries of the former belligerents.

Charles James Fox, who had replaced Shelburne as Secretary of State in charge of the peace negotiations during the latter stages, inquired of George III what the presents should be. The King, heartily disliking Fox and any conversation with him, replied shortly: "Give them whatever the French do."[13]

Even Fox, the boldest man in England, found it impossibly awkward to point out to the King that the French custom of presenting diamond-encased portraits of the monarch might not quite do in the case of the Americans. He wrote to the new British Ambassador to France, the Duke of Manchester, and to David Hartley, suggesting that the Americans might prefer a gift of money to a bejeweled portrait of the sovereign whose rule they had so fiercely resisted. A thousand pounds, it seemed to him, would be thought "a great deal." Manchester and Hartley agreed that the amount would be considered "very handsome and satisfactory."[14] Kings' gifts are never free gifts, and Franklin and his colleagues would have been expected to reward the official in charge of the present generously. It was a time of beneficent presents on all sides.

On the morning of September 3, 1783, Franklin, Adams, and Jay (Laurens having been unable to join his fellow commissioners) met at Hartley's lodgings at the Hôtel de York on the rue Jacob and signed for the United States of America. The treaty between Great Britain and France was signed at Versailles later in the day; Vergennes, ever scrupulous, held up the proceedings until word had come that the Americans had signed their treaty. Then the deeply relieved minister entertained his American friends at dinner in his Versailles residence. The Marquis de Castries and the Marquis de Lafayette were two of the pro-American French statesmen who formed part of the company.

Summing up the events of the day, John Jay put it briefly but well that same evening: "If we are not a happy People it will be our own Fault."[15]

Sally Jay had planned a ball when peace was concluded, but her last child to be born in Europe, Ann, who had been expected in July, did not make her appearance until just two weeks before the signing ceremonies, and the exuberant Mrs. Jay was still confined to her bed in Passy. To make up for it she wrote a toast:

Sarah Livingston Jay
A Toast to America and Her Friends

Paris (after September 3, 1783)

1) The United States of America, may they be perpetual
2) The Congress
3) The King and Nation of France
4) General Washington and the American Army
5) The United Netherlands and all other Free States in the world
6) His Catholic Majesty and all other Princes and Powers who have manifested Friendship to America
7) The Memory of the Patriots who have fallen for their Country—May kindness be shown to their Widows and Children
8) The French Officers and Army who served in America
9) Gratitude to our Friends and Moderation to our Enemies
10) May all our Citizens be Soldiers, and all our Soldiers Citizens
11) Concord, Wisdom and Firmness to all American Councils
12) May our Country be always prepared for War, but disposed to Peace
13) Liberty and Happiness to all Mankind[16]

John Thaxter, Jr., Adams' private secretary, reached Philadelphia at the end of November with the official copy of the treaty, and after considerable delays on the part of Congress it was ratified and returned to Paris, where, on May 12, 1784, Franklin and Jay for the United States and Hartley for Great Britain exchanged ratifications. In Philadelphia, the painter

Charles Willson Peale had been entrusted by the city fathers with six hundred pounds for the erection of a triumphal arch, a splendid thing in the style of ancient Rome, decorated with inscriptions and paintings chosen by the artist. A bust of Louis XVI and the arms of France adorned one side; on the other on a pedestal was a statue of Cincinnatus returning to his plow—his features modeled on those of General Washington. Other decorations commemorated peace and commerce, the fidelity of the army, the Christianizing of the Indians, and the arts and sciences. It was a fine effort, and the proud Philadelphians celebrated the peace treaty enthusiastically beneath it.

Jay and Laurens were the first of the peacemakers to return home, both in the summer of 1784. The former was surprised by the warmth with which he was received by his countrymen in view of the congressional criticisms that had been leveled at the diplomacy of his colleagues and himself. He was given the freedom of his native city on his arrival and learned that he was to replace Livingston as Secretary of Foreign Affairs.

Thomas Jefferson reached Paris on August 6 to succeed Franklin—modestly remarking that, while he could succeed him, he could never replace him. Mrs. John Adams at last was able to join her husband that same summer. They lived in Auteuil in a lovely rented house, seeing much of their close friend Jefferson until Adams took up his post the following spring as the first American Minister to the Court of St. James's. With Franklin's departure in July 1785, a new era in American diplomacy began, not less interesting than the ten years with which this book is concerned, but another story.

It was time for Franklin to go. While his fine mind and his gallant spirit never faltered, the pain of the stone was a torment to his nearly eighty-year-old body, and he wanted to be at home with his own people. The French did everything possible to make his journey easy—to avoid the rough motion of a coach, a royal litter from Versailles conveyed him from Passy to Le Havre. His grandson Benjamin Bache wrote that he was helped into his conveyance in the courtyard of the Hôtel de Valentinois "in the midst of a great concourse of the people of Passy; a mournful silence reigned around him, and was only interrupted by a few sobs."[17]

"When he left Passy," said Jefferson, "it seemed as if the village had lost its patriarch."[18]

Chaumont and his daughter Sophie accompanied the litter to Nanterre; Le Veillard went all the way to Le Havre and crossed the Channel to Southampton, from which port the ship was to sail. Madame Brillon could not endure seeing the actual departure, but wrote him one of her best and least affected letters: "All the days of my life I shall remember that a great man, a sage, wished to be my friend. My prayers will follow him everywhere, my heart will regret him forever."[19]

He was cheered and fêted in every village and town through which he passed. Madame Helvétius, astonishingly emotional, attempted to call him back in a letter that reached him en route. He answered sadly and sentimentally from Le Havre, and he wrote to her again from Southampton just before sailing. By now he was the old, ironical Franklin, restored, as he had always been throughout his life, by the excitement of travel.

Southampton, July 27, 1785

Our ship arrived here yesterday from London. We are sailing today. Farewell, my very, very, very dear friend. Wish me a good crossing and tell the good abbés to pray for us, that, after all, being their profession. I feel very well. If I arrive in America, you shall soon hear from me. I shall always love you. Think of me sometimes and write to your

Benjamin Franklin[20]

Before leaving Paris he had visited Versailles for the last time to say goodbye to Vergennes. It was more than a ceremonial call, for, while as Minister of Foreign Affairs Vergennes could not make an intimate friend of any ambassador without risk of mortally offending the other members of the diplomatic corps, Franklin and he had trusted one another from the beginning, and Vergennes was a lonely man. Not only had he suffered public obloquy, but his private life had been overshadowed by the contempt shown to his wife by the Court. It was years before Marie Antoinette could bring herself to receive the Comtesse de Vergennes because of her lowly birth, and her devoted husband resented this bitterly. Even when she had been officially received, Madame de Vergennes was never treated as more than an outsider, which did not greatly disturb that cheerful, placid woman but enraged her proud husband. Except for Beaumarchais, with whom he could joke and laugh in his free moments, there was very little sunshine in the life of the great statesman, and with Franklin's going such as there was was much diminished. It must have been hard for these two men to bid each other farewell.

The Philadelphians were given time to prepare a triumphal welcome for their hero, as another ship outsailed Franklin's and brought the news that he would shortly be landing. When he did so cannons announced the great event, bells pealed, and for more than a week the citizens of Pennsylvania abandoned their normal pursuits in order to pay homage to "the father of American independence," as the *Pennsylvania Packet* called Franklin. He was kept too busy receiving the public to have time to record his emotions at length, but in an official report to the Secretary of Foreign Affairs, John Jay, announcing that he had returned from his mission, he spoke of how moved he was by his reception. Both Jay and his wife responded with a warm invitation to come to New York to stay with them, and he thought that indeed he might do so. Washington sent affectionate messages from Mount Vernon, and the greetings from friends everywhere piled up at Franklin Court. It was good to be home.

It is doubtful whether even Benjamin Franklin himself could have explained why things had happened as they had. Just ten years before, the colonists assembled in Philadelphia had gathered to discuss such seemingly hopeless questions as whether, lacking gunpowder as they did, they should adopt his own proposal to employ bows and arrows against British cannons. In that same winter, the little Committee of Secret Correspondence had hurried through the dark streets to meet the obscure French spy Bonvouloir, and the hope that he gave them had led to the birth of American diplomacy. This book has been an attempt to sketch the story of our first diplomats, but by no means answers the central question asked in the prologue: How was it that the refusal of the Boston grocers to pay an extra penny for a pound of tea developed into a declaration of the Rights of Man which included Life, Liberty, and the Pursuit of Happiness? These universalist ideals for which the American colonists were prepared to fight, and if necessary to die, were very soon transformed into a strong sense of nationalism. Why, and how?

On the gloomy October day in 1777 when Franklin attempted to describe to the recalcitrant Arthur Lee what the beginning of the American Revolution had been like, he came as close to the heart of the matter as any man could, yet even his fine words beginning ". . . the manner in which the whole of this business had been conducted was such a miracle in human affairs, that had he not been in the midst of it, and seen all the movements, he could not have comprehended how it was effected . . ." still leave us wondering.

From where, for example, came the stubborn tenacity that caused the peace commissioners to battle the European powers, thereby breaking their own instructions, in order that the United States should not be "cooped up within the Allegheny Mountains"? Before the war, of the three negotiators, only Franklin had ventured much beyond his own province, and the thirteen colonies were a disparate hodgepodge without the slightest sense of unity. What made Franklin, Adams, and Jay recognize our national interests in a new frame, so wide that there was no horizon? We were poor, we were exhausted by a long war, we needed time to recover. It was most improbable that we would become what Vergennes called "masters of a massive country."

However, the brilliant British philosopher and historian Sir Isaiah Berlin has acutely pointed out "one of the distinguishing characteristics of a great man . . . his active intervention makes what seemed highly improbable in fact happen."[21]

They were great men, those founders of our country. Perhaps the explanation for their achievements may lie in the phrase used by General Washington in a letter to his wife written as he reluctantly assumed command of the army—he spoke of "a kind of destiny."

Epilogue

THE FATE OF SOME of the characters in this book not given in the text.

ADAMS, JOHN. Served as first American Minister to the Court of St. James's, 1785–88. Elected Vice-President in 1789, reelected in 1793. Elected second President of the United States 1796, running against Thomas Jefferson. Moved into still unfinished White House, Washington, D.C., Oct.–Nov. 1800; Abigail followed. December 1800, defeated for reelection to the presidency, succeeded by Jefferson. Abigail died in Quincy, Massachusetts, 1818. John died in 1826, also at Quincy, a few hours after Thomas Jefferson's death at Monticello.

ADAMS, JOHN QUINCY. Served as American Minister to the Netherlands, 1794–96. Named American Minister to Berlin. Returned to the United States in 1801; elected to U. S. Senate 1803, where he served for five years. Minister to Russia and later Great Britain, 1809–17. Served as Secretary of State under James Monroe, 1817–24. Elected sixth President of the United States, 1824; defeated by Andrew Jackson and retired to Quincy, 1829. In the last phase of his career he served in the House of Representatives until his death in 1848.

BANCROFT, EDWARD. After his successful visit to the United States, 1783–84, Dr. Bancroft surprisingly retained his British citizenship instead of the American allegiance that would have been more normal for a supposed patriot to assume. This did not appear to disturb Franklin, who, in his kindness, invited Bancroft to visit him, subscribing his letter "most affectionately." After his return to England, the traitor attempted to justify the retention of his pension in a conversation with William Pitt, in which he still advocated the policy of destroying the United States. Pitt and the new ministry were thoroughly sick of the American war and gave Bancroft short shrift. The spy therefore gave up his career as an intelligence agent and died in Margate in 1821, having spent his last years continuing his scientific investigations on the theory of colors, which he put to commercial use in the printing of calicoes. His ripe old age was a happy one, for he was prosperous and respected. It was seventy years before his perfidy was known. Unfortunately for historians, his grandson, an honorable British general, was so appalled by the discovery that his forebear had been a traitor that he destroyed the greater part of his correspondence.

BEAUMARCHAIS, PIERRE AUGUSTIN CARON DE. Beaumarchais's last years were clouded by the running dispute between him and the American Congress over the money owed to him. As has been noted, Arthur Lee had convinced the Congress that the five million livres' worth of cargoes shipped by Beaumarchais in September 1777 had been a free gift from the French government. Eventually he received 2,544,000 livres in worthless bills of exchange. Then followed years of fruitless argument in which Gouverneur Morris, Alexander Hamilton, and other distinguished Americans attempted to sort out the story. Beaumarchais died in 1799, and for the next thirty-six years every successive government in France and each of its ministers to the

United States supported the claim of the Beaumarchais heirs in vain. In 1835 the family was offered the choice of 800,000 francs to close the case or nothing. They accepted the 800,000, and the long suit was terminated. The history of the debt is a very complicated one. Readers interested in pursuing it should read *Beaumarchais et Son Temps* by Louis de Loménie.

His life during the Revolution was a difficult one. Charged with treason to the Republic, he was imprisoned during the Terror, released due to the intervention of his mistress, Madame Houret de la Marinière, and took refuge abroad. He returned to Paris in 1796 and died there three years later. Although his courage and happy nature never deserted him, his later dramas, the opera *Tarare* (1787) and *La Mère Coupable*, while very popular, are not considered worthy of his genius.

CARMICHAEL, WILLIAM. Carmichael was recognized just before the signing of the Definitive Peace Treaty of 1783 by the Spanish government as official chargé d'affaires, and later as American Minister. He served in the latter position until his recall in 1794 and died on the eve of his departure for the United States in 1795. According to Samuel F. Bemis (*American Historical Review*, Vol. XXIX, No. 3), he was a highly unsuccessful minister.

CHAUMONT, JACQUES DONATIEN LERAY DE. The Chaumont family were never repaid by the United States the very large sums owed them for munitions, clothing, and medical supplies shipped to the Revolutionary army. The only reimbursement they ever received was the rent paid by Franklin for the Hôtel de Valentinois after 1778, which he had insisted on doing instead of continuing to accept it rent free as he had since he moved in two years before. Leray de Chaumont was obliged to sell the house and in his last speculative venture he moved to America in 1797 and bought, with his sons, 500,000 acres in northern New York State at two cents an acre. Planning to develop the area, he built schools and mills in the region between Oswego and the St. Lawrence, only to go bankrupt again when the building of the Erie Canal encouraged the new immigrants to go West. He returned to France, selling his lands but retaining the rights on such mineral profits as may exist there. These are still in the hands of his descendants. Like Lafayette, Chaumont was made an honorary citizen of the United States. It would be possible today for his heirs to acquire the same claim to citizenship, but this gesture would hardly make up for the financial loss they suffered at the hands of the miserly Congress.

FRANKLIN, BENJAMIN. On his return from France, Franklin was elected president of the Supreme Executive Council of Pennsylvania, October 1785, and reelected annually until 1788 when he retired to private life. He died in 1790 in Philadelphia. When the news reached France, the National Assembly voted, on a motion moved by Mirabeau, to wear mourning for three days in his honor.

JAY, JOHN. Served as Secretary of Foreign Affairs, 1784–89. Strongly supported the Constitution and contributed five essays on foreign affairs to the *Federalist* papers as part of the campaign for ratification. Appointed first Chief Justice of the Supreme Court, 1789, where he served for five years. Sent to England 1794 as minister extraordinary to arrange a treaty of commerce and to attempt to settle various British-U.S. disputes. Resulting "Jay's Treaty" was denounced at home and barely passed Congress; today is much admired by historians. Elected governor of New York and served two terms, retiring in 1801 to his farm near Bedford, New York, where he lived until he died in 1829, aged eighty-four. His wife, Sarah, had preceded him in

1802, just as their much-looked-forward-to retirement was to begin.

LEE, ARTHUR. After his return from France, Lee served in Congress until 1784. He was unhappy in Congress, where, he declared, he could only lament what he could not prevent. He particularly opposed the adoption of the Constitution. He never married and spent the few remaining years of his life on his estate in Middlesex County, Virginia, where he died in 1792, aged fifty-two.

MURRAY, DAVID, SEVENTH VISCOUNT STORMONT, SECOND EARL OF MANSFIELD. Lord Stormont was appointed lord justice general of Scotland the same year that he left Paris, 1778, and held many important positions afterward. He lived in his beloved home, Scone Palace, near Perth, until his death in 1796. Today the tourist can admire the many magnificent art objects which he had bought in France to embellish his home.

VERGENNES, CHARLES GRAVIER, COMTE DE. Vergennes died in harness, on February 12, 1787, following one of those brief illnesses that the doctors of the day found hard to diagnose; in his case it was called inflammation of the stomach as a result of gout. Gossip at the Court of Versailles being what it was, it was immediately put about that he had been poisoned by the Austrian government, if not by Marie Antoinette herself. This was the sheerest calumny. He died of natural causes at the age of seventy.

WENTWORTH, PAUL. It will be remembered that Wentworth was the spy who was not venal. He sought recognition and respectability, a place in Parliament and a minor title. These he had been half promised by Lord North in return for his services, but nothing came of the offers on which he had counted. Thoroughly disappointed, he retired after the war to his plantation in Surinam; presumably he died there as we have no further record of him.

Appendix

TEXT OF THE PRELIMINARY AND CONDITIONAL ARTICLES OF PEACE

Preliminary Articles of Peace. Articles to be inserted in and to constitute the Treaty of Peace (with separate article which was not ratified), signed at Paris November 30, 1782. Original in English. Ratified by the United States April 15. 1783. Ratified by Great Britain August 6, 1783. Ratifications exchanged at Paris August 13, 1783. Proclaimed April 15, 1783.

Articles agreed upon, by and between Richard Oswald Esquire, the Commissioner of his Britannic Majesty, for treating of Peace with the Commissioners of the United States of America, in behalf of his said Majesty, on the one part; and John Adams, Benjamin Franklin, John Jay, and Henry Laurens, four of the Commissioners of the said States, for treating of Peace with the Commissioner of his said Majesty, on their Behalf, on the other part. To be inserted in, and to constitute the Treaty of Peace proposed to be concluded, between the Crown of Great Britain, and the said United States; but which Treaty is not to be concluded, until Terms of a Peace shall be agreed upon, between Great Britain and France; and his Britannic Majesty shall be ready to conclude such Treaty accordingly.

Whereas reciprocal Advantages, and mutual Convenience are found by Experience, to form the only permanent foundation of

Peace and Friendship between States; It is agreed to form the Articles of the proposed Treaty, on such Principles of liberal Equity, and Reciprocity, as that partial Advantages, (those Seeds of Discord!) being excluded, such a beneficial and satisfactory Intercourse between the two Countries, may be establish'd, as to promise and secure to both perpetual Peace and Harmony.

ARTICLE 1ST

His Britannic Majesty acknowledges the said United States, Viz^t New Hampshire, Massachusetts Bay, Rhode Island and Providence Plantations, Connecticut, New York, New Jersey, Pennsylvania, Delaware, Maryland, Virginia, North Carolina, South Carolina and Georgia, to be free Sovereign and independent States; That he treats with them as such; And for himself, his Heirs and Successors, relinquishes all Claims to the Government, Propriety, and territorial Rights of the same, and every part thereof; and that all Disputes which might arise in future, on the Subject of the Boundaries of the said United States, may be prevented, It is hereby agreed and declared that the following are, and shall be their Boundaries Viz^t.

ARTICLE 2D

From the north west Angle of Nova Scotia, Viz^t that Angle which is form'd by a Line drawn due north, from the Source of St Croix River to the Highlands, along the said Highlands which divide those Rivers that empty themselves into the River St Laurence, from those which fall into the Atlantic Ocean, to the northwesternmost Head of Connecticut River; thence down along the middle of that River to the 45th Degree of North Latitude; from thence by a Line due West on said Latitude, until it strikes the River Iroquois, or Cataraquy; thence along the middle of said River into Lake Ontario; through the middle of said Lake, until it strikes the Communication by Water between that Lake and Lake Erie; thence along the middle of said Communication into Lake Erie, through the middle of said

Lake, until it arrives at the Water Communication between the Lake and Lake Huron; thence along the middle of said water communication into the Lake Huron; thence through the middle of said Lake to the Water Communication between that Lake and Lake Superior; thence through Lake Superior northward of the Isles Royal & Phelipeaux, to the Long Lake; thence through the middle of said Long Lake, and the water Communication between it and the Lake of the Woods, to the said Lake of the Woods, thence through the said Lake to the most Northwestern point thereof, and from thence on a due west Course to the River Mississippi; thence by a Line to be drawn along the middle of the said River Mississippi, until it shall intersect the northernmost part of the 31st Degree of North Latitude. South, by a Line to be drawn due East, from the Determination of the Line last mentioned, in the Latitude of 31 Degrees North of the Equator, to the middle of the River Apalachicola or Catahouche; thence along the middle thereof, to its junction with the Flint River; thence strait to the Head of St Mary's River, and thence down along the middle of St Mary's River to the Atlantic Ocean. East, by a Line to be drawn along the middle of the River St Croix, from its Mouth in the Bay of Fundy to its Source; and from its Source directly North, to the aforesaid Highlands which divide the Rivers that fall into the Atlantic Ocean, from those which fall into the River St Laurence; comprehending all Islands within twenty Leagues of any part of the Shores of the United States, and lying between Lines to be drawn due East from the points where the aforesaid Boundaries between Nova Scotia on the one part and East Florida on the other shall respectively touch the Bay of Fundy, and the Atlantic Ocean; excepting such Islands as now are, or heretofore have been within the Limits of the said Province of Nova Scotia.

ARTICLE 3D

It is agreed, that the People of the United States shall continue to enjoy unmolested the Right to take Fish of every kind on the Grand Bank, and on all the other Banks of Newfoundland; Also in the Gulph of St Laurence, and at all other Places in the Sea where the Inhabitants of both Countries used at any time heretofore to fish. And also that the Inhabitants of the United States shall have Liberty to take Fish of every kind on such part of the Coast of Newfoundland, as British Fishermen shall use, (but not to dry or cure the same on that Island,) and also on the Coasts, Bays, and Creeks of all other of his Britannic Majesty's Dominions in America, and that the American Fishermen shall have Liberty to dry and cure Fish in any of the unsettled Bays Harbours and Creeks of Nova Scotia, Magdalen Islands, and Labrador, so long as the same shall remain unsettled; but so soon as the same or either of them shall be settled, it shall not be lawful for the said Fishermen to dry or cure Fish at such Settlement, without a previous Agreement for that purpose with the Inhabitants Proprietors or Possessors of the Ground.

ARTICLE 4TH

It is agreed that Creditors on either side, shall meet with no lawful Impediment to the Recovery of the full value in Sterling Money of all bonâ fide Debts heretofore contracted.

ARTICLE 5TH

It is agreed that the Congress shall earnestly recommend it to the Legislatures of the respective States, to provide for the Restitution of all Estates, Rights, and Properties which have been confiscated, belonging to real British Subjects; and also of the Estates Rights and Properties of Persons resident in Districts in the Possession of his Majesty's Arms; and who have not borne Arms against the said United States; And that Persons of any other Description shall have free Liberty to go to any part or parts of any of the thirteen United States, and therein to remain twelve months unmolested in their Endeavours to obtain the Restitution of such of their Estates, Rights and Properties as may have been confiscated; And that Congress shall also earnestly recommend to the several States a Reconsideration and Revision of all Acts or Laws regarding the premises, so as to render the said Laws or Acts perfectly consistent not only with Justice and Equity, but with that spirit of Conciliation which on the Return of the Blessings of Peace should universaly prevail. And that Congress shall also earnestly recommend to the several States, that the Estates Rights and Properties of such last mention'd Persons shall be restored to them; they refunding to any Persons who may be now in Possession the bonâ fide Price, (where any has been given,) which such Persons may have paid on purchasing any of the said Lands, Rights, or Properties since the Confiscation.

And it is agreed that all Persons who have any Interest in confiscated Lands, either by Debts, Marriage Settlements or otherwise, shall meet with no lawful Impediment in the prosecution of their just Rights.

Article 6th

That there shall be no future Confiscations made, nor any prosecutions commenced against any Person or Persons, for or by reason of the Part which he or they may have taken in the present War, and that no person shall on that account suffer any future Loss or Damage either in his Person, Liberty or Property; and that those who may be in confinement on such charges, at the time of the Ratification of the Treaty in America, shall be immediately set at Liberty, and the Prosecutions so commenced be discontinued.

Article 7th

There shall be a firm and perpetual Peace, between his Britannic Majesty and the said States, and between the Subjects of the one and the Citizens of the other, Wherefore all Hostilities both by Sea and Land shall then immediately cease: All Prisoners on both sides shall be set at Liberty, & his Britannic Majesty shall, with all convenient speed, & without causing any Destruction or carrying away any Negroes, or other Property of the American Inhabitants withdraw all his Armies Garrisons and Fleets from the said United States, and from every Port, Place, and Harbour within the same; leaving in all Fortifications the American Artillery that may be therein: And shall also order and cause all Archives, Records, Deeds and Papers belonging to any of the said States, or their Citizens, which in the Course of the War may have fallen into the hands of his Officers to be forthwith restored and delivered to the proper States & Persons to whom they belong.

Article 8th

The Navigation of the River Mississippi from its Source to the Ocean, shall for ever remain free and open to the Subjects of Great Britain and the Citizens of the United States.

Article 9th

In case it should so happen that any Place or Territory belonging to Great Britain, or to the United States, should be conquered by the Arms of either, from the other, before the Arrival of these Articles in America, It is agreed that the same shall be restored, without Difficulty, and without requiring any Compensation.

Done at Paris, the thirtieth day of November, in the year One thousand Seven hundred Eighty Two

Richard Oswald	[Seal]
John Adams.	[Seal]
B Franklin	[Seal]
John Jay	[Seal]
Henry Laurens.	[Seal]

[On the page of the original next after the above signatures is the following, the brackets being in the original:]

Witness

The Words [and Henry Laurens] between the fifth and sixth Lines of the first Page; and the Words [or carrying away any Negroes, or other Property of the American Inhabitants] between the seventh and eighth Lines of the eighth Page, being first interlined

Caleb Whitefoord
Secretary to the British Commission.
W. T. Franklin
Sec^y to the American Commission

[On the last written page of the original appears the separate article, which was not ratified.]

Separate Article

It is hereby understood and agreed, that in case Great Britain at the Conclusion of the present War, shall recover, or be put in possession of West Florida, the Line of North Boundary between the said Province and the United States, shall be a Line drawn from the Mouth of the River Yassous where it unites with the Mississippi due East to the River Apalachicola.

Done at Paris the thirtieth day of November, in the year One thousand Seven hundred and Eighty Two.

Attest	Richard Oswald	[Seal]
Caleb Whitefoord	John Adams.	[Seal]
Sec^y to the British		
Commission	B Franklin	[Seal]
Attest		
W. T. Franklin	John Jay	[Seal]
Sec^y to the American	Henry Laurens.	[Seal]
Commission		

Source Notes

PROLOGUE

1. Brodie, Fawn M., *Thomas Jefferson: An Intimate History*, p. 109.
2. Morison, Samuel Eliot, *The Oxford History of the American People*, p. 172.
3. Ibid., p. 182.
4. Commager, Henry Steele, Morison, and Leuchtenburg, William E., *The Growth of the American Republic*, p. 170.
5. Morison, *The Oxford History of the American People*, p. 191.
6. Commager, Morison, and Leuchtenburg, *The Growth of the American Republic*, p. 159.
7. Morison, *The Oxford History of the American People*, p. 182.
8. Clark, William, Talk II, BBC, June 1976.
9. Ibid.
10. Ibid.
11. Butterfield, L. H., ed., *The Adams Papers*, Vol. II, p. 96.
12. Ibid., p. 97.
13. Smyth, Albert H., ed., *The Writings of Benjamin Franklin*, Vol. VI, p. 458.
14. Van Doren, Carl, *Benjamin Franklin*, p. 540.
15. Flexner, James T., *Washington: The Forge of Experience*, p. 243.
16. Butterfield, ed., *The Adams Papers*, Vol. II, p. 156.

CHAPTER I

1. Nicolson, Harold, *The Age of Reason*, pp. 264, 268.
2. Raynal, Thomas François, *Histoire Philosophique et Politique des Établissements et du Commerce dans les États-Unis*.
3. Abbé de Pauw, *Recherches Philosophiques sur les Anglo-Américains*.
4. Kimball, Marie, *Jefferson: The Scene in Europe, 1784–1789*, p. 40.
5. Nicolson, *The Age of Reason*, p. 396.
6. Faure, Edgar, *La Disgrâce de Turgot*, p. 7.
7. Ibid., p. 17.
8. Faÿ, Bernard, *Louis XVI, or the End of a World*, p. 187.

9. Faure, *La Disgrâce de Turgot.*
10. Marquise de La Tour du Pin, *Journal d'une Femme de Cinquante Ans.*

CHAPTER II

1. Castelot, André, *Marie Antoinette*, p. 137.
2. Chambrun, Charles de, *Vergennes*, p. 292.
3. Ibid., p. 292.
4. Doniol, Henri, *Histoire de la Participation de la France à l'Établissement des États-Unis d'Amérique*, Vol. I, p. 167.
5. Ibid., pp. 154 ff.
6. Castelot, *Marie Antoinette.*
7. All material about Bonvouloir's personal life comes from Joseph Hamon, *Le Chevalier de Bonvouloir.*
8. Doniol, *Histoire de la Participation . . .*, Vol. I, p. 286.
9. Aldridge, Alfred O., *Benjamin Franklin: Philosopher and Man*, p. 256.
10. Hamon, Joseph, *Le Chevalier de Bonvouloir*, p. 43.
11. Mitford, Nancy, *Madame de Pompadour*, p. 7.
12. Ibid., p. 6.
13. Doniol, *Histoire de la Participation . . .*, Vol. I, p. 244.
14. Ibid., p. 372.

CHAPTER III

1. Butterfield, ed., *The Adams Papers*, Vol. II, p. 96.
2. Ibid., p. 97.
3. Ibid., p. 99.
4. Ibid.
5. Ibid., p. 100.
6. Ibid., p. 107.
7. Ibid., p. 109.
8. Auckland MSS, King's College, Cambridge.
9. Central Intelligence Agency, *Intelligence in the War of Independence*, p. 29.
10. Isham, Charles, ed., *The Deane Papers*, Vol. I, pp. 121, 122.
11. Morris, Richard B., ed., *John Jay: The Making of a Revolutionary, Unpublished Papers, 1745–1780*, p. 325.
12. Boyd, Julian P., *William and Mary Quarterly*, April 1959, Part I, p. 183.
13. Bemis, Samuel F., "British Secret Service and the French-American Alliance," *American Historical Review*, Vol. XXIV, April 1924, p. 477.
14. Doniol's account of the meeting, Vol. I, pp. 486–502.
15. Einstein, Lewis, *Divided Loyalties*, p. 6.
16. Ibid., p. 13.
17. Ibid., p. 14.
18. Bemis, *The Diplomacy of the American Revolution*, p. 37.
19. Ibid.
20. Conversation with Mr. Lucius Wilmerding, Jr. 1979.
21. Boyd, "Silas Deane," Part I, p. 184.
22. Loménie, Louis D., *Beaumarchais et Son Temps*, Vol. I, pp. 226 ff.

23. Ibid., p. 357.
24. Ibid., p. 358.
25. Ibid., p. 366.
26. Ibid., p. 369.
27. Faÿ, *L'Esprit Révolutionnaire en France et aux États-Unis*, p. 38.
28. Author's conversation with Monsieur Jacques de Beaumarchais, October 1979.

CHAPTER IV

1. Conversation with Monsieur Jacques de Beaumarchais, owner of the letters, 1979.
2. Stevens, B. F., *Facsimiles of Manuscripts in European Archives Relating to America, 1773–1783*, ⚹240, Library of Congress, Manuscript Division.
3. Kunstler, Charles, *La Vie Quotidienne sous Louis XVI*, p. 94.
4. Ibid., p. 192.
5. Ibid., p. 188.
6. Monsieur Olivier Bernier, conversation with the author, 1979.
7. Watson, Elkanah, *Men and Times of the Revolution*, p. 80.
8. Ibid., p. 93.
9. I am indebted to David Schoenbrun, from whose *Triumph in Paris* I have taken the description of the *Reprisal*'s crew and voyage.
10. Lewis, W. S., ed., *Horace Walpole's Correspondence*, Vol. VI, p. 380.
11. Ibid., p. 385.
12. Adams, C. F., ed., *The Works of John Adams*, Vol. I, p. 660.
13. I owe this anecdote to Claude-Anne Lopez's splendid *Mon Cher Papa: Franklin and the Ladies of Paris*, p. 17.
14. Auckland MSS. Stevens, *Facsimiles . . .* , ⚹235, Library of Congress, Manuscript Division.
15. Stormont Papers, Scone Palace, Scotland, Dispatch of January 1, 1777.
16. Ibid.
17. Ibid.
18. Stormont Papers, Dispatch of January 8, 1777.
19. Ibid.

CHAPTER V

1. Doniol, *Histoire de la Participation . . .* , Vol. II, pp. 118 ff.
2. Ibid., p. 124.
3. Morison, *The Oxford History of the American People*, p. 244.
4. Doniol, *Histoire de la Participation . . .* , Vol. II, p. 319.
5. Ibid., p. 325.
6. Stevens, *Facsimiles*, Subject Matter Index, p. 319.
7. Stormont Papers, Dispatches of July 9, August 6, September 3, 1777.
8. Bemis, *The Diplomacy of the American Revolution*, p. 53.
9. Bailey, Thomas A., *A Diplomatic History of the American People*, p. 11.
10. Chambrun, *Vergennes*, Letter of 23 August 1774.

11. Doniol, *Histoire de la Participation* . . . , Vol. II, pp. 460–69.
12. Deane, Silas, Peter Force Papers, December 29, 1777.
13. Morison, *John Paul Jones*, p. 36.
14. Van Doren, *Benjamin Franklin*, p. 611.
15. Ibid., p. 584.
16. Ibid., p. 585.
17. Lee, Richard Henry, *Life of Arthur Lee*, Vol. I, pp. 343 ff.
18. Deane, Peter Force Papers.
19. Van Doren, *Benjamin Franklin*, p. 589.
20. Fleming, Thomas, ed., *Benjamin Franklin: A Biography in His Own Words*.

CHAPTER VI

1. Einstein, Lewis, *Divided Loyalties*, p. 16.
2. Stevens, *Facsimiles*, ⚹315.
3. Einstein, *Divided Loyalties*, p. 19.
4. Stevens, *Facsimiles*, ⚹1781.
5. Bemis, "British Secret Service and the French-American Alliance," p. 480.
6. Stevens, *Facsimiles*, ⚹248.
7. Doniol, *Histoire de la Participation* . . . , Vol. II, pp. 336 ff.
8. Stevens, *Facsimiles*, ⚹675.
9. Ibid.
10. Einstein, *Divided Loyalties*, p. 30.
11. Doniol, *Histoire de la Participation* . . . , Vol. II, p. 744.

12. Van Doren, Carl, *Secret History of the American Revolution*, p. 87.
13. Chambrun, *Vergennes*.

CHAPTER VII

1. Van Doren, *Benjamin Franklin*, p. 599.
2. Ibid., p. 579.
3. Fleming, ed., *Benjamin Franklin in His Own Words*, p. 307.
4. Lopez, *Mon Cher Papa*, p. 9.
5. For the description of the Hôtel de Valentinois, I am indebted to Madame Meredith Frapier, "Benjamin Franklin's Residence in France," *Antiques*, August 1977.
6. Lopez, *Mon Cher Papa*, p. 132.
7. Van Doren, *Benjamin Franklin*, p. 639.
8. Ibid., pp. 635–36.
9. Lopez, *Mon Cher Papa*, p. 182.
10. Castelot, André, *Queen of France*, pp. 131 ff.
11. Butterfield, ed., *The Adams Papers*, Letter to R. H. Lee, Vol. IV, p. 172.

CHAPTER VIII

1. Shepherd, Jack, *The Adams Chronicles: Four Generations of Greatness*, p. 92.
2. Butterfield, ed., *The Adams Papers*, Vol. IV, pp. 66, 67.
3. Ibid., p. 56.
4. Ibid., p. 66.
5. Ibid., pp. 58, 59.
6. Ibid., p. 120.

7. Ibid., p. 49.
8. Ibid., p. 50.
9. Mongrédien, Georges, *La Vie de Société aux XVII et XVIII siècles*, p. 297.
10. Ibid., p. 50.
11. d'Haussonville, Le Vicomte, *Le Salon de Madame Necker*, pp. 121 ff.
12. Mongrédien, *La Vie de Société . . .* , p. 248.
13. Ibid., p. 247.
14. Lewis, ed., *Horace Walpole's Correspondence*, pp. 406 ff.
15. Ibid.
16. Vigée-Lebrun, *Souvenirs de Madame Vigée-Lebrun*, pp. 67 ff.
17. *Memoirs de Talleyrand*, p. 47.
18. Ibid., p. 149.
19. Vigée-Lebrun, *Souvenirs de Madame Vigée-Lebrun*, Vol. I, p. 102.
20. Mongrédien, *La Vie de Société . . .* , pp. 56, 57.
21. Marquise de La Tour du Pin, *Journal d'une Femme de Cinquante Ans*, Vol. I, p. 160.
22. Butterfield, ed., *The Adams Papers*, Vol. IV, p. 63.
23. Ibid., pp. 118, 119.
24. Ibid., p. 150.
25. Ibid., pp. 151, 152.
26. Ibid., p. 144.
27. Van Doren, *Benjamin Franklin*, p. 611.
28. Ibid., p. 612.

CHAPTER IX

1. Bemis, *The Diplomacy of the American Revolution*, p. 35.

2. Morris, *The Peacemakers*, p. 8.
3. Ibid., p. 10.
4. Ibid., p. 9.
5. Ibid., p. 11.
6. Boyd, "Silas Deane," *William and Mary Quarterly*, Third Series, Vol. XVI, October 1959, Part III, p. 531.
7. Ibid., p. 532.
8. Ibid.
9. Morris, *The Peacemakers*, p. 11.
10. Ibid., p. 12.
11. Ibid.
12. Bemis, *The Diplomacy of the American Revolution*, p. 59.
13. Boyd, "Silas Deane," Part I, p. 169.
14. Ibid.
15. All quotes from the Deane-Jay correspondence are taken from Richard B. Morris, *John Jay: The Winning of the Peace*, pp. 49–51, 54, 56, 58, 84, 620.
16. Boyd, "Silas Deane," Part I, p. 185.
17. Einstein, *Divided Loyalties*, p. 48.
18. Boyd, "Silas Deane," Part III, p. 535.
19. Ibid., p. 536.
20. Bemis, "British Secret Service and the French-American Alliance," p. 495.
21. Boyd, "Silas Deane," Part I, p. 185.
22. Ibid, I, p. 187.
23. Ibid., II, p. 332, *William and Mary Quarterly*, July 1959.
24. Ibid., II, pp. 332, 333.

25. Ibid., I, p. 172.
26. Ibid.
27. Ibid., I, p. 173.
28. Ibid.
29. Ibid., I, p. 176.
30. Ibid., III, p. 549.
31. Ibid., I, pp. 185, 186.
32. Bemis, "British Secret Service . . . ," p. 492.
33. Auckland MSS. William Eden was created the first Baron Auckland.
34. Bemis, *The Diplomacy of the American Revolution,* p. 59.
35. Central Intelligence Agency, *Intelligence in the War of Independence,* p. 19.
36. Boyd, "Silas Deane," Part II, pp. 337, 338.

CHAPTER X

1. Van Doren, *Benjamin Franklin,* p. 627.
2. Faÿ, *L'Esprit Révolutionnaire en France et aux États-Unis,* p. 72.
3. Butterfield, ed., *The Adams Papers,* Vol. IV, p. 80.
4. Morison, *The Oxford History of the American People,* p. 256.
5. Flexner, *Washington: The Indispensable Man,* p. 28.
6. Ibid., p. 134.
7. Schoenbrun, *Triumph in Paris,* p. 275.
8. Faÿ, *L'Esprit Révolutionnaire . . . ,* p. 95.
9. Van Doren, *Benjamin Franklin,* p. 618.

10. Morison, *John Paul Jones,* p. 200.
11. Ibid., p. 187.
12. Van Doren, *Benjamin Franklin,* p. 622.
13. American Philosophical Society, "One Christmas Season in the Life of Benjamin Franklin."
14. Ibid., p. 376.
15. Loménie, *Beaumarchais et Son Temps,* p. 273.
16. Morris, ed., *John Jay: The Making of a Revolutionary,* pp. 531, 532.
17. Loménie, *Beaumarchais et Son Temps,* p. 323.
18. Whitridge, Arnold, *Rochambeau,* p. 147.
19. Ibid., p. 94.
20. Faÿ, *L'Esprit Révolutionnaire . . . ,* p. 78.
21. Ibid., p. 92.
22. Whitridge, *Rochambeau,* p. 132.
23. Ibid., p. 133.
24. Morison, *The Oxford History of the American People,* p. 262.
25. Ibid., p. 265.
26. Ibid.

CHAPTER XI

1. Davis, Curtis Carroll, *The King's Chevalier,* p. 32.
2. Morris, *The Peacemakers,* p. 2.
3. Akers, Charles W., *Abigail Adams: An American Woman,* p. 80.
4. Morris, *The Peacemakers,* p. 4.
5. All Mrs. Jay's letters are taken from Morris, ed.,

John Jay: The Making of a
Revolutionary.

6. Ibid., p. 693.
7. Morris, The Peacemakers,
p. 223.
8. Morris, ed., John Jay: The
Making of a Revolutionary,
p. 716.
9. Ibid., p. 753.
10. Monaghan, Frank, John
Jay, p. 145.
11. Ibid., pp. 145, 146.
12. Ibid., pp. 147, 148.
13. Morris, The Peacemakers,
p. 66.
14. Bemis, The Diplomacy of
the American Revolution,
p. 107.
15. Morris, ed., John Jay: The
Making of a Revolutionary,
p. 775.
16. Morris, John Jay: The
Winning of the Peace, p.
109.
17. Ibid., p. 197.
18. Ibid., p. 192.
19. Morris, ed., John Jay: The
Making of a Revolutionary,
p. 770.
20. Bemis, The Diplomacy of
the American Revolution,
p. 109.
21. Morris, John Jay: The
Winning of the Peace, p.
108.
22 Ibid., p. 117.
23. Ibid., p. 120.
24. Monaghan, John Jay, p.
181.

CHAPTER XII

1. Morris, The Peacemakers,
p. 251.
2. Ibid.

3. Ibid., p. 253.
4. Ibid., p. 255.
5. Ibid.
6. Ibid., p. 253.
7. Namier, Sir Lewis,
England in the Age of the
American Revolution,
p. 217.
8. Dictionary of National
Biography, p. 1,007.
9. Ibid., p. 1,008.
10. Ibid., p. 1,011.
11. Bailey, A Diplomatic
History of the American
People, p. 28.
12. Van Doren, Benjamin
Franklin, p. 683.
13. Ibid., pp. 682, 683.
14. Morris, The Peacemakers,
p. 276.
15. Ibid., p. 281.
16. Ibid., p. 286.
17. Ibid.
18. Bailey, A Diplomatic
History of the American
People, p. 26.
19. Ibid., p. 26.
20. Ibid., p. 27.
21. Morris, The Peacemakers,
p. 276.
22. Ibid., p. 285.
23. Ibid., p. 289.
24. Ibid.
25. Ibid., p. 301.
26. Van Doren, Benjamin
Franklin, pp. 683, 684.
27. Morris, The Peacemakers,
p. 303.
28. Ibid., p. 302.
29. Ibid.
30. Morris, John Jay: The
Winning of the Peace, p.
311.
31. Morris, The Peacemakers,
p. 305.

32. Ibid., p. 306.
33. Ibid.
34. Bemis, *The Diplomacy of the American Revolution*, p. 220.
35. Morris, *The Peacemakers*, p. 308.
36. Ibid., p. 310.
37. Bailey, *A Diplomatic History of the American People*, p. 30.
38. Ibid.
39. Doniol, *Histoire de la Participation . . .* , Vol. III, p. 56.
40. Bailey, *A Diplomatic History of the American People*, p. 28.
41. Van Doren, *Benjamin Franklin*, p. 688.
42. Ibid.
43. Morris, *John Jay: The Winning of the Peace*, p. 324.
44. Ibid., p. 336.
45. Van Doren, *Benjamin Franklin*, p. 690.
46. Ibid., p. 691.
47. Ibid., p. 697.
48. Ibid.
49. Bailey, *A Diplomatic History of the American People*, p. 31.
50. Ibid., p. 32.
51. Ibid.
52. Ibid.
53. Doniol, *Histoire de la Participation . . .* , Vol. III, p. 561.
54. Morris, *John Jay: The Winning of the Peace*, p. 549.
55. Duc de Castries, *La France et l'Indépendance Américaine*, pp. 314 ff.
56. Ibid.

57. Gayet, Robert Lacour, *Histoire des États-Unis*, p. 32.
58. Salinger, Pierre, *La France et le Nouveau Monde*, p. 176.

CHAPTER XIII

1. Van Doren, *Benjamin Franklin*, p. 703.
2. Ibid., p. 636.
3. Ibid., p. 707.
4. Lopez, *Mon Cher Papa*, p. 251.
5. Ibid., p. 258.
6. Malone, Dumas, *Jefferson and the Rights of Man*, p. 19.
7. Monaghan, *John Jay*, p. 217.
8. Ibid., p. 218.
9. Morris, *John Jay: The Winning of the Peace*, p. 171.
10. Chambrun, René de, *Les Prisons des la Fayettes*.
11. Morris, *John Jay: The Winning of the Peace*, p. 570.
12. Ibid., p. 670.
13. Morris, *The Peacemakers*, p. 434.
14. Ibid., p. 435.
15. Morris, *John Jay: The Winning of the Peace*, p. 580.
16. Ibid., p. 581.
17. Van Doren, *Benjamin Franklin*, p. 725.
18. Ibid.
19. Ibid.
20. Lopez, *Mon Cher Papa*, p. 300.
21. Berlin, Sir Isaiah, *Personal Impressions*, p. 33.

Bibliography

Adams, C. F., ed. *The Works of John Adams.* Vol. I. Boston: Little, Brown, 1856.

Adams, James Truslow. *The Living Jefferson.* New York: Scribner's, 1941.

Adams, John. *The Adams Family in Auteuil, 1784–1785.* Introduction and Notes by Howard C. Rice, Jr. Boston: Massachusetts Historical Society, 1956.

Akers, Charles W. *Abigail Adams: An American Woman.* Boston: Little, Brown, 1980.

Albion, Robert Greenhaugh, and Pope, Jennie Barnes. *Sea Lanes in Wartime: The American Experience.* New York: W. W. Norton, 1942.

Aldridge, Alfred O. *Benjamin Franklin: Philosopher and Man.* Philadelphia: Lippincott, 1965.

———. *Franklin and His French Contemporaries.* New York: New York University Press, 1957.

American Philosophical Society. "One Christmas Season in the Life of Benjamin Franklin," *Proceedings,* Vol. 121, No. 5 (September 1977).

Bailey, Thomas A. *A Diplomatic History of the American People.* Stanford: Stanford University Press, 1945.

Bemis, Samuel Flagg. "British Secret Service and the French-American Alliance," *American Historical Review,* Vol. XXIV, April 1924.

———. *The Diplomacy of the American Revolution.* New York, 1935. Reprinted Bloomington: Indiana University Press, 1967.

Berlin, Isaiah. *Personal Impressions.* London: The Hogarth Press, 1980.

Berthier, Alexandre. *Journal de la Campagne d'Amérique*. Edited by Gilbert Chinard. Institut Français de Washington, 1951.

Bizardel, Yvon. *Les Américains à Paris Pendant la Révolution*. Paris: Calmann-Levy, 1972.

Boigne, Comtesse de. *Mémoires*. Paris: Librairie Plon, 1908.

Bonsal, Stephen. *When the French Were Here*. New York: Doubleday, Doran, 1945.

Bowen, Catherine Drinker. *The Most Dangerous Man in America*. Boston: Atlantic–Little, Brown, 1974.

Boyd, Julian P. "Silas Deane: Death by a Kindly Teacher of Treason?" *William and Mary Quarterly*, April 1959, Part I.

———. "Silas Deane: Death by a Kindly Teacher of Treason?" *William and Mary Quarterly*, July 1959, Part II.

———. "Silas Deane: Death by a Kindly Teacher of Treason?" *William and Mary Quarterly*, Third Series, Vol. XVI, October 1959, Part III.

Brodie, Fawn M. *Thomas Jefferson: An Intimate History*. New York: W. W. Norton, 1974.

Butterfield, L. H., ed. *The Adams Papers: Diary and Autobiography of John Adams*. Vols. II–IV. Cambridge: Harvard University Press, 1961.

Cambridge Modern History. Vol. VIII: *The French Revolution*. Cambridge: The University Press, 1902–12.

Castelot, André. *Marie Antoinette*. London: Vallentin, Mitchel, 1957.

———. *Queen of France*. New York: Harper & Bros., 1957.

Castries, Duc de. *La France et l'Indépendance Américaine*. Paris: Librairie Académique Perrin, 1975.

Central Intelligence Agency. *Intelligence in the War of Independence*. Washington, D.C., 1976.

Chambrun, Charles de. *Vergennes*. Paris: Librairie Plon, 1944.

Chambrun, René de. *Les Prisons des la Fayettes*. Paris: Librairie Académique Perrin, 1977.

Chinard, Gilbert. *Thomas Jefferson: The Apostle of Americanism*. Boston: Little, Brown, 1929.

Commager, Henry Steele; Morison, Samuel Eliot; and Leuchtenburg, William E. *The Growth of the American Republic*. New York: Oxford University Press, 1962.

Davis, Curtis Carroll. *The King's Chevalier*. Indianapolis: Bobbs-Merrill, 1961.

Deane, Silas. The Peter Force Papers, Series VII-E-6 & 7. Library of Congress.

Doniol, Henri. *Histoire de la Participation de la France à l'Établissement des États-Unis d'Amérique.* Vols. I–V. Paris: Imprimerie Nationale, 1886.

Einstein, Lewis. *Divided Loyalties.* New York: Books for Libraries Press, 1933.

Ellet, Mrs. *Court Circles of the Republic.* Philadelphia Publishing Co., 1872.

Elliott, Grace Dalrymple. *Journal of My Life During the French Revolution.* London: Rodale Press, 1955.

Faure, Edgar. *La Disgrâce de Turgot.* Paris: Gallimard, 1961.

Faÿ, Bernard. *Franklin: The Apostle of Modern Times.* Boston: Little, Brown, 1929.

——. *L'Esprit Révolutionnaire en France et aux États-Unis.* Paris: Librairie Édouard Champion, 1925.

——. *Louis XVI, or the End of a World.* London: W. H. Allen, 1968.

Fisher, H. A. L. *A History of Europe.* London: Edward Arnold, 1936.

Fleming, Thomas, ed. *Benjamin Franklin: A Biography in His Own Words.* New York: Newsweek, 1972.

Flexner, James T. *George Washington: A Biography.* Vol. I: *The Forge of Experience, 1732–1775.* Boston: Little, Brown, 1965.

——. *Washington: The Indispensable Man.* Boston: Little, Brown, 1969.

Franklin, Benjamin. *The Autobiography of Benjamin Franklin.* Edited by Leonard W. Labaree et al. New Haven: Yale University Press, 1965.

——. *Benjamin Franklin's Autobiographical Writing.* Edited by Carl Van Doren. New York: Viking, 1945.

——. *The Complete Works of Benjamin Franklin.* Edited by John Bigelow. 10 vols. New York: Putnam, 1887–89.

——. *The Founding Fathers.* Edited by Thomas Fleming and Joan P. Kerr. New York: Newsweek, 1972.

——. *The Papers of Benjamin Franklin.* Vols. I–XIV, edited by Leonard W. Labaree et al. Vol. XV, edited by William B. Willcox et al. New Haven: Yale University Press, 1959.

——. *The Works of Benjamin Franklin.* Edited by Jared Sparks. 10 vols. Boston: Hilliard, Gray, 1836–40.

———. *The Writings of Benjamin Franklin*. Edited by Albert H. Smyth. 10 vols. New York: Macmillan, 1905–07.

Frapier, Meredith. "Benjamin Franklin's Residence in France." Meredith Martindale, Assistant Historian, Société Historique d'Auteuil et de Passy, *Antiques*, August 1977.

Freeman, Douglas S. *George Washington*. Vol. IV. New York: Scribner's, 1948.

Gayet, Robert Lacour. *Histoire des États-Unis*. Paris: Fayard, 1976.

Gottschalk, Louis. *Lafayette Comes to America*. Chicago: University of Chicago Press, 1935.

Hamon, Joseph. *Le Chevalier de Bonvouloir*. Paris: Jouve et Cie, 1953.

d'Haussonville, Le Vicomte. *Le Salon de Madame Necker*. Paris: Calmann Levy, 1885.

Herold, J. C. *Mistress to an Age: A Life of Madame de Staël*. Indianapolis: Bobbs-Merrill, 1958.

Hobart, Lois. *Patriot's Lady*. (Life of Sarah Jay.) New York: Funk & Wagnalls, 1960.

Isham, Charles, ed. *The Deane Papers*. Vol. I. Deane to Elizabeth Saltonstall Deane, March 3, 1776.

Jay, William. *The Life of John Jay*. New York: J. & J. Harper, 1833.

Kaplan, Lawrence S. *Jefferson and France: An Essay on Political Ideas*. New Haven: Yale University Press, 1967.

Kimball, Fiske. *The Life Portraits of Jefferson*. Philadelphia: American Philosophical Society, 1944.

Kimball, Marie. *Jefferson: The Scene in Europe, 1784–1789*. New York: Coward, McCann, 1950.

Kunstler, Charles. *La Vie Quotidienne sous Louis XVI*. Paris: Hachette, 1950.

La Tour du Pin, Marquise de. *Journal d'une Femme de Cinquante Ans*. Editeurs: Imhaus et Chapelot. Paris: Librairie Chapelot, 1916.

Lee, Richard Henry. *Life of Arthur Lee*. Vols. I and II. Boston: Wells and Lilly, 1829.

Lewis, Wilmarth S. *Horace Walpole*. New York: Pantheon, 1961.

Loménie, Louis de. *Beaumarchais et Son Temps*. Paris: Michel Lévy Frères, 1856.

Lopez, Claude-Anne. *Mon Cher Papa: Franklin and the Ladies of Paris*. New Haven: Yale University Press, 1966.

Loth, David. *Lafayette*. London: Cassell, 1952.

Maclay, Edgar Stanton. *A History of American Privateers*. New York: D. Appleton, 1899.

Malone, Dumas. *Jefferson and His Time*. Vol. II: *Jefferson and the Rights of Man*. Boston: Little, Brown, 1951.

Manceron, Claude. *Le Bon Plaisir 1782/1785*. Paris: Robert Laffont, 1976.

——. *Le Vent d'Amérique 1778/1782*. Paris: Robert Laffont, 1974.

Maurois, André. *Adrienne*. New York: McGraw-Hill, 1961.

Mercier, Sebastien. *Paris Delineated*. London: H. D. Symonds, 1802.

Mitford, Nancy. *Madame de Pompadour*. New York: Random House, 1953.

Monaghan, Frank. *John Jay*. Indianapolis: Bobbs-Merrill, 1935.

Mongrédien, Georges. *La Vie de Société aux XVII et XVIII Siècles*. Paris: Hachette, 1950.

Morison, Samuel Eliot. *The Oxford History of the American People*. New York: Oxford University Press, 1965.

——. *John Paul Jones*. Boston: Atlantic–Little, Brown, 1959.

Morris, Gouverneur. *A Diary of the French Revolution*. Edited by Beatrix Davenport. Freeport, N.Y.: Books for Libraries Press, 1939.

Morris, Richard B., ed. *John Jay: The Making of a Revolutionary*. New York: Harper & Row, 1975.

——. *The Peacemakers: The Great Powers and American Independence*. New York: Harper & Row, 1965.

——. *John Jay: The Winning of the Peace*. New York: Harper & Row, 1980.

Namier, Sir Lewis. *England in the Age of the American Revolution*. New York: St. Martin's Press, 1930.

Nicolson, Harold. *The Age of Reason*. London: Constable, 1960.

Orieux, Jean. *Talleyrand*. Paris: Flammarion, 1970.

Padover, Saul K. *A Jefferson Profile*. New York: John Day, 1956.

Pauw, Abbé de. *Recherches Philosophiques sur les Anglo-Américains*. Berlin, 1770–71.

Pennypacker, Morton. *General Washington's Spies on Long Island and in New York.* Long Island Historical Society, 1939.

Peterson, Merrill D. *Adams and Jefferson: A Revolutionary Dialogue.* Athens: University of Georgia Press, 1976.

———. *Thomas Jefferson and the New Nation.* New York: Oxford University Press, 1970.

Pulley, Judith P. *An Agent of Nature's Republic Abroad: Thomas Jefferson in Pre-Revolutionary France.* Essays in History published by History Dept., University of Virginia, Vol. 11, 1966.

———. *Thomas Jefferson at the Court of Versailles: An American Philosophe and the Coming of the French Revolution.* Ph.D. dissertation, University of Virginia, 1966.

Raynal, Thomas François. *Histoire Philosophique et Politique des Établissements et du Commerce dans les États-Unis.* Paris, 1770.

Salinger, Pierre. *La France et le Nouveau Monde.* Paris: Robert Laffont, 1976.

Schoenbrun, David. *Triumph in Paris: The Exploits of Benjamin Franklin.* New York: Harper & Row, 1976.

Shepherd, Jack. *The Adams Chronicles: Four Generations of Greatness.* Little, Brown, 1975.

Stevens, B. F. *Facsimiles of Manuscripts in European Archives Relating to America, 1773–1783.* Issued to subscribers only. London, 1889.

Stormont Papers, Scone Palace, Scotland.

Memoires de Talleyrand. New York: G. F. Putnam & Sons, 1891.

Van Doren, Carl. *Benjamin Franklin.* New York: Viking, 1938.

———. *Secret History of the American Revolution.* New York: Viking, 1941.

Vigée-Lebrun. *Souvenirs de Madame Vigée-Lebrun.* Vol. I. Paris: G. Charpentier et Cie, n.d.

Walpole, Horace. *Correspondence.* Edited by W. S. Lewis. Vol. VI. New Haven: Yale University Press, 1939.

Watson, Elkanah. *Men and Times of the Revolution.* New York, 1856.

Whitridge, Arnold. *Rochambeau.* New York: Macmillan, 1966.

SUSAN MARY ALSOP *is a true stylist, keen observer and indefatigable researcher. With a heritage of two hundred years of diplomacy behind her, she is especially qualified to write the story of our first Yankees at the Court. She is a direct descendant of John Jay and has had access to private collections of journals, diaries, letters, documents and artwork. She knows the French intimately, having lived among them for fifteen years. Her last book,* Lady Sackville, *prompted the Washington* Star *to declare that she "belongs in the select company of André Maurois, Lord David Cecil and Nancy Mitford. There's more than a touch of the 18th century in her sophistication; and her perspective is so broad and classically balanced that she is never tempted to fit people from the past into a context of now-fashionable values." Mrs. Alsop lives in Washington, D.C.*

Index